The Political Economy of the Kimberley Process

In the late 1990s, the issue of diamonds contributing to conflict began to receive global attention. In response, the Kimberley Process, an international agreement drawn up in 2003, was implemented to reduce the trade of conflict diamonds and provide a way to certify the global diamond trade. This study looks at the political economy of resource-wealthy states in Africa to understand responses to the Kimberley Process, asking why some African states have higher levels of compliance and co-operation than others. Using cross-country comparisons to explain differing state policies and outcomes, Nathan Munier explores whether domestic, private economic actors matter in how international agreements operate. In doing so, he asks why states that regularly ignore international agreements will use scarce resources to raise their level of compliance with the Kimberley Process. Focusing on the domestic political economy of states, in contrast to past theories of state responses to international agreements, Munier finds that economic dependence and the preferences of private actors are essential in understanding the variation of state responses to international agreements.

NATHAN MUNIER is Assistant Professor of International Relations at Tokyo International University where his research areas focus on international political economy, international agreements, African Politics, conflict resources, and migration. He is the author of articles in journals including *Resources Policy, Review of African Political Economy and African Security.*

The Political Economy of the Kimberley Process

NATHAN MUNIER
Tokyo International University

CAMBRIDGE
UNIVERSITY PRESS

CAMBRIDGE
UNIVERSITY PRESS

Shaftesbury Road, Cambridge CB2 8EA, United Kingdom

One Liberty Plaza, 20th Floor, New York, NY 10006, USA

477 Williamstown Road, Port Melbourne, VIC 3207, Australia

314–321, 3rd Floor, Plot 3, Splendor Forum, Jasola District Centre, New Delhi – 110025, India

103 Penang Road, #05–06/07, Visioncrest Commercial, Singapore 238467

Cambridge University Press is part of Cambridge University Press & Assessment, a department of the University of Cambridge.

We share the University's mission to contribute to society through the pursuit of education, learning and research at the highest international levels of excellence.

www.cambridge.org
Information on this title: www.cambridge.org/9781108813587

DOI: 10.1017/9781108884877

First published 2020
First paperback edition 2024

A catalogue record for this publication is available from the British Library

ISBN 978-1-108-83970-9 Hardback
ISBN 978-1-108-81358-7 Paperback

Contents

Tables

Acknowledgments

There are many institutions and individuals I want to thank here. Western Illinois University, where I received my BA and MA degrees, has an excellent political science department that allowed me to grow as a scholar. The members of my master's thesis committee, Vincent Auger, Daniel Ogbaharya, and Julia Alberaccin, deserve special recognition for their ongoing support. The University of Nebraska–Lincoln, where I received my PhD, has an oustanding political science program and I have many fond memories of both researching and teaching there. Specifically, I would like to thank the members of my doctoral dissertation committee: Ross Miller, Alice Kang, Courtney Hillebrecht, and Wayne Babchuk. Tokyo International University has provided an exceptional intellectual environment and support to complete this manuscript. I would like to thank the journals *Review of African Political Economy* and *Resources Policy* for giving permission to use parts of previously published articles in Chapters 4 and 5 of this book respectively. Finally, Alma Jeftic, my *sova* (owl), my everything.

1 *Diamonds after Blood?*

Explaining State Responses to the Kimberley Process in Africa

In October 2008, government troops descended upon the diamond-rich Marange region in eastern Zimbabwe. Their goal was to clear the area of illegal miners who only a few years before had arrived in the region to search for diamonds, in what has been one of the most significant diamond discoveries in decades. Allegedly at least 200 miners died in these attacks, although the Zimbabwean government denies that this happened. The conflict led the Kimberley Process, a diamond certification scheme that had been created to prevent "conflict diamonds," to place a ban on diamonds originating from the Marange region. In turn, the Zimbabwean government agreed to follow a joint work plan in which a series of steps would have to be followed for the ban to be lifted.

Despite the ban, diamonds continued to be traded from the Marange region in violation of the agreement. Even more troubling, at least to some observers, is that in 2011 all sanctions preventing the trade of Zimbabwean diamonds ended. These dynamics prompted the influential nongovernmental organization Global Witness to leave the Kimberley Process. Others argued that the Kimberley Process was unable to stop the trade in conflict diamonds and concluded that the institution was too weak and ineffective.

In contrast, some participant countries in the Kimberley Process, especially Zimbabwe's politically allied neighbors, claimed that Zimbabwe had complied with the joint work plan. Since decisions in the Kimberley Process are based on consensus, this made Zimbabwe eligible to participate in the diamond trade. States that see the Kimberley Process as working point to potential successes and argue that many countries have invested scarce resources in complying with the Kimberley Process. For instance, it is telling of the motivations of domestic policymakers that the Zimbabwean government decided to comply with the Kimberley Process at all; given that it has ignored other international regimes and that the Kimberley Process appeared unable to act forcefully in this case.[1]

The controversy surrounding the diamond trade in Zimbabwe illustrates how the domestic political economy matters when looking at cooperation and compliance with international agreements. Since the Kimberley Process is indecisive in many cases, it is a paradox why states such as Zimbabwe will use scarce resources to stay in compliance. Furthermore, it is an interesting puzzle why comparable states in Africa, such as those examined in this study – Angola, Central African Republic, Namibia, Sierra Leone, and Zimbabwe – have varied significantly in their levels of compliance and cooperation with the Kimberley Process. This puzzle is essential to understanding the nature of the postconflict/postapartheid states that emerged in Africa and the central role that private diamond companies have played in the political economy of these states.

The Kimberley Process

In the late 1990s, there were ongoing conflicts in Africa that started to be tied to diamonds, especially in Sierra Leone and Angola, leading nongovernmental organizations to publish reports on the diamond trade and demand action (Global Witness 1998).[2] Also, in academia scholars were beginning to argue that a state's risk of experiencing a civil war can rise considerably if it is wealthy in natural resources and resource extraction provides a funding opportunity for rebel groups (e.g., Collier and Hoeffler 1998).[3] On July 1, 1998, the United Nations made the first attempt to ban conflict diamonds by placing an embargo on diamonds from areas that were being held by the National Union for the Total Independence of Angola (UNITA), a rebel group that

[1] Information on the Kimberley Process in Zimbabwe was drawn from Global Witness (2010, 2011a, 2011b); Kimberley Process reports (2009, 2011); Nyamunda and Mukwambo (2012); Towriss (2013).

[2] Accounts of the role that diamonds played in African conflicts can be found in Campbell (2002); Cleveland (2014); Le Billon (2008, 2012); and Smille (2010a, 2014).

[3] Collier and Hoeffler (1998) found a strong correlation between the level of resource wealth a state has and the onset and duration of civil war. While the findings of this study have been heavily debated (Fearon 2005), it influenced a significant amount of research on the relationship between a state's economic activity and the risk for civil war.

used diamonds for funding (Global Witness 1999). This ban was somewhat successful in that it did force rebels to sell their diamonds for less as it raised the costs of trafficking these diamonds, even though it did not necessarily make diamond mining itself more difficult (Cater 2003). The issue of conflict diamonds started to get far more coverage in the media and the potential for a reduction in demand for diamonds and even a boycott forced actors to pay attention to an issue that was once overlooked.

The threat of a consumer boycott and the possibility of declining demand for diamonds led to the creation of the Kimberley Process in 2000 (Bieri 2010a). According to the Kimberley Process agreement, states would be responsible for passing domestic legislation that complied with the Kimberley Process regulations.[4] Compliance with the Kimberley Process is straightforward, in that all diamonds that are produced within a state or enter a state's borders are supposed to be accompanied with a certificate of origin and held in a "tamper-resistant container" (Kimberley Process 2013a). It is up to the states to print the certificates and to enforce the certification process. A state that complies at a high level is successful in certifying most of the diamonds that either originate or enter its territory. On the other hand, where diamonds either originate in a country that does not provide certification or enter its territory without certification there are low levels of compliance. Since the Kimberley Process deals directly with the transborder trade of a resource, cooperation between states is a necessary, but not always sufficient, condition for a high level of compliance. Primarily, cooperation between states involves coordination between law enforcement agencies to prevent uncertified diamonds from being smuggled across a border. Other instances of cooperation involve sharing technology, expertise or other resources to make it easier for a state to comply.

Most states had diamond regulation systems in place before the Kimberley Process, mainly for taxation purposes and to stop smuggling that led to tax evasion. These systems were often unsuccessful, especially in states where diamonds contributed to conflict.[5] The Kimberley Process did change policy in virtually all member states

[4] For instance, in 2003 the United States passed the "Clean Diamond Trade Act" and joined the process (Public Law 108-19 2003).

[5] See Reno (1995, 1998).

because under the process they must address the issue of diamonds that originated from outside their borders and entered the legitimate trade without being accounted for (Bockstael 2008). This had not been a prominent issue before the process, but because most major diamond importers joined the Kimberley Process, these regulations became de facto requirements for countries that wanted to access most of the world's market. The Kimberley Process decided on consensus decision-making, in which each member state or "participant" would have a vote.

In an idyllic scenario, Kimberley Process certification would be able to trace diamonds from where they were mined to their final export destination, but this has proven difficult (Bockstael 2008). Since the beginning of the Kimberley Process in January 2003, the ability for the process to deal with the problem of conflict diamonds and create a reliable certification scheme for all diamonds is a matter of debate (Bieri 2010a). Some argue that conflict diamonds are not nearly as prevalent as they once were and that the Kimberley Process has been able to accomplish international cooperation on this challenging issue.[6] The Kimberley Process has come under increased scrutiny as several observers have argued that the process is deeply flawed and does not have a decision-making structure that allows for effective regulation of the global diamond trade.[7]

While most critics of the Kimberley Process see it as not going far enough in regulating conflict diamonds, some argue that the project of certifying the global diamond trade to prevent "conflict diamonds" is inherently problematic. For instance, Siegel (2009) argues that the Kimberley Process is misguided in that it is dominated by Western countries that do not understand local dynamics in Africa, it may hurt poor diamond miners in Africa if consumers are less likely to buy their diamonds, and trying to certify diamonds for countries that have never been tied to conflict diamonds is a waste of resources. Thus, according to this view, the Kimberley Process is an example of what Easterly (2006) has termed the "white man's burden," in which Western states

[6] For instance, the World Diamond Council (2013) portrays the very existence of the Kimberley Process as being a success. See also Taylor (2012).

[7] This has been a particularly common line of criticism from nongovernmental organizations that helped create the Kimberley Process, such as Global Witness (2011a) and Partnership Africa Canada (2006, 2013), and some activists and scholars, see Murphy (2011); Smille (2010b).

try and "help" poor states by imposing policies that do not consider local factors. According to this perspective, this can leave the people who are supposed to benefit from these policies worse off than if Western states had never interfered in the first place.[8]

Anatomy of a "Weak" Regime

To situate this study in the overall literature of international agreements and to understand the nature of the Kimberley Process as an institution, we will look at the nature of the agreement here. Two central points need to be made about the institutional history of the Kimberley Process. First, it is a weak agreement with little ability to use sanctions or other mechanisms to shape state responses. This illustrates that Kimberley Process interaction with states alone is insufficient to understand variation between states and temporally in a single state. Second, the decision-making process and relative influence that the Kimberley Process has had, in its ability to influence state behavior, has been relatively constant since its implementation in 2003. Thus, changes in state response to the Kimberley Process over time have little to do with changes in the institutional nature of this agreement.

The Kimberley Process is based on consensus decision-making in which every "participant" country has a vote. With fifty-four participants in the Kimberley Process, any one of them can block a resolution. A useful theory in understanding how institutions function is the "veto players" theory developed by Tsebelis (2002). According to this theory, the more actors there are that can block a resolution the smaller the "win set" or the acceptable range of outcomes to all actors will be. It follows from this that the more actors there are that have a veto over changing policy the harder it will be to change it significantly. Furthermore, in institutions where there are several veto players, change to a "status quo" policy is usually slow and changes to current policy are more incremental because this is usually acceptable to more actors.[9] It

[8] See also Easterly (2013); Moyo (2009).

[9] Another important political organization that used consensus decision-making was the General Agreement on Tariffs and Trade (GATT), in which votes on an issue were a possibility but almost never happened (Scott and Watal 2000). This was one of the factors that caused the GATT to decline or become impractical over time. Scott and Watal (2000, 284) describe how consensus worked under the GATT: "the system worked by consensus: no votes on senseless resolutions, no

could be predicted from veto player theory that the United Nations, which has five veto players, would be able to act far more efficiently in regulating conflict diamonds than the Kimberley Process, although this has never been looked at in a study. This theory applies to a wide variety of institutions. As Tsebelis (2002) argues, the number of veto players is more important in looking at decision-making than how these veto players are selected.[10]

Given the number of veto players, the Kimberley Process has had difficulty in acting forcefully as an institution. Nevertheless, the agreement has been under constant pressure to appear relevant. These dynamics have led to a situation where sanctions have been imposed on some countries, and the goal has been to appear to be taking a hard line while still ignoring larger violators or countries with issues of noncompliance that the process would have a harder time pursuing politically. A good example of these dynamics is Ghana, a country where diamonds had been banned from November 24 to December 5, 2006, and February 17 to March 7, 2007. Through interviews with miners, Hilson and Clifford (2010, 449) found that

> reflecting on the impacts of the ban, many miners and buyers interviewed in Akwatia expressed concern over why Ghana was targeted and not countries

decisions by majority rule. The consensus rule was not abused. Developed countries, particularly the United States and European Community, drove the GATT agenda and negotiations but did not insist on full participation by all countries." When GATT expanded into the World Trade Organization (WTO), consensus no longer worked because there were too many members, and more was at stake for all members, so that "free riding" off other decisions became more impractical (Schott 1994). Therefore, the GATT trading system reached a point where consensus decision-making was no longer efficient. By looking at the GATT we can see a weaker international organization that was able to use consensus for a while, but this system broke down when there was more at stake for specific countries. Given how the GATT worked for many years, it seems as though there would be disincentives for actors to try and push forward any change that would clearly fall well short of consensus, even if this is what they wanted. Thus, it is easy to see how this decision-making system affected both the boundaries of what would be decided and the influence that the GATT had over trade in general. The history of consensus in the GATT trade regulations would seem to predict that institutions that use consensus decision-making, such as the Kimberley Process, will have difficulty making controversial decisions or significant change in policy over a short time.

10 For instance, according to Tsebelis (2002), the number of veto players a government has is more important to the study of policymaking than whether a government is presidential or parliamentary.

such as Sierra Leone, Guinea, or the DRC – where diamond smuggling is arguably a far more pressing concern. Did Kimberley officials target Ghana because of the potential to make a more visible impact – and in the process, appease critics such as Amnesty International and Global Witness?

While the diamond sector is vital for some areas of the economy in Ghana, it is not pivotal to the economic or political structure of the society as a whole, at least in comparison to several countries in sub-Saharan Africa. Thus, this might be a case where the Kimberley Process could pursue sanctions that may change policy to some extent by showing countries that the process has some coercive power, which they would not want to challenge. However, it does not set a direct precedent in which a larger diamond producer is suspended.[11]

From reviewing the few cases in which sanctions have been implemented, listed in Table 1.1, two central claims can be made. First, the consensus nature of decision-making in the Kimberley Process results in suboptimal policy outcomes that rarely impose sanctions on diamond-producing countries. Second, the Kimberley Process does appear to have some ability to impose sanctions for one type of state:

[11] After some smaller producers were found to have smuggled coffee into other countries that had not exceeded their quota, the International Coffee Organization instituted a certification mechanism that was to be collected by importing countries. Countries that exceeded their quota could be penalized by "excess shipments from one year be deducted from the quota for the next; that excess shipments in a second year be penalized by a doubling of the deduction in the next; and that a third violation lead to the loss of voting rights and the possibility of expulsion from the International Coffee Organization" (Bates 1997, 145–146). These rules only constrained the behavior of small producers who had little influence on the decision-making process of the organization. Voting structures in the organization followed the market share, so Brazil and Columbia dominated the decision-making process by being able to outvote the smaller producers. Given the power distribution in the International Coffee Organization, rules were set up so that the major voters would be unlikely to break them and would not face sanctions if they did. Compliance among the large producers was taken as a given, especially since they set the rules themselves and there was a clear economic incentive to do so. However, the International Coffee Organization did have the potential to affect the production levels of smaller producers that lacked political influence in the organization. While some countries did consistently violate their quotas, the organization lacked the capacity and political will to enforce them. Smuggled coffee made up a small enough share of the global market that it was not crucial to change the behavior of small producing countries, even if they produced well beyond their quota. Therefore, sanctions by the International Coffee Organization only existed for one type of member and had no record of enforcing compliance.

Table 1.1 *List of countries in the Kimberley Process and sanctions*

All members[3]	Problematic countries	Review visits[3]	Missions[3]	Indirect sanctions	Suspension	Expulsion	UN sanctions[7]
Angola	Angola[1]	Angola	CAR (June 8–15, 2003)	Ivory Coast (United Nations Ban 2005–present[7])	Central African Republic (March 17–July 15, 2003[4] and May 23, 2013–present[5])	Congo (ROC) 2004–2007[7]	Angola (1998–2002),
Armenia	Brazil[1]	Armenia	Republic of Congo (May 31–June 3, 2004)	Venezuela ("self-suspended" 2008–present)[7]	Lebanon (April 1, 2004–June 2006[6])		Sierra Leone (2000–2003),
Australia	CAR[2]	Australia	Zimbabwe (June 30–July 4, 2009 and August 9–14, 2010)		Ghana (November 24–December 5, 2006 and February 17–March 7, 2007[8])		Liberia (2000–2007)
Bangladesh	Congo (DRC)[1]	Bangladesh					Ivory Coast (2005–present)
Belarus	Congo (ROC)[1]	Belarus					
Botswana	Côte d'Ivoire[1, 2]	Botswana					
Brazil	Ghana[1, 2]	Brazil					
Cambodia	Guinea[1]	Canada					
Cameroon	Guyana[1]	CAR					
Canada	Lebanon[2]	China					
CAR	Liberia[1]	Cote d'Ivoire					
China	Sierra Leone[1]	DR Congo					
Congo (DRC)	Togo[1]	EU					
Congo (ROC)	Venezuela[1, 2]	Ghana					
Côte d'Ivoire	Zimbabwe[2]	Guinea					
Croatia		Guyana					
EU		India					
Ghana		Israel					
Guinea		Japan					
Guyana		Laos					
India		Lebanon					
Indonesia		Lesotho					
		Liberia					
		Malaysia					

Israel
Kazakhstan
Japan
Laos
Lebanon
Lesotho
Liberia
Malaysia
Mauritius
Mexico
Namibia
New Zealand
Norway
Panama
Russia
Sierra Leone
Singapore
South Africa
South Korea
Sri Lanka
Swaziland
Switzerland
Tanzania
Thailand
Togo

Mauritius
Namibia
New Zealand
Norway
Republic of Congo
Russia
Sierra Leone
South Africa
South Korea
Sri Lanka
Switzerland
Tanzania
Thailand
Togo
Turkey
UAE
Ukraine
USA
Zimbabwe

Table 1.1 (*cont.*)

All members[3]	Problematic countries	Review visits[3]	Missions[3]	Indirect sanctions	Suspension	Expulsion	UN sanctions[7]
Turkey							
Ukraine							
UAE							
USA							
Venezuela							
Vietnam							
Zimbabwe							

1 Partnership Africa Canada (2006).
2 Smille (2010b).
3 Kimberley Process (2013b).
4 International Crisis Group (2010).
5 International Crisis Group (2010).
6 Kimberley Process (2013c).
7 Partnership Africa Canada (2013).
8 Bieri (2010a).
9 Hilson and Clifford (2010).

those that do not have a high level of domestic diamond production but serve as smuggling centers.

Examining the weakness of the Kimberley Process as an institution, especially in terms of dealing with countries that have a large amount of diamond wealth, raises the question of why states take this regime seriously at all. Furthermore, why do some states not just comply at a basic level that would avoid sanctions, which from the history of the Kimberley Process is very low, but instead spend extensive resources to implement Kimberley Process regulations? This is an important question because, as Knill and Lehmkuhl (2002, 42) point out, "the development, formulation, and implementation of international policies are generally a highly time-consuming and complex process." Thus, the study of state responses to the Kimberley Process is an ideal case for understanding state behavior in relation to international agreements in general, especially those that have weak enforcement mechanisms. Furthermore, it is a goal of this study to uncover the complexity that leads to variation in state responses to international regimes.

The Domestic Political Economy of International Regimes

In the study of international agreements there has been a long debate between scholars who argue that international agreements seldom change state behavior (Goldsmith and Posner 2005; Mearsheimer 2004) and those that view international agreements as having the ability to make states pursue policies that they would not otherwise (Alter 2014; Hillebrecht 2014; Keohane 1984; Keohane and Nye 1977; Simmons 2009).[12] This approach assumes the latter in that under some conditions international agreements can constrain state behavior. However, this is not necessarily because of the nature of the international agreement itself, as some agreements if not most are notorious for having little independent power to constrain states. Instead, when examining international agreements, especially those with clear economic aspects, it can be domestic private actors that shape state responses to international agreements and get states to pursue policies that they would be unlikely to pursue otherwise.

[12] A useful overview of the theoretical debate on international regimes is given by Haggard and Simmons (1987).

The first area of inquiry in the domestic political economy approach is to look at how dependent a state is on an economic sector that could potentially influence the decision-making process around a regime. This part of the theory draws from the "dependency school," which argues that government actors in states where resource exports dominate the economy are often dependent on this sector for revenue and thus constrained in the policy options that are available to them (Frank 1966, 1978; Rodney 1974; Smith and Lee 2018; Taylor 2016; Wallerstein 1974, 2004). This theory also draws on the idea of political survival, in that governments are likely to form policy preferences in economic governance that improve their ability to hold onto state power regardless of what is best for the average citizen or prior ideological predispositions (Bueno De Mesquita et al. 2005).

In many relevant economic sectors, preferences around state responses to international regimes vary. In states where private economic firms have considerable influence over policy preferences, which increases according to how dependent a government is on the economic sector, it is essential to figure out what the preferences of these actors are. Preferences of private actors can often differ in terms of their preferred policies concerning international agreements. For example, Robert Falkner (2008) examines how the conflict between firms that have numerous different interests and viewpoints over regulation can partially explain why cooperation around environmental issues varies considerably in different regimes. This is an important point because usually private firms in the same economic sector do not have the same goals. In this approach, the preferences and relative power distribution between private economic actors are used to explain variation in state-level responses to the Kimberley Process, across countries and across time within the same country.

The influence of private actors is an understudied area in the literature on regimes, especially in terms of explaining variation in state responses in a single regime. However, international agreements have the potential for economic actors to lock in favored policy preferences at an international level and support regulations that improve their market position against competitors. The desire of private firms to influence regulatory policy has long been observed on a domestic level by neoclassical economists. These scholars argue that regulation can be a good way for large firms to maximize profit against competitors and convince governments to take on regulatory costs that the firm would have to pay in the absence of regulation (Akerlof 1970; Bates 1998a; Peltzman 1976; Stigler 1971).[13] Furthermore, multiple scholars have found that a motivating factor behind participation in international agreements around human rights issues is to lock in policy preferences for future government administrations (Cardenas 2007; Hillebrecht 2014; Simmons 2009). According to this logic, future government administrations will face more constraints in changing state policy at an international level than they would if the policy process only took place domestically. Thus, there is good reason to believe that economic actors see the potential for international agreements to lock in policy preferences. This may particularly be the case if firms anticipate a future decline in power relative to competitors and desire to maintain preferred policy preferences well into a future where they are likely to have less control over the domestic decision-making process.

Diamonds, Geography, and State Capacity

In addition to making an argument about the political economy of state responses to international agreements, this research also draws on past studies in both the political geography and "resource curse" literature. It may be the case that some states intend to comply with the Kimberley Process, but the distribution of diamonds in the country and an overall lack of state capacity could make compliance difficult.[14] Weak states may require cooperation from members of the Kimberley Process to maintain higher levels of compliance given the challenges to certifying diamonds in that state. Thus, while examining diamond dependence and the preferences of private actors can give us an

[13] A classic example of the complexity of regulatory policy is the support that some large meat-packing companies gave to government regulation of the industry after *The Jungle* by Upton Sinclair (1906) was published. Some large meat-packing companies calculated that they could better pay the costs of regulation in comparison to smaller competitors, thus allowing them to gain an advantage in the competition over market share. For more information on the role of regulation in the meat-packing industry see Azzam and Anderson (1996). The global chemical sector has experienced some of these dynamics as well. Garcia-Johnson (2000) argues that large American chemical companies have pushed for more environmental regulations in South America to secure a comparative advantage and have raised their own environmental standards in anticipation of policy changes.

[14] This idea draws from the "managerial school" developed by Chayes and Chayes (1993, 1998).

understanding of what leads to cooperation with the Kimberley Process, political geography becomes a crucial intervening variable in understanding compliance. Alternatively, even if the level of domestic diamond dependence, the preferences of private actors and cooperation would predict a high level of compliance with the Kimberley Process, it is possible that this might not be the case because of a political geography that makes regulation of the diamond trade difficult. Minimally it would seem as though an explanation for compliance with the Kimberley Process would be incomplete if geography were not examined, given that this has been a prominent part of the civil war literature.

There is a significant amount of literature on the role that diamonds play in civil wars.[15] This literature makes a distinction between two types of diamonds: alluvial and primary. Alluvial diamonds are usually found in the dirt or a riverbed and can be mined by individuals with little equipment, whereas primary diamonds require expensive extraction procedures and significant capital investments. The former is more tied to conflict and diamond smuggling in general, as it provides an opportunity for rebel groups to get immediate funding since all that is needed is the control of a region where diamonds are found, and individuals to mine for them. Ross (2003) points out that the most common way for rebel groups to finance themselves is looting and to Le Billon (2008) diamonds are the "ultimate loot" for a rebel group.

In the civil war literature, scholars have debated whether alluvial diamond wealth makes a country more at risk for civil war.[16] There is little debate that in some cases rebel groups have acquired a substantial amount of funding from diamond mining. For instance, in Sierra Leone the Revolutionary United Front made about $25–75 million a year from diamonds, and in Angola the National Union for the Total Independence of Angola (UNITA) made about $200–500 million a year (Le Billon 2012). Therefore, under some conditions, diamonds can provide a lucrative funding source for rebels. Challenges with regulating illegal mining are prominent in the literature that looks at local diamond mining, as even if diamonds are not tied to conflict there

[15] Some of the most influential studies are: Humphreys (2005); Le Billon (2008, 2012); Lujala, Gleditsch, and Gilmore (2005); Ross (2004a, 2004b, 2006).

[16] For a meta-analysis of research on the influence diamond wealth has on conflict, see Le Billon (2008).

can still be an incentive to escape taxation (Gooch 2008).[17] The interest that conflict diamonds received led to more research on alluvial diamond mining in general.[18] Thus, looking at the dynamics caused by the geographical location of diamonds and the type of diamonds a country has are essential in studying state responses to the Kimberley Process.

Diamond Mining in Independent Africa

From the discovery of diamonds in South Africa in 1866 until the end of 2013, Africa is estimated to have produced almost 3.2 Bct out of a total global production of 5.03 Bct, or 63.6% of all diamonds that have ever been mined.

(de Wit et al. 2016, 199)

Anyone who visits the Namibian coast today is likely to encounter "ghost towns" that have been completely abandoned. Towns such as Pomona or Kolmanskop were once vibrant mining communities, around the time of World War One, but today they are silent, with only tourists visiting.[19] These towns are witness to the changing nature of diamond mining in Namibia, as over half of diamond mining since the early 2000s takes place offshore, and most mining otherwise is centered around Oranjemund, a restricted city on the far southern coast. While the "diamond rush" may be long over, the diamond sector in African states is still as important as ever, if not more so. Understanding the political economy of the modern diamond sector in sub-Saharan Africa is vital to understanding the region more generally and the variation that exists between states that have some important similarities.

In 1867 diamonds were first discovered in Southern Africa and would play an essential role in the development of the modern

[17] This has been documented in Sierra Leone (Wilson 2011), Ghana (Banchirigah 2008), Cameroon, and the Central African Republic (International Crisis Group 2010; Schure et al. 2011).

[18] For example: Le Billon (2008, 2012); Munier (2016b); Snyder and Bhavnani (2005).

[19] De Juan, Krautwald, and Pierskalla (2017) demonstrate that during German colonization the police force was mostly concentrated on ensuring resource extraction, especially of diamonds.

Southern African state.[20] From the late 1800s onward, De Beers essentially held a monopoly on the legal rough diamond trade as the founder, Cecil Rhodes, bought all competitors in Southern Africa. This gave De Beers a dominance over the diamond industry that was mostly unrivaled by any other company in any other major economic sector worldwide. More important for the socioeconomic development of African states, this gave De Beers a wide range of influence not just on mining sector policy but on economic policy more broadly.

Diamonds entering the global market outside of De Beers' control caused a constant challenge to the company's near monopoly over the global diamond trade. This led De Beers to either buy these diamonds or convince governments to secure the diamond trade. In some weak African states with large deposits of alluvial diamonds, this led to longstanding political engagements with local governments to secure the diamond fields or allow De Beers to use private security to prevent smuggling and police local areas. In some regions that were particularly difficult to govern, in states where De Beers had a high level of influence, such as Angola or Sierra Leone, De Beers was able to take over many of the local administrative functions usually associated with states.[21] These arrangements became difficult to continue after independent African states replaced colonial regimes. Furthermore, in the 1990s arrangements that were made between De Beers and some of the larger diamond producers would break down altogether. Diamonds from conflict zones, particularly in Angola and Sierra Leone, presented a challenge to the De Beers monopoly, as these diamonds accounted for as much as 15 percent of the global trade (Global Witness 2006). Thus, at the end of the 1990s, De Beers faced a situation in which its near monopoly over the global diamond trade was no longer sustainable, and change became inevitable.

Change and Competition in the Global Diamond Trade

Changes in the global diamond trade, particularly since the early 2000s when the Kimberley Process first came into effect, have had a

[20] Comprehensive historical accounts of diamond mining in Southern Africa are given by Meredith (2008); Roberts (2016).

[21] Examples of historical mining communities under the control of De Beers are the Luanda province of Angola (Cleveland 2015) and the Kono district of Sierra Leone (Reno 1995).

significant influence on the domestic political economy of states in Africa. De Beers' share of the global value in rough diamonds has dropped considerably, from about 85 percent in the late 1980s to about 65 percent when the company decided to give up on price fixing the global market in 2000 (Stein 2001). In 2010 De Beers' market share was at about 45 per cent and in 2018 at about 37 percent (Zimnisky 2018). While this decline is notable, it is important to point out that De Beers continues to be the largest company in the diamond sector globally and when looking at Southern Africa it still occupies a position of dominance, especially in Botswana, Namibia, and South Africa.

The investor who would be able to capitalize on changes in the global diamond sector, and ultimately be the first to mount a credible challenge De Beers in Africa, was an Israeli citizen who once had close ties to De Beers. Lev Leviev was born in Tashkent, Uzbekistan in 1956 and immigrated to Israel in 1971.[22] In Israel, Leviev opened a diamond-cutting factory in 1977 and quickly expanded to twelve factories. Leviev became a sightholder for De Beers in 1987. The system of being forced to blindly buy boxes of diamonds at any price De Beers wanted gave Leviev a desire to challenge this system. Forming a joint company with the Soviet-owned firm Alarosa gave Leviev a chance to supply rough diamonds directly to polishing companies without De Beers' involvement. When mass privatization took place

[22] Largely through changes in global diamond trade, Leviev has become one of the world's wealthiest and most influential people. In 2004, Leviev was worth about US$2 billion (The Economist 2004). In 2007 he had an estimated wealth of $4.1 billion although some suspect that it may be double this (Chafets 2007). Leviev is known for extensive spending on charity, possibly around $50 million a year (Chafets 2007). Through this immense wealth Leviev has been able to gain an influence on global politics in many different contexts. Most of Leviev's giving has been for Jewish charities, especially in the former Soviet Union where he grew up (Chafets 2007). He has been known to fund the Orthodox Jewish Hasidic Chabad group in many endeavors and is seen as a leader in the movement. Leviev has also been a consistent supporter of right-wing Israeli politics and was long suspected of investing in Jewish settlements in the Palestinian territory. Bowing to international pressure in 2014, Leviev disbanded a plan to build 935 apartments in West Jerusalem and stopped building in Palestinian territory (Mezzofiore 2014). Leviev has been a longtime friend of Russian president Vladimir Putin and has had some economic and political influence in Russia (Green 2017). Leviev also gained publicity for alleged ties to Donald Trump and his son-in-law Jared Kushner through New York real estate deals (Green 2017).

after the fall of the Soviet Union Leviev would emerge as the sole private owner of Alarosa in a joint agreement with the Russian government.

In 1996 Leviev first entered the Angolan diamond market with an investment of US$60 million. The People's Movement for the Liberation of Angola (MPLA) government had long resented De Beers' control of the Angolan diamond trade and the firm's willingness to buy any rough diamonds that became available in the country, including those that originated in UNITA-controlled areas. In 2001 De Beers suspended operations in Angola altogether, leaving Leviev as the sole active partner with the MPLA government in the diamond sector. Although De Beers did continue to maintain negotiations and some ties with the MPLA government in this period, when the Angolan civil war ended in 2002 Leviev had access to all the countries diamond mines, worth around $850 million. However, in 2003 the Angolan government moved beyond allowing Leviev to have a near monopoly over the state's legal diamond trade when it canceled over half of the mining contracts that had been signed the year before. Leviev's inability of to pay miners market value for rough diamonds may have been a significant factor in the loss of some licenses; this led to widespread smuggling as miners knew they could get more for diamonds in illegal channels. Nevertheless, Leviev was able to operate successfully in a region where De Beers had long monopolized the legal diamond trade.

By the early 2000s, Lev Leviev had become a direct challenge to De Beers across Southern Africa. He started making inroads into the rough diamond trade in Namibia, in return for a promise to beneficiate some of the diamonds locally. On June 28, 2004 Lev Leviev opened the largest diamond polishing plant in Africa at the time in Namibia. Lev Leviev's involvement in Namibia would have important implications for establishing Kimberley Process regulations in the country and became a way for the Namibian government to leverage influence with De Beers. In the early 2000s, Leviev tried to attract interest from Botswana to allow him to mine for diamonds in the country. Government officials showed interest and even toured some of his operations in Namibia. However, allowing Leviev to invest in the country never materialized, and De Beers maintained its critical monopoly in Botswana. Leviev has been willing to set up local diamond beneficiation plants in Angola and Namibia, even if this does not turn a profit directly, in order to get governments in the region to provide him with more access to mining rough diamonds.[23]

For many years Leviev has had ties to the Hong Kong-based company the 88 Queensway Group. This group has extensive mining investments in Angola and Zimbabwe.[24] While Leviev does not appear to own any diamond mines in Zimbabwe directly, it is likely he has invested in companies that do. However, given the secretive nature of the diamond contract in Zimbabwe, ownership can be hard to determine.

Beyond Leviev, the significant challenge for De Beers came with the massive discovery of diamonds in the Marange region in eastern Zimbabwe. De Beers had long dominated mining in Zimbabwe but had fallen out with the Mugabe regime over the push for indigenization policies. Until 2006 De Beers had exploration rights in the Marange region and was allegedly mining for diamonds without public knowledge (Katsaura 2010a; Southhall 2013). After 2006 De Beers was removed from the diamond fields and a government monopsony was set up. However, De Beers continues to claim a right to the diamond fields (Nyamunda and Mukwambo 2012).

The absence of De Beers from the Zimbabwean mining sector has allowed a large number of rough diamonds to be produced in Southern Africa outside of the company's control. Private diamond companies did not gain access to the Marange diamond fields until 2009, and most did not start mining until 2011. Previously, the government had tried a monopsony until 2008, when the military took over the diamond fields directly. From 2011, until the government nationalized diamond mining in 2016, many private diamond companies had joint extraction agreements with the Zimbabwean government through the Zimbabwe Mining Development Corporation (ZMDC).

The most prominent diamond companies were Anjin, a partially Chinese-owned company, and Mbada Diamonds. Both diamond companies had secretive ownership structures and are believed to have had ties to factions within Zimbabwe African National Union-Patriotic

[23] Information about Lev Leviev was drawn from Smith (2007); Stein (2001). See also a profile published by *Forbes*, which can be found at www.forbes.com/global/2003/0915/046.html#7f3374bc4567 and *The Economist*, which can be found at www.economist.com/node/2921462

[24] For more about the 88 Queensway Group and alleged connections with Lev Leviev, see Lee, Ross, and Warner (2009); Mailey (2015); Melman (2010).

Front (ZANU-PF).[25] While neither of these companies had any real chance of challenging De Beers in other African states, it is telling that they exist at all. Without the changes that the global diamond industry went through in the early 2000s, it is likely that the Zimbabwean government would have turned to De Beers to mine the Marange diamond fields out of necessity.

With challenges to De Beers' dominance in Africa since 2000, other options that do not involve De Beers in the mining sector have become an increasing possibility for states. Furthermore, the threat of ending or modifying longstanding agreements with De Beers has given states more bargaining power. These dynamics have had important implications for how these states responded to the Kimberley Process after 2003, as will be demonstrated in depth in the case study chapters.

Talking Left and Walking Right

At the dawn of independence in Africa, Algerian writer Franz Fanon (1963) predicted that the new elite would obscure the same exploitive policies that existed under colonialism with leftist rhetoric. The global economy has changed dramatically since this time but when the diamond trade is examined Fanon's prediction has been accurate. From all the cases examined in this study, "liberation" movements promised transformative change in mining policy after independence yet for the most part once in power they found themselves trying to justify aspects of the former status quo. While these governments had far more legitimacy than their predecessors, in many cases there was continuity in policy, at least in the sense that mining wealth was rarely used for public goods provision.

The African diamond trade can be viewed as a mode of exchange. Lie (1992, 510) defines a mode of exchange as "an ensemble of traders engaged in commodity exchange under historically specific technological and socio-institutional constraints. Exchange relations among traders, while central in this framework, stem from the underlying dynamic of macrostructural change. Macrostructural changes create opportunities for groups to construct exchange networks and to establish social organizations with an infrastructure, rules and norms." This definition is useful for examining the African states in general because

[25] See Global Witness (2012a, 2017a) and Chapter 5.

if new opportunities for exchange are not being created and rules and norms are relatively similar then this means that "macrostructural" change is not taking place. This research presents the current mode of exchange that exists in the African diamond sector because of a complex bargaining process between private firms and African governments. When examining the African state, it is important to note that in some cases private firms can have "power" comparable to the state itself, if not more, in deciding policies in some sectors.

Several observers, including Fanon (1963), mainly focused on the "mode of production" in postindependence Africa. What we can see from examining the diamond trade is that as important is the "mode of exchange" in which Africans at all levels, including government elites, get systematically shortchanged in the bargaining process. The clearest example of this is that, despite multiple efforts by African governments not just to produce rough diamonds but also to participate in the beneficiation process, and thus keep far more of the country's diamond wealth within its borders, these attempts have always failed.[26] Thus, sub-Saharan Africa remains at both the bottom of both the production process and the exchange process where both local producers and states only receive a fraction of what their diamond wealth is worth. In fact, in 2014 the overall value of legal diamonds traded from India was US$17,000 billion according to Kimberley Process (2014) statistics. This is from a country that has very little production but serves as the world's major polishing center. Furthermore, Israel. which had no domestic diamond production in 2014, traded almost US$5 billion worth of diamonds according to Kimberley Process (2014) statistics. These increases in diamond value may however pale in comparison to how much dealers eventually get for selling them in Western countries, especially when it comes to diamonds that can be used for jewelry, most of which originally came from Africa.

While African countries are often portrayed as being aid dependent, it is notable that the value of aid is only worth a small fraction of what they export in diamonds, gold, oil and other minerals every year.

[26] Botswana, Namibia, and South Africa have all made attempts to beneficiate more diamonds locally (Grynberg 2015). Interestingly, Botswana has been most successful in creating opportunities for local beneficiation, whereas the most "powerful" state in the region, South Africa, has been least successful. Increasing political pressure in these states is likely to make diamond benefaction an important political issue.

Burgos (2015) referred to this as a "looting machine" in which local government leaders in Africa are often complacent with this process but are also constrained in their ability to change this reality without facing state collapse or a backlash from powerful global actors. It is within this context that the Kimberley Process was first implemented and continues to operate. As we will see from this study, in practice the Kimberley Process has reinforced the position of De Beers, and large multinational companies in general, with little benefit to the local population. While the Kimberley Process was implemented under the auspices of change, it has served to reinforce an unequal "mode of exchange" in the global diamond trade that has little to do with its original intent.

At a time when the process of exchanging goods is getting increased attention from political economists across the political spectrum, this study of the Kimberley Process is ideal for understanding the role of international agreements in either reinforcing past patterns of exchange or facilitating new ones.[27] Furthermore, with the growth of international agreements in regulating or reinforcing traditional patterns of exchange, a function that once fell solidly in the realm of state behavior, it is essential to examine what this means for these patterns and the actors involved. When more of the decision-making process in terms of domestic policy is outsourced to international agreements, does that enhance the higher level of democracy and positive cooperation between states that this is supposed to facilitate? Alternatively, is this a way of reinforcing already existing patterns of economic behavior in a changing world in which domestic governments are no longer capable of providing the context in which the same patterns can be followed? It is these crucial questions that this project hopes to understand better.

Compliance, Cooperation, and Cases

In this study, I use a most-similar comparative case study design to examine Angola, Central African Republic, Namibia, Sierra Leone, and Zimbabwe.[28] These five cases are similar in many respects except

[27] See Collier (2010); Karatani (2014); Yifu Lin (2012).

[28] This research relies predominantly on case study research. Creswell (2013, 97) defines a case study as "a qualitative approach in which the investigator explores a real-life, contemporary bounded system (a case) or multiple bounded systems

for their level of compliance and cooperation with the Kimberley Process (Basedau 2005a, 2005b; Geddes 2003; King, Keohane, and Verba 1994; Landman 2003). These cases provide a significant amount of variation in their response to the Kimberley Process, both in comparison to each other and within single states over time. All five cases I have chosen are alluvial diamond producers in sub-Saharan Africa that have a significant diamond trade and have emerged from conflict. Therefore, it is an interesting puzzle why these states that have several similarities have nevertheless varied in their response to the Kimberley Process.

This research uses a most-similar method of case selection. For this purpose, cases need to be similar except for the dependent variable, which should vary (Basedau 2005a, 2005b; Geddes 2003; King, Keohane, and Verba 1994; Landman 2003). With a most-similar design "the researcher looks for cases that differ on the outcomes of theoretical interest but are similar on various factors that might have contributed to that outcome" (Gerring 2007, 131). For this research, I have selected a small-*N* of five countries: Angola, Central African Republic, Namibia, Sierra Leone, and Zimbabwe. These cases were chosen because they are similar in several ways, but the dependent variable – compliance/cooperation with the Kimberley Process – varies. The most important similarity for these countries is that the diamond industry is pivotal to the economic and political nature of the countries. Table 1.2 shows some characteristics of these states.

over time, through detailed, in-depth data collection involving multiple sources of information (e.g. observations, interviews, audiovisual material, and documents and reports), and reports a case description and case themes." Here I will focus on textual analysis of documents to build a thick description of the cases and interviews to better understand the Kimberley Process. A major benefit of the case study approach is the potential for thick analysis of the cases. According to Merriam (2009, 50), "the case study offers a means of investigating complex social units consisting of multiple variables of potential importance in understanding the phenomena." Along the same lines, Creswell (2013, 100) says "a hallmark of a good qualitative case study is that it presents an in-depth understanding of a case." Thus, in-depth discussion of many important variables and contextual factors are what case studies are best for. As Creswell (2013, 100) goes on to say, "relying on one source of data is typically not enough to develop this in-depth understanding." Therefore, it will be a goal of this study to approach the research question from as many angles as possible, as this is consistent with case study methodology.

Table 1.2 *Country indicators*

Country name	State fragility (2017)[1]	HDI Index (2018)[2]	Diamond-related conflict[3]	Type of diamonds[3]	Production in carats (2017)[4]	Value in dollars (2017)[4]
Angola	16	0.581	Yes	Both	9,438,802.06	1,104,622,553
Central African Republic	23	0.367	Yes	Alluvial	47,636.70	6,505,304.82
Namibia	5	0.647	No	Alluvial	1,948,412.28	1,010,716,178
Sierra Leone	13	0.419	Yes	Alluvial	289,141	122,316,627
Zimbabwe	17	0.535	No	Both	2,507,604	175,379,664

1 Marshall and Elzinga-Marshall (2017).
2 United Nations Development Program (2018).
3 Le Billon (2008).
4 Kimberley Process Diamond Statistics (2017).

One could argue that any country that is a Kimberley Process member could have been chosen. However, these countries are selected because they represent a variety of cases in which the effectiveness of the Kimberley Process matters. Thus, they are all large producers of diamonds, have a history where diamond wealth has been influential, and will continue to have large diamond sectors well into the future. Participants that are large importers of diamonds, such as the United States or the European Union, are unlikely ever to face sanctions from the process and while their compliance might not be perfect, it is not controversial. Therefore, all cases have been chosen from sub-Saharan Africa, a region where diamonds have often been tied to conflict, where compliance with the Kimberley Process has been the most difficult, but at the same time most important.

In terms of setting up a useful most-similar case study it is notable that, at least in terms of formal decision-making, the Kimberley Process has varied little as an institution since its founding. Therefore, the amount of pressure the institution places on states and the type of response it expects in return is to a large degree constant. Thus, this is an important constant across all cases that make the explanatory potential of these cases greater than if compliance and cooperation were examined across different agreements or a single agreement that had undergone significant institutional change.

Sierra Leone and Angola are essential to look at as they are the countries in which diamonds have been most clearly tied to conflict in the past.[29] Despite some similar challenges, how these countries have implemented Kimberley Process rules and interacted with the process varies significantly as Sierra Leone has been inclined to cooperate with the process whereas Angola has argued that it can certify its diamonds on its own (Grant 2012). The Central African Republic is a crucial case for this study because it is the only country where most observers can agree that "conflict diamonds" have originated since the Kimberley Process was implemented in 2003.[30] Furthermore, the Central African

[29] In fact, these cases are often used as examples of diamonds contributing directly to conflict (Le Billon 2008, 2012; Ross 2004a, 2004b, 2006; Snyder 2006; Snyder and Bhavnani 2005).

[30] See Global Witness (2017b); International Peace Information Service (2018); Kimberley Process (2015c).

Republic probably has the lowest level of compliance with the Kimberley Process of any country that has been part of the agreement. Zimbabwe is chosen because it has become a large producer of diamonds and is the most controversial case for the Kimberley Process.[31] As discussed in the introduction, this case presents an interesting puzzle. While the Zimbabwean government has ignored numerous human rights regimes, it has at least attempted to expend resources to stay in compliance with the Kimberley Process and has attracted help from other states to do so. Namibia adds to the representativeness of the sample because it is a large producer of alluvial diamonds in sub-Saharan Africa and is not usually seen as having trouble complying with the Kimberley Process.

I analyze documents from several sources for this project. The Kimberley Process has reports of review missions and administrative decisions on specific countries. This has proven to be a useful source for measuring a state's level of diamond production, the value of exports, and insight into the role that the Kimberley Process has played in a specific state. Many governments publish reports on the diamond sector and compliance with the Kimberley Process. These documents are useful to find information on diamond production, tax structures, and challenges that countries are having with compliance domestically. Furthermore, government sources often outline which companies are operating within the country and give information about the location of diamonds. Nongovernmental organizations, particularly Global Witness and Partnership Africa Canada, frequently publish reports, often critical, on the Kimberley Process and issues related to regulating the diamond trade. These organizations are invaluable sources because they publish information that is difficult to find elsewhere. Also, nongovernmental organizations often publish reports that are country-specific and are based on local-level research. Newspapers, relevant academic scholarship, and media sources are analyzed as well. Newspapers, in particular, are useful in tracking changes in diamond policy over time.

[31] The case of Zimbabwe created a legitimacy crisis for the Kimberley Process that has never been fully resolved. One of the major sources of legitimacy for the Kimberley Process was the participation of NGOs and many left over the perceived mishandling of the Zimbabwe case (Global Witness 2011b).

Outline of Chapters

This study will proceed as follows. Chapter 2 outlines theories of compliance and cooperation with international regimes and discusses how these theories would predict state responses to the Kimberley Process. Next, the domestic political economy approach is defined, and an explanation is given of why it has more potential than past approaches to account for variation in compliance and cooperation in response to the Kimberley Process . Finally, specific hypotheses that result from this approach will be presented along with an outline of how they will be tested in the case studies.

The following chapters examine the cases of Angola, Central African Republic, Namibia, Sierra Leone, and Zimbabwe. Chapter 3 presents a case study of Angola. Of all the states examined in this research, the case of Angola best illustrates how state responses to the Kimberley Process can be a result of competition for market share. Angola was an initial member of the Kimberley Process in 2003 but was mostly indifferent to the agreement until De Beers reentered the country in 2005 after the resolution of a court case (Grant 2012; Munier 2014). De Beers' main competitor in Angola, Lev Leviev, had a monopoly over the legal trade until then. This company is known for ignoring the Kimberley Process (Globes 2011, 2012; Wall Street Journal 2010). Since De Beers has gained in market share continuously since 2005, the Angolan state has become more responsive to the Kimberley Process and served as president in 2015 (Grant 2012; Munier 2014).

Chapter 4 examines Namibia, the state with the highest level of compliance in the study. It is also the clearest example of compliance with the Kimberley Process reflecting diamond dependence, specifically the Namibian government's longstanding dependence on De Beers. Other companies have tried to enter the Namibian market, but the Kimberley Process has played an essential role in creating a regulatory environment within Namibia that is advantageous to De Beers.

Chapter 5 examines Zimbabwe, the state with the most in-country variation in response to the Kimberley Process. Zimbabwe has had five different regulatory strategies, which are defined in this study. This research argues that variation in regulatory policy is due to the political economy of factional rivalries in which Kimberley Process regulations are used as a political instrument to gain market share.

Chapter 6 emphases that the state administration in Sierra Leone is too weak to comply with the Kimberley Process at a high level, despite a preference for compliance. This shows how cooperation is a necessary but not always sufficient condition to bring about a high level of compliance. The case of Sierra Leone also brings up interesting questions over whether complying with the Kimberley Process should be a priority of a state at a low level of institutional development and is an excellent example of how Kimberley Process regulations can become a "moving target" over time.

Chapter 7 examines whether or not the Kimberley Process has been successful in preventing conflict diamonds from reaching the global market by looking at a country where "conflict" diamonds exist: the Central African Republic. The lack of any private diamond companies with a preference for compliance with the Kimberley Process means that there is almost none. Furthermore, the political geography of the country makes enforcing Kimberley Process regulations almost impossible.

The final chapter ties the findings of the case studies into the theoretical framework. Here the different cases are compared both within cases over time and with each other. The chapter ends by discussing what the findings of this study mean for understanding the big picture of state responses to international regimes, regulatory policy in the diamond sector, and the economic future of African states.

2 *The Domestic Political Economy of International Agreements*

Chapter 1 described the puzzle of compliance with the Kimberley Process, outlined the basic ideas of this study and discussed the importance of this study for understanding the role of private economic actors in international agreements. This chapter focuses systematically on the theoretical framework used in this study. It begins by defining the core concepts employed. Then multiple theories of compliance with international agreements are examined, with a focus on the predictions that can be derived from these approaches for understanding state responses to the Kimberley Process and how they compare and contrast to the approach used in this research.[1] Next is an in-depth outline of the domestic political economy approach. The chapter ends with a list of hypotheses resulting from the theory used in this study to explain variation in compliance and cooperation with the Kimberley Process.

Core Concepts

Domestic dependence, an independent variable, deals with the level of dependence on the diamond trade that could potentially constrain state actors in policymaking, thus allowing private actors more "influence" or "power." For this study, the influence actors have over decision-

[1] When examining the different theoretical schools that try and explain compliance with international agreements scholars have divided them into different categories. For instance, Simmons (1998) divides the theoretical schools up into four categories: realism, rational functionalism, domestic, and normative, whereas Hasenclever, Mayer, and Rittberger (1997) use three distinctions between those based on interest, power, and knowledge. Here I will use the terms: realism, liberalism, constructivism, critical theory, and rational functionalism. When choosing any categorization of different theories in international political economy there is always a potential that some could be oversimplified, or nuances could be overlooked. However, my goal in discussing the major theories is to examine the central ideas and identify how they are incomplete in their ability to understand state responses to international agreements, particularly the Kimberley Process.

making, or "power," will use a conceptualization from Strange (1996, 17): "the ability of a person or group of persons so to affect outcomes that their preferences take precedence over the preferences of others." This definition is useful because it includes material resources or "capabilities" but is not limited to just this. By and large, the more revenue that is gained by the government through the private diamond industry or through a joint extraction process in which the government has ownership the more dependent the state is on the private diamond trade. In some cases, there may be more to dependence than just pure material dependence, as private diamond companies may provide positive externalities such as infrastructure, access to education, or healthcare in regions where they are a dominant actor. Furthermore, they may provide jobs to a specific part of the population that would have difficulty finding them otherwise, thus filling in where the state might have to be active. Even in terms of security, an issue area that is usually seen as being up to the state, there are examples where private diamond companies have provided this on behalf of the state.[2] Given the historical role that diamond companies have played in several states, there could be a level of policy constraint that has developed over policy surrounding the diamond trade that is not just dependent on material considerations. Furthermore, diamond dependence also matters in relation to the overall economic profile of the country and how the importance of diamond wealth is viewed in the future.

Preferences of private actors, an intervening variable that is of interest in this study, examines how, given the level of state diamond dependence, private economic actors can have their policy preferences reflected in state policy. Some domestic actors may have a high preference for cooperation and compliance with the Kimberley Process, even spending their resources to this effect and making sure that in areas where they mine all diamonds are certified to the best of their administrative ability. Others may be mostly indifferent to the process or choose to avoid complying outright, as in some cases this could bring about higher profits through tax avoidance or sidestepping local administrative regulations. Given the level of influence and market share these private actors have domestically, these dynamics can be useful for explaining preferences that are reflected at the state level. Where states are very dependent on the diamond trade, it might be the

[2] See Cleveland (2015); Reno (1995, 1998).

case that private actor preferences surrounding compliance and cooperation dominate decision-making and that states matter very little. In a state where one or a few companies dominate, and they are supportive of the Kimberley Process, it is likely to lead to a high level of cooperation; the reverse may be true in states where preferences are different. If states are not very dependent on the diamond trade, it is likely that state responses to the Kimberley Process will reflect those of state actors. As these dynamics differ, as state actors gain more influence in comparison to private actors or some private actors gain more influence over the domestic political economy of a state in comparison to others, this is likely to bring about variation in cooperation and compliance with the Kimberley Process.

Political geography, an independent variable, deals with the type and distribution of diamonds that are found in a region. For a type of diamonds, there are two distinctions, alluvial and primary, the former of which has been more tied to conflict in the civil war literature.[3] Alluvial diamonds are found in the dirt or a riverbed and usually only require cheap equipment such as a shovel to extract.[4] Primary deposits are found underneath the ground and require expensive equipment and high levels of capital investment to extract. Distribution of diamonds draws upon Le Billon's (2001a) theory in which whether diamonds are distributed over a vast region or a more centrally located area leads to different political dynamics, and in this case different challenges for compliance with the Kimberley Process. This variable is important for understanding compliance because geographic characteristics are likely to vary even among states that have similar preferences for complying with the Kimberley Process; thus it has the potential to explain some of the variation.

Cooperation, a dependent variable, is explained in this study by the domestic political economy of states and is an intervening variable on the level of compliance a state has with the process. Given the global nature of Kimberley Process regulations, cooperation is necessary for a state to have a high level of compliance with the Kimberley Process, but may not be sufficient.

[3] See Humphreys (2005); Le Billon (2008, 2012); Lujala, Gleditsch, and Gilmore (2005); Munier (2016b); Ross (2004a, 2004b); Snyder and Bhavnani (2005).

[4] See Vlassenroot and Bockstael (2008).

The level of domestic diamond dependence and the preferences of private actors are predictive of the level of cooperation a state will have with the Kimberley Process, but in these cases a state may still have low levels of compliance because of difficult political geography. On the other hand, if a state's level of domestic diamond dependence and the preferences of private actors do not facilitate a state to cooperate with the Kimberley Process then a high level of compliance is not feasible given the transborder nature of Kimberley Process regulations.

Sharing technical information in order to raise a state's level of compliance with Kimberley Process regulations is necessary for many states that lack both the expertise and resources to develop or obtain this technology on their own. An essential part of cooperation deals with review missions by Kimberley Process inspectors. If a state allows review missions, cooperates when inspectors are there, and follows through on the findings of the inspectors then a state can be said to have a high level of cooperation in this regard. Cooperation also constitutes playing a role in the Kimberley Process, by participation in working groups that are important for different aspects of regulating the diamond trade, attending meetings, and serving in leadership roles. Countries that do not cooperate will try and certify diamonds without any assistance from the Kimberley Process, despite challenges they may face. Countries that do cooperate will admit to challenges they have in complying with the process, will allow inspectors/assistance from the process, and will attempt to put recommendations into government policy. If countries lack the capacity to comply with the Kimberley Process on their own, they may require "side payments" from other actors to make their level of compliance higher.[5] Some countries may go beyond taking compliance seriously within their borders and provide assistance and financial backing to states that are having trouble complying with Kimberley Process regulations on their own. Also, it is important to examine why some countries may be better able to attract cooperation from other members to comply at a higher level. Thus, it is

[5] In a seminal study on state cooperation in the water sector in Central Asia, Weinthal (2002) finds that nonstate "third parties" such as nongovernmental organizations and international institutions provided "side payments" for states that may otherwise have rejected local cooperation. Furthermore, nonstate actors were influential in creating the institutional framework in which cooperation in the water sector could take place in Central Asia. This process helped build state capacity in the region after the fall of the Soviet Union.

a goal of this study to explain why states may go "above and beyond" a minimal level of cooperation and spend scarce resources to enhance the viability of the Kimberley Process overall and why states may vary in their ability to attract assistance.

Compliance, the dependent variable, is straightforward in that the goal of the Kimberley Process is for every diamond that originates or is imported into a country to be certified. Countries that can comply certify most if not all of their diamonds and do not have much of an issue with uncertified diamonds smuggled through their borders. Countries that are unable to comply are either unable effectively to certify diamonds that originate in their borders and/or have issues with uncertified diamonds being smuggled into the country that originate from somewhere else. Kimberley Process regulations are clear in that for a country to comply fully all diamonds need to be certified. The straightforward nature of the Kimberley Process allows states participating in the Kimberley Process to avoid confusion over the basic rules and regulations that constitute compliance. Confusion over what constitutes compliance has led to noncompliance with other international agreements.[6] It is worth noting that an essential part of compliance with the Kimberley Process is that diamonds entering a state need to be certified. This presents a challenge that most states were less concerned with before the process was implemented and a dynamic that makes cooperation between states necessary for compliance.[7]

[6] Chayes and Chayes (1993, 1998) argue that often it is unclear which regulations brought about through a state's participation in an international agreement constitute compliance on a local administrative level. Furthermore, international agreements change and what constitutes compliant behavior in one time period may be viewed as no longer compliant in another. Thus, what is considered compliant behavior often represents a discourse between multiple stakeholders and not any measurable reality that is independent of this discourse.

[7] In comparison to diamonds mined domestically, diamonds that originate in a foreign state are generally less likely to attract attention from local government. Reasons for this may be because state capacity to regulate the cross-border trade in diamonds is low in many states, it is more difficult to tax them at a high level, and there is less of a sense of ownership. The Kimberley Process has changed this calculation, as now there can be consequences for failing to regulate the cross-border trade in diamonds and all states that are members have formal laws against allowing noncertified diamonds from entering their territory. See Vlassenroot and Bockstael (2008).

International Agreements as a Reflection of State Power

Realists have long argued that compliance with international agreements reflects the power distribution in the international system. States will comply with agreements that encourage behavior that they would have pursued regardless of whether the agreement existed or not. Therefore, while states usually comply with international agreements, this is more a reflection of political dynamics and when states see these agreements as no longer reflecting their calculated best interests then this will quickly lead to noncompliance. A modern realist view of compliance is given by Goldsmith and Posner (2005, 225), who argue that "the best explanation for when and why states comply with international law is not that states have internalized international law, or have a habit of complying with it, or are drawn by its moral pull, but simply that states act out of self-interest." According to this theory, international agreements have little potential to change state behavior. Instead, they are ways of institutionalizing how states would act even if the agreement did not exist, and they provide convenient rhetoric for policymakers to justify decisions.

Most research that draws from the realist perspective on international agreements focuses on mechanisms through which Western states impose compliance on weaker states. For instance, Andreas and Nadelmann (2006), trace the development of "global policing" and argue that it is largely a Western-dominated enterprise in which weaker states are pressured to take up the norms surrounding illegal activity that had already been well accepted in the West. Furthermore, weaker states are pressured to accept Western standards that surround policing domestically. Threatening to withhold monetary aid to a state, even in cases where cooperation was politically difficult, is a major mechanism to enforce compliance with international courts.[8]

Realism is overly state centered in its approach to international regimes, in a way that has overlooked economic change, often relegating this to "low politics" whereas security concerns are "high politics." This focus on the state and security overlooks numerous critical political decisions in which these categories may not prove useful.

[8] An example of this is in the former Yugoslavia where Western states conditioned monetary aid on state compliance with international courts. See Lamont (2016); Peskin (2008).

Furthermore, much evidence clearly shows that regimes can constrain states, in some instances even powerful states (Alter 2014; Cardenas 2007; Hillebrecht 2014; Lamont 2016; Peskin 2008; Simmons 2009). Since most realist studies of international regimes tend to argue that they do not matter, and it is an assumption of the domestic political economy approach that regimes can constrain state behavior, it is a theory that challenges realism by going beyond its assumptions about regimes altogether.

With the Kimberley Process, there is reason to believe that realist assumptions about international regimes are incorrect. Several states spend scarce resources to comply with the Kimberley Process. Given that many Kimberley Process members are weak states, it is improbable that they would focus on diamond certification in the absence of the Kimberley Process. Also, contrary to realist predictions, some states that have a significant amount of influence over decision-making in the Kimberley Process are far from being major powers, notably Botswana, Namibia, and South Africa.[9] Furthermore, there is evidence that Kimberley Process members have complied with resolutions even when they thought it was not in their best interests.[10] Thus, realist predictions about the Kimberley Process do not hold.

International Agreements as a Cost-Benefit Response by States

The most common theory used for the study of compliance with international regimes is often called "neoliberalism." This approach argues that states often make choices that are not directly affected by power relations and that international regimes can exist without a dominant state maintaining them (Keohane 1984; Keohane and Nye 1977). Furthermore, states often comply with international regimes largely because cooperation will lead to better policy outcomes than if the regime did not exist and certain international issues could not be effectively addressed at the domestic level. Simmons (2009, 125) discusses how international agreements can matter, saying: "treaties are causally meaningful to the extent that they empower individuals, groups, or parts of the state with different rights preferences that were

[9] Grant (2013a, 2018) shows that "middle power" states, such as Canada and South Africa, have more influence in the Kimberley Process than their place in the global power structure would predict.

[10] See the example of Ghana given by Hilson and Clifford (2010).

not empowered to the same extent in the absence of the treaties." Some are more pessimistic about the role of human rights regimes, arguing that human rights treaties only help under certain conditions and the number of rule breakers that are in various treaties undermines their effectiveness (Hafner-Burton 2013). Many studies from this perspective, especially in environmental politics, focus primarily on institutional-level explanations for compliance outcomes (Keohane and Victor 2011; Mitchell 1994; Young 2010). While this is part of the picture, usually these explanations do not explain variations in compliance beyond a basic level, such as to avoid sanctioning or negative costs, and do not explain variations of compliance within the same regime.

By looking at the nature of international agreements, Guzman (2005) argues that interstate dynamics account for the fact that compliance measures are often weak in relation to domestic law. According to his theory, when an agreement is broken in domestic law one party usually pays the other but with international agreements a state may be sanctioned or shamed for breaking an agreement. This generally does not give any direct benefit to the other states in the agreement. With agreements that have an economic dimension, this dynamic may be especially common as other states may not gain or lose because they sanction a participant. Guzman (2008) goes on to use a rational choice model to show that international agreements are not distinct commitments, but that reputation and reciprocity are essential concepts for understanding states' utility calculations about when to comply or cooperate with an agreement.[11]

In one of the few book-length projects on cooperation around the transborder trade of illicit goods, Efrat (2012) argues that cooperation takes place when the "benefits" of cooperation outweigh the "costs" to states.[12] This project examines state cooperation aimed at preventing the global trade in illicit arms, rare antiques, and human trafficking.

[11] Some ways in which liberal theorists such as Keohane (1984) or Guzman (2008) conceive of rationality may not work when looking at actors surrounding some economic sectors, especially those such as the diamond industry that some would argue are built on irrationality. Diamonds are not particularly rare in nature and the high cost of jewelry-quality diamonds is largely due to successful marketing schemes and attempts at price fixing. See Hart (2001).

[12] As Andreas (2015) points out, Efrat's study uses conventional cooperation theory to look at an unconventional topic and thus provides a good basis to improve upon understanding of state behavior surrounding illicit trade.

A significant finding of this study is that interest groups, such as legal arms dealers or museums, can raise the costs associated with different state responses to illicit trade. This is especially the case if these interest groups are in influential states. This study provides a good comparison of challenges associated with cooperation around different types of illicit trade, but raises the question of why we see variation between states in dealing with illicit trade. Thus, it is a primary goal of this study to provide the first account of state-level variation in cooperation with a single illicit commodity, specifically uncertified diamonds.

The domestic political economy approach draws from some aspects of liberalism and also departs from it in some areas. The liberal approach to understanding international regimes has gone a long way in showing how regimes can matter. Liberals are right about the ability for international regimes to constrain states, but their focus is still overly state-centered and ignores how in several cases states are beholden to economic interests. Furthermore, they often focus on economic interdependence and how freer markets have lessened political conflict between states. This may be true to a large extent, but increasingly some of the most important political conflicts are between economic actors, often international actors, with different interests, the outcomes of which can have implications for states. It is also true that interdependence has become a defining element of global capitalism and a mechanism that has brought about regimes that facilitate this. However, political conflict has continued between firms seeking more global market share. International agreements are reflective of this dynamic or, put another way, international regimes just like domestic politics are an arena where political conflict between firms takes place.

In a seminal work, Keohane (1984) argued that hegemonic states try and lock in policies through international agreements and international law, especially if they know that a relative decline in power is inevitable. The approach used in this study applies this idea to powerful economic actors as well. For private actors, there is an incentive to lock in preferable policies when their relative advantage is substantial, and this can take place at both the domestic and international level. These preferences may not necessarily be a top choice for powerful economic actors, as is true with states, but with the possibility of an eventual decline in relative power, there is an incentive to lock in policy that will maintain some of their gains both now and in the future. This is especially true in cases where "the shadow of the future is long." Pursuing policies at the international level may have the added benefit to economic actors in that policy at this level is difficult to change and is not subject to reconsideration by changes in domestic regimes, democratic pressures, or a situation in which other competing actors could take advantage of local politics. The difficulty in changing policy from international regimes has been seen as a reason why countries decide to join them in initially.[13] While a future government or actors may want to change policy enforced by an international agreement, it is usually more difficult to do this procedurally at the international level with the calculations states make about reputation.[14]

Liberalism is a state-centered approach, in that it is state preferences that are the primary determinate of policy in the international arena. For instance, in his study of the International Coffee Organization Bates (1998b) explains how cold war politics and the desire of Brazil and Columbia to maintain a high market share account for the existence of the regime and its decline after the cold war ended. These state-level dynamics are essential to understand, but this study overlooks the role of significant coffee companies in decision-making. As has been a feature of Bates's (1981, 1987) work, it is state actors that dominate the decision-making process and act in accordance to their interests at the expense of private economic interests.

In contrast to state-centered theories, the domestic political economy approach is open to the possibility that preferences that are ultimately enacted at the international level may be more in line with those held by private economic actors. This is not always the case, but there is reason to believe that when looking at the policies that are enacted at the international level private economic interests will usually have some influence over decision-making. This influence might range from consultation, to what amounts to veto power, or even having the ability to more or less get their preferences enacted regardless of what

[13] See Cardenas (2007); Hillebrecht (2014); Simmons (2009).

[14] Drawing from Guzman (2008), cost-benefit calculations by states on whether to comply with an international regime need to be viewed in the overall context of a state's interaction with other states. Reputation matters, and if this means complying with a suboptimal policy in response to a specific regime, states can still see this as being in their interests when all interactions between states are considered.

state actors would most prefer if the state is heavily dependent on an economic sector or a single economic actor.

Liberalism would generally predict that compliance and cooperation with the Kimberley Process take place when state actors see the benefits of complying and cooperating as outweighing the costs, taking into consideration the repeated interactions that states have. This may be a partial explanation, but it overlooks the process by which states view their costs and benefits in responding to regimes and the prominent role that important economic actors play in this process. In examining the Kimberley Process there is a repeated interaction that takes place between state actors and private diamond companies, an interaction that is likely to change over time. Furthermore, the influence that domestic diamond actors have in multiple states can influence the interactions between these states. It may also be the case that states miscalculate their costs and benefits when taking decisions, make decisions that empower one group in society while disadvantaging others, and indeed some states value how decisions will influence the future more than others.

Another prediction about the Kimberley Process that would flow from liberal theory is that compliance and cooperation with the Kimberley Process would be a result of domestic or international political support. This prediction would primarily come from the study of implementing human rights regimes, as some authors have found that the ability for human rights regimes to work with domestic actors who have the same goals is key to explaining compliance and cooperation (Cardenas 2007; Hillebrecht 2014; Keck and Sikkink 1998; Lamont 2016; Peskin 2008; Simmons 2009). For instance, in explaining compliance with international law Alter (2014, 19) argues:

> The existence of an international legal remedy empowers those actors who have international law on their side, increasing their out of court political leverage. ICs then alter political outcomes by giving symbolic, legal, and political resources to compliance constituencies, ever-changing groups of actors that for a variety of reasons may prefer policies that cohere with international law.

Studies to this point have often focused on activists or domestic political opinion in democratic regimes but have frequently overlooked private firms except when a regime deals directly with regulating them, as is the case with some environmental regulations. Most studies examine how private economic actors have reacted to them, not how they could play a role in a state's attempt to enforce compliance in the first place, or how the influence of private economic actors could influence state responses to international regimes over time.

Ideas, Discourse, and Nongovernmental Organizations

In the study of international relations constructivism has become increasingly influential, especially in the study of international agreements. Ruggie (1998, 867) gives a common definition of constructivism: "social constructivists have sought to understand the full array of roles that ideas play in world politics, rather than specifying a priori roles based on theoretical presuppositions." Constructivists argue that international agreements can be agenda setters that have an authority of their own outside the power of states, largely through their ability to control dialogue or get their ideas accepted (Barnett and Finnemore 2004). The problem with this is that it is unclear why "ideas" should have such a privileged position when looking at regimes. To the proponents of constructivist theory, the mental world of "ideas" or "meaning" has a life of its own, which is more important than the material world but at the same time is presumably supposed to derive significance by its shaping of the material world. This outlook ignores that fact that constructivism itself is the product of changing socio-economic conditions and the questions, theories, and explanations that these conditions give rise to. It could just as easily be argued that it is a material reality that gives rise to "ideas" or "dialogue" or at least there is no reason a priori to assume one over the other. Constructivism is based on at least one theoretical assumption, and that is that there should be no theoretical assumptions. Thus, the epistemology used for constructivist theory is inherently circular and vague.

NGOs have been cited as an essential part of international agreements, especially those that are working within a "constructivist" or "global governance" framework. While they do play a role, there is reason to believe that they do not have influence independent of their potential usefulness for state and economic actors. At times when their goals are similar, and there are indeed examples where this is the case, NGOs or similar advocacy groups can have an influence.[15] However,

[15] Spar and La Mure (2003) find that most calculations of businesses in response to NGO activity can be understood in terms of cost-benefit analysis. However, in some cases personal preferences of private actors that go beyond narrow economic calculations may play a role. This is similar to Kantz's (2007)

this is mostly because the state or economic actors co-opt their message or use it to their advantage. When this is no longer possible, or NGOs no longer play a role that important economic actors find useful, then they are often pushed to the sidelines. This is not to say that the goals of NGOs and powerful economic actors are always or even often at odds in several issue areas, just that NGOs exist mostly in an area that is separate from the actual decision-making process. However, NGOs can be used by influential actors when they feel as though this will be useful to their goals. This may make it appear as though NGOs have influence, but this is only true on a purely selective basis, is primarily based on current conditions that could change, and rarely are NGOs a deciding factor in getting states or private actors to pursue policies that lie outside their preferences. Alternatively, NGOs have agenda-setting power in some cases and may be influential in a coalition with other powerful actors but are almost never given anything approaching veto power.

The constructivist theory has been used to explain how nongovernmental organizations changed norms about conflict diamonds as an explanation for how the process started (Bieri 2010a, 2010b). Also, Kantz (2007) uses Ruggie's (2002) theory of a social learning process to describe how diamond companies became concerned with the issue of "conflict diamonds" and changed their behavior because of the Kimberley Process.[16] This research is contradicted by a significant amount of literature that finds that corporate socialization in the mining sector is rare. A study by Santiago (2014) shows that "norms" around the diamond trade do not appear to have a high degree of influence in how diamonds are sold and marketed at the retail level. This is similar to a central finding in the literature on "mineral certification schemes," in which consumers may think that they are buying a more "ethical" or "fairly" produced product but in reality these attempts are about traceability of where minerals are originally mined and do not necessarily produce positive changes in local mining conditions (Hilson 2014; Schroeder 2010). This is especially the case in

portrayal of diamond companies as socialized agents that have taken on some of the same goals and values of NGOs.

[16] A social learning process can be defined as a "learning approach to inducing corporate change, as opposed to a regulatory approach; and it comprises a network form of organisation, as opposed to the traditional hierarchic/bureaucratic form" Ruggie (2002, 27).

many sub-Saharan countries where the legal status of miners is unclear, and they are marginalized by government policy in favor of large companies that have closer ties to the formal state structure (Childs 2008, 2014a, 2014b).[17] This study builds on prior "certification" scheme research by emphasizing the notion that the reality of these attempts is far from how both private companies and governments usually portray them. The Kimberley Process is different from "fair trade" or other "ethically" motivated attempts at mineral certification in that to reach most of the "legal" diamond market states need to be members. However, past research illustrates that different actors such as the government, large diamond companies, or small-scale miners stand to gain or lose considerably by the influence of certification schemes in the market and that the level of "power" over decision-making varies between actors in the mining sector.

Constructivists would generally predict that compliance and cooperation with the Kimberley Process is a result of changing "ideas" or "dialogues" around conflict diamonds and as this varies across states so does compliance and cooperation. This line of thinking does not go deeply enough into the motivations and material interests inherent in the diamond industry. Ideas do play a role in this area and can change the conversation around what sort of responses states should have to the Kimberley Process, but this does not work on its own for explaining outcomes as there is always an underlying material reality that is more important. For instance, actors may have to change their dialogue or rhetoric around the diamond trade because of ideas that activists or NGOs push for; maybe some policies could be changed as well, but that is constrained by those who influence decision-making, and is shaped by material interests. More likely is that if discourse surrounding the diamond industry does change policy that is because it is in the interests of at least some state and economic actors who can get their preferences reflected in policy. Some groups may use rhetoric to advance their interests, but this does not mean that the rhetoric influences the decision-making process independent of these interests.

The most heavily researched areas of the Kimberley Process are in the role that nongovernmental organizations have played in starting

[17] Ironically, some governments will buy from "illegal" small-scale miners, benefiting from their lack of formal legal status (Hilson 2008).

the agreement. This is the focus of the only book-length project on the Kimberley Process, Bieri's (2010a) *From Blood Diamonds to the Kimberley Process*,[18] which examines how nongovernmental organizations, states, and the diamond industry were able to form the Kimberley Process despite differing views and interests. In-depth interviews are used to show how all actors had incentives to create the process and how they viewed different events. Some analysis was also done of newspaper sources to see how often they discussed conflict diamonds, building an argument for how publicity influenced some actors, especially those in the diamond industry, to become more inclined to approve regulation of the diamond trade. In a different study Bieri (2010b) portrays NGOs as "experts" on certain issues surrounding conflict diamonds, providing useful information to the Kimberley Process. Nongovernmental organizations have served the role of "watchdogs" in that they have documented and critiqued actions taken.[19]

As research shows, nongovernmental organizations are essential in looking at the creation of the Kimberley Process.[20] They can be agenda

[18] Bieri's (2010a) study provides a great deal of documentation about how the Kimberley Process started and has developed over time but does not seek to describe in much detail how effective it has been in specific cases or what explains variation in how the Kimberley Process makes decisions.

[19] It should be noted that many of the NGOs that were influential in starting the Kimberley Process have left it. Global Witness (2011a) left over many issues including the Zimbabwe case. Another major NGO, Partnership Africa Canada, stayed in the process. However, in 2017, after changing its name to IMPACT, the NGO left the Kimberley Process. Executive director of IMPACT Joanne Lebert said that "We have come to the conclusion that the Kimberley Process has lost its will to be an effective mechanism for responsible diamond governance. The Kimberley Process – and its certificate – has lost its legitimacy. The internal controls that governments conform to do not provide the evidence of traceability and due diligence needed to ensure a clean, conflict-free, and legal diamond supply chain." Quoted in Bates (2017).

[20] It is notable that campaigns by nongovernmental organizations and activists have had less success in managing other resources compared to diamonds. Looking at why this is the case, Tamm (2004) compares attempts at regulating conflict diamonds with Sudan's oil trade. A diverse coalition of actors from across the political spectrum wanted to outlaw US companies from buying oil from Sudan in the late 1990s, as several human rights abuses had been documented in the southern part of the country. Tamm (2004) argues that it was the focus on security after 9/11 that largely explains different outcomes in attempts to regulate conflict resources, as campaigners for regulation of diamonds were able to argue that there may be a connection between terrorist groups and using diamond wealth for profit. On the other hand, the government

setters, influencing what sort of issues become important through publishing reports on the Kimberley Process. When examining the Kimberley Process nongovernmental organizations do have power over which country cases gain more attention than others, but it is unlikely they have a direct influence on decision-making. Nongovernmental organizations have no vote on Kimberley Process regulations; it is up to member states to accept their recommendations. It is also unlikely that nongovernmental organizations have much influence on domestic decision-making, beyond possibly drawing attention to specific issues, but they do not play a role in deciding whether these issues are addressed or not.

While there are some interesting articles on the Kimberley Process they are mostly journalistic, in that they describe events or the origin of the process but do not explore in depth how the process operates or tie it into the literature on international agreements. Many of the studies that exist are somewhat similar or talk briefly about the same cases. Thus, there is a need for an in-depth study on the Kimberley Process that compares how it has operated in different countries and explains why it has led to different outcomes, as this study does.

A theory that is often associated with early constructivist thought and is of interest for the study of international regimes is the "managerial school" developed by (Chayes and Chayes 1993, 1998). The central argument of this perspective is that states usually join international agreements intending to comply and that noncompliance is usually due to failures in state capacity, public administration, or confusion over what constitutes compliance. Thus, better cooperation between states to assist those that lack the capacity to comply is needed in order to get states to comply with international agreements at a higher rate.[21] For this project, given that there will be a focus on fragile

of Sudan became a potential ally against terrorist groups and human rights violations became a secondary concern. Furthermore, while some in the diamond trade saw regulation as a way to uphold their image and help financially, few companies in the oil trade supported a ban on Sudanese oil. Attempts to regulate conflict oil have lacked the same interests that surround the diamond trade, as the dominance of De Beers has made for a situation in which the diamond industry has fewer actors than most other sectors.

21 This theory has received some criticism; Downs, Rocke, and Barsoom (1996) argue that the reason it appears states are inclined to comply with international agreements is because they only enter into agreements with which they are already inclined to comply. Furthermore, they argue that noncompliance is often

states, a major reason for noncompliance could be that states and private economic actors lack not the will but the capacity to comply under certain conditions. Therefore, while the assumption is not that states join the Kimberly Process intending to comply, there is reason to think that a major factor in explaining variation in compliance is the lack of state capacity or the need for some states to receive assistance in order to comply with regulations at a higher level. Thus, aspects of "managerial school" theory are useful for understanding compliance with the Kimberley Process. The hypothesis section will draw on this, along with some of the civil war literature, to hypothesize about Kimberley Process compliance.

Critical Theory

It is often argued that theories generally associated with "critical theory" or other terms such as "dependence" or "Marxism" have less explanatory power than in the past, especially since the end of the cold war.[22] This is ironic: with the growth of global capitalism to most areas of the globe, the growing power of economic actors in relation to states, and the high level of influence private interests have on political choices, a theoretical school that takes the ability of economic forces to influence political outcomes seriously is indeed still relevant. The significant contribution of the critical theory perspective in terms of understanding state responses to international regimes is that it recognizes the potential primacy of economic actors in domestic decision-making, especially in states that are dependent on primary commodities.[23] Its weakness is that those from this perspective are too quick to overlook the ability of international regimes to constrain states or

a function of states calculating that it is not in their best interests to comply, thus negative sanctions are needed to raise the costs to states to enforce compliance. This perspective is not well suited when examining the Kimberley Process, especially since several of the states that joined knew they lacked the capacity to comply on their own and the institutional structure of the Kimberley Process makes it unlikely to effectively sanction states.

22 A major criticism of those from the "critical theory" perspective is that they are overly deterministic and dogmatic, and in some cases this is certainly true, although it should be noted that this is also a feature of adherents to other theories.

23 This is the idea from dependency theory that this study will focus on. It does not attempt to make an argument about other ideas associated with dependency theory, such as whether import substitution industrialization is a good idea, etc.

economic actors independent of state or economic power and how economic actors, especially those operating in many states, might want to use policies flowing from international agreements for their benefit.

In studying the global economy several scholars associated with "critical theory" have come up with a series of explanations to describe global inequality between states, often termed "dependency theory." There are multiple formulations of dependency theory, but the most influential is Wallerstein's (1974, 2004) "world systems theory." According to this perspective, the global economy is broken up into different spheres, the core of which is made up of wealthy economically advanced states, the semiperiphery are middle powers that are economically exploited by the core but also can exploit peripheral states which are seen as having a low level of development and basing their economy on the export of primary commodities. This perspective has some important insights into how the global economy and economic dependence can constrain the economic decisions that state actors make. However, this is more of a state-level theory that might explain some aspects of the "big picture" of the global economy but lacks the depth to explain specific decisions and behaviors in global politics. Furthermore, those who have worked with this theory have never had much to say about international regimes. They usually see them as being simply a new face on the old order or as a way to get support for exploitative policies under the guise of "democracy," "conflict prevention," or "human rights" – in fact just new ways of reinforcing historical patterns of domination and exploitation. While there may at times be a grain of truth to the analysis of the global economy from those in the dependency school, it tends to overlook extensive transformative changes that have taken place both in the global economy and in major political arrangements that have developed at the international level.

Similar to realists, some associated with "critical theory" tend to see international regimes as another way for powerful countries to enforce their economic dominance. This also leads to a similar state-centered approach. For instance, Cox and Jacobson (1973, 27) justify their use of a state-centered approach to examine influences of policy in eight international organizations by saying "states are the principal units in world politics, the dominant mode for organizing human and physical resources." It should come as no surprise that their findings confirm that states are the principal actors in influencing international outcomes.

Other critical theorists have argued that the "state is withering" to economic interests, and this is often the case, but they have been too quick to overlook the influence of international regimes (Strange 1982, 1996, 1998). They argue that multinational corporations have undermined state sovereignty but have overlooked how international agreements have done this as well and have ignored how powerful economic actors can use international agreements to their advantage or as an organizing mechanism, something that those in this tradition have often seen the state as performing. Critical theorists are right about the "withering" of the state in relation to powerful economic interests but are too quick to ignore that the influence of states has declined in relation to international agreements as well, in some cases because of the former process. While critical theorists have some interesting insights about the importance of examining powerful economic actors and their relationships to state interests, they provide no coherent theory to explain the role of international regimes, how economic factors may influence them, or how states are likely to respond to regimes. Their impulse has been to largely underestimate and overlook the influence international regimes have in global politics, thus overlooking some of the most important political institutions that exist today. The domestic political economy approach draws from critical theory by taking seriously several of its claims regarding how state dependence on primary resources or a particular economic sector can constrain state actors' choices, in some instances forcing them to pursue policies that are very different from what they would prefer.

Rational Functionalism

Rational functionalism mostly assumes that regimes and the form regimes take exist to solve a common action problem in the international system (Hass 2008). This overlooks much complexity in the behavior and state responses to international regimes. It may be the case that the goals of the state when building a regime and the role that the same regime plays in the state domestically are very different. Some "solutions" that advantage certain actors in the political world are in constant search of a "problem" or the conditions under which a new set of rules or regulations could be implemented. The incentive then is to create a problem or overstate certain conditions regardless of whether the "solution" will address any real objective problem or serve to perpetuate or enhance certain actors' interests. It may be the case that certain actors do not initially see an international agreement as being to their benefit, or they pretend that they will not comply in order to increase their bargaining power. However, over time they can manipulate the regime or change it to their advantage. The longer actors expect the regime to be in place the more incentive they have to bargain early to make sure that the structure of the regime is likely to support their interests and to withhold their support if it does not (Fearon 1998). Thus, it is too much to assume that the creation, behavior, or state responses to an international regime serve to overcome a collective action problem, although this may often be the case. It could be that the regime, in reality, exists more to empower specific interests or advantage certain actors. Furthermore, this theory mostly seeks to explain why regimes are created but does not give much of an explanation of the significant variation in state cooperation and compliance with a regime.

The Domestic Political Economy Approach: International Agreements as an Outgrowth of Domestic Economic Power

In any international agreement with an economic element, which is most if not all international agreements, the domestic political economy of states shapes the creation, behavior, and state responses to these agreements. There is a need to get beyond a narrow set of questions that have for too long dominated the study of international regimes. This is especially the case with the question of whether international regimes matter or if they can constrain states – in many cases they do – but instead ask largely understudied questions such as: What shapes state responses to international agreements after they are enacted? Furthermore, why do state responses to international regimes change over time and vary considerably among otherwise similar states? Why is it that some states spend scarce resources to comply and cooperate with an international agreement but ignore or put no effort into responding to other agreements? The study of international agreements has to this point been overly state-centric and has focused too much on how changing "ideas" or "norms" drive state behavior while ignoring significant economic changes associated with globalization that have been a driving force for both the increase in international agreements and their level of influence. It is the goal of the domestic political economy approach to take seriously private economic actors, economic change, and the influence of these forces on state responses to international agreements.

Private economic actors largely influence international agreements and state responses to them. The level of influence by private economic actors, the distribution of power between them, and their relationship with government actors are all essential in understanding state behavior concerning international agreements. International agreements can be a way for economic actors to achieve policy goals, pass costs on to states, or increase their market advantage compared to other actors. While this might primarily be done procedurally by "state actors," in some states private economic actors have considerable, if not a dominating, influence over a country's domestic political economy. Thus the preferences of private economic actors will also be reflected at the international level. Therefore, understanding the domestic political economy, what private economic actors are important, their relationship with other competitors, or the balance of power between them can help explain their preferences toward international agreements and in turn what constitutes state preferences because of the domestic decision-making process. These preferences toward international agreements are likely to change over time as the domestic political economy of states changes.

Just as private economic actors can benefit from political policies pursued at the domestic level, and at times focus on the government sphere to gain profits and competitive advantage over competitors, the same is true on the international level. With the growth of globalization and the decline of state power in relation to economic actors, this process is more likely (Gale 1998; Garcia-Johnson 2000; Strange 1982, 1996, 1998). Just as international agreements present an opportunity for government actors to make it more difficult for future governments to undo their preferred policies, they also provide this opportunity to private economic actors. The ability to constrain state behavior in the future is likely to make economic actors interested in influencing international agreements. This can be a way for economic actors to consolidate gains and make sure that they will have a certain level of predictability of government policy in the future. At the very least it will be much more difficult for future governments to significantly depart from past policies that are a response to complying and cooperating with international agreements.

The more dependent a state is on a single economic sector, the more the policies of the state at the international level will reflect the policies of the important economic actors in this sector. Furthermore, change in the level of dependence on a single economic sector is likely to result in a change of economic policy both domestically and at the international level. A significant part of dependence is directly material, or the ability to gain tax revenue from a sector.

The state could also rely on technology or other positive externalities from businesses. Dependence plays a role in that states often need to pursue policies that keep firms within their borders or attract firms from abroad. The "shadow of the future" matters, especially in a more globalized world where firms can move while states are tied to a particular location. This is another way in which firms have bargaining power. Furthermore, the geographical characteristics of an economic sector are vital in understanding the bargaining influence that state and private economic actors have.

As private economic actors have different policy preferences and their relative influence in comparison to other actors changes, so will state policy or responses to relevant economic agreements. Private economic actors are key to understanding compliance and cooperation with international agreements because often they are responsible for complying directly and cooperation between states can frequently involve them as well. Thus, some private economic actors may comply as doing so is mostly in line with their interests, possibly going beyond a minimal level of compliance. Other actors may only comply because they fear legal sanctions or may choose deliberately not to comply at all as they calculate that the economic benefits of noncompliance outweigh the costs. In some cases, noncompliance may become the norm or third-party payments can be used to induce compliance, which would then often involve cooperation.[24] It could also be the case that certain local private economic actors may lack the capacity outright to comply; thus they are disadvantaged by the existence of the agreement in the first place. Given environmental or geographical constraints this may be an issue with many agreements, calling for either sanction of the noncompliers or cooperation

[24] See Weinthal (2002).

from other actors to make compliance feasible. Which path is chosen is an inherently political decision and is likely to vary significantly given the context. To understand compliance with international agreements it is necessary to examine in depth examples where actors have the intention of complying but lack the means and then what sort of political decisions lead to either cooperation or sanctioning. Furthermore, it is essential to understand why some actors have the incentive to go beyond just a basic level of compliance and spend resources on raising compliance with an international regime in an overall sense.

Decision-making in international agreements often reflects the disproportionate influence of powerful states, but in some agreements where economic actors have more influence rules can be written so that weaker states have more influence, mainly as a function of these private actors' high level of influence over state-level decision-making. In international regimes where economic motivations are central the level of influence a state has may have more to do with its share of the global market and the influence of multinational corporations on its domestic decision-making structure, in contrast to more traditional ways of thinking about power in terms of overall economic and military capability. Thus, in many cases, the level of influence over decision-making in international regimes, by different states, is likely to vary considerably given these dynamics and may not necessarily reflect the distribution of power in the international system more broadly.

Understanding compliance with international agreements according to the domestic political economy approach is an interrelated three-part process. First is understanding the level of dependence of a state on a particular economic sector, which can vary and largely explains how beholden a state is to the preferences of private economic actors. Second is understanding the policy preferences of the relevant economic actors in this sector, often conflicting, and their relative level of economic control or political influence in the political decision-making process. Finally, what sort of political geography may influence choices about compliance and the relative influence over decision-making between state actors and private economic actors? For instance, some economic sectors are more dependent on operating in a particular territory, possibly advantaging the state, whereas other sectors allow more movement thus often enabling private economic actors to have more choices. Also, state capacity in several cases is uneven in different geographical regions; preferences the state has surrounding compliance may be beholden to local actors as a result. By understanding these factors, we can better understand the dynamics of compliance and cooperation with international regimes and what policies this leads to domestically.

While states often are the ones that directly make decisions in international regimes, the domestic political economy approach emphasizes that state preferences which express themselves at the international level are in fact the result of a complex and conflictual domestic decision-making process. In this process, the goals and preferences of some economic actors win out over others and, given the level of state dependence, in some cases private economic actors have more bargaining power over states than others. Whether policies that are the preferences of states or private economic actors are implemented at the international level is a result of domestic decision-making and calculations, even if state interests appear to have the "upper hand" in procedurally deciding preferences. However, it is likely that this is often not the case as there are several states where private economic actors have traditionally had and have continued to gain power and influence over major decisions in society. In recent decades it is undeniable that the bargaining power of private economic actors has grown and that to some degree both the nature and the growth of international agreements reflect this dynamic.

Hypotheses

In this section, three interrelated hypotheses are presented that seek to understand compliance and cooperation with the Kimberley Process. The first two are derived from the domestic political economy approach. Here is a description of how this approach builds on prior theoretical thought and diverges from it to arrive at these hypotheses.

Hypothesis 1: Government Diamond Dependence

There is great variation in how much influence governments in diamond producing countries have over the extraction of diamonds and how much revenue they gain from it. Some governments have a direct joint extraction agreement in which they get a certain amount of revenue; in others, the diamond industry has been taxable, while other countries have a hard time taxing the diamond industry at all as diggers may smuggle diamonds instead of paying taxes. While there is no research on how diamond dependence effects compliance with the Kimberley Process there is some on diamond dependence.

Dependency theory influences this area of inquiry: specifically, states that are dependent on primary commodities as a source of revenue will face policy constraints from more advanced economies to sell their goods.[25] Also, this draws upon the theory of political survival developed by Bueno De Mesquita et al. (2005). In this theory, government actors may have to implement policies that they do not prefer ideologically or that lead to dismal results for most of the population in order to satisfy powerful groups that are essential to them staying in power and to economic activity that is a source of revenue. An excellent example of this is Namibia, as the South West Africa People's Organization (SWAPO) had long argued that the fifty-fifty partnership with De Beers was incompatible with its socialistic goals. However, when the apartheid government was overthrown, and SWAPO came to power it signed a similar fifty-fifty agreement with De Beers in 1994 (Stein 2001). More than ten years before the political transition, De Beers Chairman Harry Frederick Oppenheimer argued that no government in Namibia could last without the money that could be made through a partnership with De Beers (Epstein 1982). This research suggests that in some states diamond wealth matters a lot; also, these states have more to lose if the Kimberley Process fails to convince consumers that the diamond trade does not include conflict diamonds. The country in which the role of diamond wealth has often been seen as the greatest is Botswana.[26] This literature generally argues that Botswana has been prosperous in comparison to most resource-wealthy countries in that Botswana has used its diamond wealth to

[25] See Frank (1966, 1978); Rodney (1974); Smith and Lee (2018); Taylor (2016); Wallerstein (1974, 2004).

[26] Botswana is a sparsely populated land-locked state in Southern Africa that has been one of the world's largest producers of diamonds. In fact, Botswana has become almost synonymous with De Beers, as the state owns 15 percent of the company. Botswana has also been used as an example of a successful African state and an exception to the issues surrounding the "resource curse." Although to what extent it has avoided these issues and whether the state can perpetuate its current institutional base when diamond wealth declines is subject to debate. See Acemoglu, Johnson, and Robinson (2002); Dunning (2008); Holm (1987); Poteete (2009, 2012).

build a one-party "democracy." Namibia's diamond wealth has also been a central element in the political trajectory of the country.[27]

The domestic political economy approach builds on past theories about how dependence on primary commodities constrains state behavior. However, Hypothesis 1 departs from this school of thought by viewing international regimes as having the ability to at times constrain states and important economic actors. It contends that economic dependence is an integral part of any explanation as to why international regimes have power independent from the preferences of states and private economic actors. This approach argues that state dependence can have important implications for the creation of international regimes, how these regimes develop, and, most importantly for this study, how state responses to international regimes are shaped. Thus this leads to:

Hypothesis 1. *The higher the level of government dependence on the private diamond industry, the more states will be inclined to accept the preferences of private economic actors that relate to compliance and cooperation with the Kimberley Process.*

Hypothesis 2: Influence of the Diamond Industry

There has been little theoretical development on how the Kimberley Process operates, but one exception is Haufler (2009b), who uses it as an example of Potoski and Prakash's (2009) "Club Theory Approach to Voluntary Programs." According to this theory, voluntary programs are joined by companies that then adopt rules that are not compulsory. The incentive for companies to join voluntary agreements is that they will get benefits that they would not otherwise receive, such as a better reputation, reduced costs in transactions, or greater likelihood of investment. Haufler (2009b) uses this theory to describe the Kimberley Process as a "double club" in which both states and the

[27] To a large extent reading about the history of twentieth-century Namibia is reading about the diamond trade. The diamond trade has influenced most areas of life in Namibia and has had a consistent influence on the political economy of the country since the early 1900s. In fact, even in areas of Namibia where diamonds are not found, the trade has still had a major impact through the "contract labor system" that developed and the unions these workers created. See Bauer (1998); Boer and Sherbourne (2003, 2004); Cooper (1999, 2001); Pisani (2003); Schneider (2008).

diamond industry get the benefit of a better reputation for being part of a system that is seen as lessening the chance of conflict diamonds making it to the market. Also, large diamond producers, especially De Beers, have been able to use the Kimberley Process to retain their disproportionate share of the diamond industry; thus it is clear that some members of the process may benefit more than others. This approach describes why states would want to enter the Kimberley Process, how it may be expected to operate as an institution, and why states would not want to get expelled from the "club." It does not explain state responses to the regime and why compliance and cooperation vary considerably between states and over time in a single state, simply noting that states would not want to get expelled. Furthermore, since most of the diamond trade takes place within states that are members of the Kimberley Process its membership is compulsory to states that want to access the global market; at the very least, membership in practice would seem to be less than "voluntary" even if this might be theoretically true.

The neoclassical school of economics theorizes about the role of private businesses in allowing or even pushing for regulation, often as part of a critique of government intervention in the market. Bates (1998a, 206) says that this school of regulation

> stresses that cartels are inherently unstable; producers face grave difficulties in restricting entry and in restraining competition. In response, the argument holds, producers shift their efforts from the marketplace to the political arena. By marshaling public-interest arguments – such as the need to enhance the quality or protect public health – private firms secure government regulation of an industry. By thus bending the regulatory process to their ends, they employ public power to secure private objectives: the cartelization of the market and the redistribution of income from consumers to themselves.

Other research makes this argument by looking at how in some cases private firms may welcome regulation to lessen competition or to pass expenses on to the public sector that they may have had to pay themselves (Akerlof 1970; Peltzman 1976; Stigler 1971). If we look at the Kimberley Process through this lens it could be argued that the process is primarily a public provision of a private good where most of the benefits go to large diamond companies, notably De Beers. While certifying that diamonds did not originate in conflict zones may prove costly but necessary to maintain the same level of profit for diamond companies, passing this responsibility to certify diamonds on to states is one way of assuring consumers that their product is clean.[28] These theories have more predictive power about the creation of institutions to regulate the market and have rarely been applied systematically to the study of international regimes or state responses to these regimes. However, they do paint a picture of market regulation that describes how there can be winners and losers and how private actors that push for regulating a specific market may see it as being to their economic benefit.

Some theories often associated with what could be called "critical theory" go further than the neoclassical school's view. They argue that economic actors may be more powerful in causing policy outcomes than states, view international agreements as being weak in their ability to constrain powerful economic actors or states, and that often in the domestic political decision-making process economic actors are more influential in policy outcomes than states are (Strange 1982, 1996, 1998). One example of using some of this theory along with a Gramscian perspective is Gale (1998), who contends that tropical timber regimes have been dominated by economic actors as a way for them to institutionalize their policy preferences but does not examine how this shaped state responses to the regime.[29] It seems clear that there is a theoretical basis for believing that diamond companies are important actors when it comes to policies relating to the Kimberley Process. By looking at "club theory," "neoclassical economics," and "critical theory" we can see that when regulating market transactions there are those who stand to benefit economically despite the altruistic rhetoric that may surround regulatory behavior. This is not to say that economic actors do not at times have altruistic motivations or that

[28] A somewhat similar logic is used by Akerlof (1970) to look at the used car market. According to this theory the used car market faces a problem of incomplete information between buyers and sellers. Often buyers are unclear whether the car they are buying is a "lemon" that has many problems; thus some "lemons" can hurt the used car market in general. Government regulation or certification schemes are ways to ensure buyers are not buying a "lemon" and raise consumer confidence in the sector overall.

[29] This would seem to have the potential to apply to the Kimberley Process; however, to give a counterargument, Kantz (2007) argues that diamond companies have become "socialized agents" and have taken on some of the same goals as nongovernmental organization and human rights campaigners on this issue.

their preferences are always contrary to the "greater good." The point is that private economic actors have a stake in policy outcomes and certain private actors often have a higher level of influence over regulatory decisions than others in their sector. Therefore, influencing government regulation can become an arena for competition or in some cases can supplant competition in the market. Building on this past research, this study uses the logic about how economic actors will use regulations to their advantage at the domestic level and applies it to understanding state responses to international agreements.[30]

Hypothesis 2. *Given the level of diamond dependence in a state, the higher the level of influence over the domestic political decision process by private economic actors that have preferences for complying and cooperating with the Kimberley Process, the higher the level of state compliance and cooperation with the Kimberley Process.*

Hypothesis 3: Political Geography of Diamond Mining

The third hypothesis draws on the civil war literature and the managerial school of compliance and cooperation. The attention that conflict diamonds have received has prompted scholars to place more of a focus on diamond mining in general, especially the alluvial variety that has been more tied to conflict.[31] Furthermore, while a domestic political economy that leads to preferences for state cooperation with the Kimberley Process is necessary for a high level of compliance, this may not be sufficient if the political geography of a state makes compliance difficult.

[30] The domestic political economy approach builds on the idea that the "state is withering" regarding domestic economic actors (Strange 1982, 1996, 1998), but departs from this approach in arguing that in some cases the "state is withering" regarding international agreements as well, largely as a consequence of the increased role of private economic actors in the domestic decision-making process.

[31] An edited volume titled *Artisanal Diamond Mining: Perspectives and Challenges* looks mostly at alluvial diamonds and discusses how the Kimberley Process has influenced this sector at every level (Vlassenroot and Bockstael 2008). The central focus of the volume is to describe how the diamond trade has evolved in postconflict countries and what local laws have been put in place, many of them dealing with diamond regulation and compliance with the Kimberley Process. See also Le Billon (2008); Snyder and Bhavnani (2005).

Among countries where there are issues with noncompliance the Kimberley Process may have more incentive to pressure states if the geographical distribution of diamonds will make policy changes easier to obtain than others. One example of this dynamic is Ghana. As Hilson and Clifford (2010, 449) say: "With more localized diamond production, it is far easier to monitor, and institute change in Ghana than, for example, the DRC, where borders are more porous, deposits are more diffuse, and criminal networks are potentially entrenched." Thus, countries with certain types of diamond mining will have both a variety of different challenges when it comes to Kimberley Process compliance and the ability for the process to act more forcefully; in some cases this may also change the calculations that states make domestically.

Others have looked at the geographic distribution of alluvial diamonds and have found that the location of diamonds may be a better indicator of conflict risk than overall countrywide production.[32] Furthermore, natural resource wealth within a conflict zone can play a role in shaping how geographically large a conflict is. Thus, while none of these studies looks at attempts to regulate diamonds, they do show that the geographic distribution of alluvial diamonds can cause challenges for states and is politically relevant.

A framework that will help to explain the difficulty in regulating diamonds under some geographic conditions is given by Le Billon (2001a), who builds a theory for what sort of conditions make natural resources more likely to lead to conflict. Le Billon (2001a), breaks up the geographical distribution of natural resources into two different categories: "proximate," which is near the capital city or power center of the country, and "distant," which is in rural, less populated areas where the state is weaker. If natural resources are "proximate" this might lead to the formation of groups that want to take over the government to control the revenue outright or to urban unrest. On the other hand, if natural resources are "distant" then secessionist movements that want to form their own political entity, and other types of opportunistic warlords or rebel groups, may emerge. It flows from Le Billon's (2001a) theory that since alluvial diamonds are often spread out over a large geographical area dynamics associated with

[32] Buhaug and Gates (2002); Buhaug and Lujala (2005); Buhaug and Rod (2006).

"distant" resource wealth is more likely and under these conditions regulating diamond wealth would be inherently more difficult.[33]

Hypothesis 3. *Countries that have alluvial diamond deposits will have a lower probability of complying/cooperating with Kimberley Process regulations than those that have primary deposits. The geographical distribution of alluvial diamonds matters, as in countries where they are more widely distributed compliance will be more difficult than those in which they are located in a limited area.*

These hypotheses, which flow from the domestic political economy approach discussed above, are aimed at understanding the economic basis of state responses to international agreements. This theoretical framework is tested with the Kimberley Process in this project but should have widespread applicability to comprehending state responses to international agreements in which there is an economic element. By testing these hypotheses, this study will gain a better theoretical understanding of the mechanisms behind state compliance and cooperation with international agreements than state-centered, or constructivist-based approaches have done in the past.

[33] To look in depth at how the type and distribution of diamonds in a country has influenced compliance, studies that map the global distribution of diamonds are examined. Some of the major studies on the geography of diamonds and their influence on conflict that are used throughout this study are: Gilmore et al. (2005); Le Billon (2008, 2012); Lujala, Gliditsch, and Gilmore (2005). These studies uncover some of the contextual challenges that states have faced in terms of their diamond wealth fueling conflict. These same contextual challenges are also important for understanding state responses to the Kimberley Process.

3 *From Passiveness to the Presidency*

The Changing Nature of Angola's Responsiveness to Conflict Diamond Regulation

The Angolan civil war, possibly more than any other conflict, brought worldwide attention to the issue of "blood diamonds" during the 1990s.[1] Although an initial member to the Kimberley Process in 2003, Angola showed little interest in cooperating with other members or participating in the process at first, but increasingly has cooperated extensively with neighboring countries to prevent diamond smuggling. While institutional decision-making by the Kimberley Process and the predilections of policymakers partially explain Angola's responses to the Kimberley Process, this chapter argues that changes in the domestic political economy of Angola are the most persuasive explanation for why Angola's level of cooperation and compliance with the Kimberley Process has varied. The experience of the Kimberley Process within the country has had little to do with regulating "conflict diamonds" per se but has become a terrain in which both regulatory decisions from the agreement and the state-level responses to these regulations have been primarily a function of private diamond companies implementing their preferences in policy.

While much attention in both the popular media and academic literature has centered on the role that diamonds played in funding Angola's war,[2] which ended in 2002, little attention has been paid to the importance of the diamond trade since and the role that the Kimberley Process has played in the country. This study of Angola intends to explain why attempts to regulate the diamond trade have varied considerably over time since the Kimberley Process was created. What can account for Angola's initial indifference to the Kimberley Process and then subsequent participation?

[1] See Cillers and Dietrich (2000); Fowler (2000); Malaquias (2001).

[2] Books and academic studies that discuss the role of diamonds in Angola's civil war: Campbell (2002); Cillers and Dietrich (2000); Cleveland 2014; Fowler (2000); Le Billon (2008, 2012); Malaquias (2001); Smillie (2010a; 2014).

The story of diamonds after blood is essential to examine because although the Angolan state has the potential to fund social programs and build infrastructure with resource wealth, this has mostly not been the case. The attempt by the Kimberley Process to certify the global diamond trade is undoubtedly ambitious, but there are few countries in which it would be as difficult, or as potentially important given recent history, as in Angola. To understand Angola's changing responses to the Kimberley Process, this chapter applies the domestic political economy approach and the hypotheses that were outlined in Chapter 2. To summarize, this chapter on Angola will highlight three critical aspects of understanding compliance and cooperation with the Kimberley Process. First, it looks at domestic diamond dependence, precisely how much a state relies on a particular industry, and if as a condition of its dependence it is beholden to the preferences of private economic actors when making decisions. Second, it is important to understand what the preferences of private actors are concerning an international agreement as this can certainly vary with different actors and over time with the same actor. Finally, it may be the case that a state has a desire to comply with an international agreement or may push for specific policies but have administrative and environmental constraints in getting these policies implemented effectively. Thus, it is crucial to examine how a state may vary over time in its capacity, but not the desire, to comply.

This chapter will proceed as follows. The first part will examine the history of the diamond sector in Angola as the relationship between the state and private actors is important for understanding how Angola was likely to respond to the Kimberley Process when it was first implemented in 2003. The following section will discuss the period from 2003 to 2005 when Angola had little cooperation with the Kimberley Process, especially in comparison to other countries that were emerging from large-scale conflicts and were having difficulty complying, such as Sierra Leone and the Democratic Republic of the Congo. Then the discussion will focus on the changing political economy in Angola's diamond sector that emerged after 2005. The emphasis will be on the last few years in which Angola has cooperated extensively with the Kimberley Process and other neighboring countries to minimize the flow of illicit diamonds. Finally, the study will examine Angola's place as vice president of the Kimberley Process in 2014 and then president in 2015.

Historical Development of the Diamond Sector in Angola

Most literature on diamonds in Angola has focused on how UNITA was able to use diamond wealth to continue the war against the MPLA government (Cillers and Dietrich 2000; Le Billon 2001b; Malaquias 2001). However, the most significant part of the history of the diamond sector in Angola for understanding Angola's response to the Kimberley Process when it was implemented in 2003 is the historical relationship between the MPLA government and private diamond companies. This section focuses on the role that diamond companies have played in relation to the MPLA government. This is important for understanding how the state has responded to the Kimberley Process since its implementation, especially in the first few years.

As with most diamond-producing countries in Africa, De Beers has had a long and controversial history in Angola. Diamonds were first found in eastern Angola in 1912, and by 1917 a joint agreement had been set up between the Portuguese colonial government and De Beers to create the company Diamang (Hodges 2004). In the mining regions, De Beers became the de facto government with the ability to enforce laws and control security (Cleveland 2015; Gordon and Ngolo 2004). While many Portuguese leaders, especially the Salazar regime, were hesitant to allow foreign-owned companies to gain a foothold in Angola, De Beers was allowed to mine out of pragmatic considerations. From 1957 to 1967 diamond mining rose by 50 percent and became a crucial source of revenue for the colonial government, which was facing challenges from independence movements (Newitt 2008).

Even though opposition to the monopolistic role of De Beers in Angola's mining sector was part of the overall movement against colonialism, the MPLA signed a contract with De Beers in 1977, only two years after independence from Portugal (Gordon and Ngolo 2004). The MPLA had the stated goal of building socialism in Angola, and it gained extensive support from Cuba and the Soviet Union. However, given the financial constraints of fighting a large-scale war, a contract with De Beers was a way to provide essential funding. While the MPLA held onto the capital city of Lunda, its main rival for power, UNITA, had extensive foreign support from China, South Africa, and the United States (Polack 2013). Allies of UNITA saw the conflict in Angola as a frontline in stopping the influence of the Soviet Union in Africa, and the South African government wanted to maintain control over Namibia and continue its policy of racial segregation domestically. Both of these goals were endangered by the MPLA, as the government allowed rebel groups with the aim of overthrowing the apartheid South African state to set up bases and organize in Angola.

Initially, the relationship between De Beers and the MPLA was successful, in that diamond output went up considerably. However, by 1985 the agreement broke down as UNITA constantly tried to sabotage the diamond trade by attacking mines (Gordon and Ngolo 2004). Diamond smuggling became common in Angola. The entry of these diamonds into the global market created a problem for De Beers, as it became difficult to continue the practice of price fixing the diamond market and releasing diamonds into the market only when it was most advantageous for De Beers. Having a large number of diamonds being smuggled and placed on the global market outside of De Beers' control had long been an issue in weak states such as Sierra Leone (Reno 1995). Informal markets in the diamond sector were challenging for a large company like De Beers to gain a share in, especially in comparison to local private groups with political connections, although there are some cases where De Beers was able to gain a share in "illegal" diamond mining (Reno 1995, 1998).

Smuggling from UNITA became one of its biggest challenges to the dominance of De Beers over the diamond market. According to some estimates, this represented 10–15 percent of the global diamond trade during the 1990s (Hodges 2004). In the past, De Beers had been able to use a virtual monopoly over the global diamond trade to deal with challenges from those who would try and market diamonds outside of their control. Over several decades De Beers had spent millions on preventing diamond smuggling, often through coercive means approved by governments (Smillie 2014).[3]

In the early 1990s, the funding structure of UNITA changed, as it lost most of its foreign supporters after the cold war and the end of

[3] An example of De Beers' ability to use its advantage in the diamond market, to coerce governments to enforce its policy preferences, happened in 1981. Mobutu Sesa Seko, the longtime ruler of the Democratic Republic of Congo, tried to sell diamonds outside of De Beers' control. De Beers responded by flooding the market with similar diamonds, deeply depressing prices and forcing Mobutu to negotiate a new agreement with De Beers in 1983, which gave Mobutu far less revenue (Spar 2006).

apartheid in Namibia and South Africa.[4] Thus, UNITA found the diamond trade to be one of the few ways to fund the conflict. UNITA would sell the diamonds for well under market value; in fact, it had few other choices. It is likely that after the UN banned the trade of diamonds that originated in UNITA-controlled areas in 1998, the prices that UNITA could get for its diamonds were depressed; however, some were still willing to take the associated risks and buy them for lower prices. Since it was uncommon for someone to be charged with buying or trading in diamonds from UNITA-controlled areas, actors involved in the diamond trade probably calculated the risk as not being much higher than before the ban; the only real cost was likely to be reputational. Allegedly, some heads of state continued their economic ties with UNITA, allowing diamonds to be smuggled through their territory (Smillie 2014).

While many smaller diamond traders and those who operate in the informal economy have less reputational concerns, De Beers is often associated with the diamond trade overall. Thus, a loss to reputation is of paramount concern. By the end of the 1990s, when NGOs and the popular media began to expose how diamonds were fueling conflict, De Beers had to pay attention. De Beers and the Angolan government signed a new agreement in 1991, but this became difficult to maintain because UNITA never disarmed and still controlled vast amounts of territory (Gordon and Ngolo 2004). Under this contract several top MPLA generals joined the board of De Beers in Angola, gaining direct access to any profits that were made (Polack 2013).

The war in Angola was a nightmare for De Beers, and is one of the reasons behind its relative decline from the early 1990s.[5] While it may be the case that De Beers was not directly purchasing diamonds from UNITA, it is likely that its local diamond-buying offices in Africa were.[6] Giving in to pressure from the international community in the late 1990s, De Beers shut down all of its local buying offices in Africa

[4] An exception is the Democratic Republic of Congo led by Mobutu Sesa Seko, who continued to support UNITA until being overthrown in 1997.

[5] Despite challenges in Angola, De Beers was able to maintain a position in which it still dominated the global diamond trade but for the first time viable competitors started to emerge.

[6] Allegedly, De Beers tried to deal with the problem of UNITA-produced diamonds going to market by buying them up locally but the extent to which this took place is unclear (Hodges 2004).

and had left Angola by 2000 (Gordon and Ngolo 2004). The smuggling of diamonds outside of the De Beers market in Angola was making the ability to set prices on the global diamond trade difficult for De Beers and at the same time the company was being blamed for the conflict. Given the reputational costs that the entire industry was paying for the role that diamonds played in funding conflict in Angola and the dominance of De Beers over the industry, the company had to change course. This is not necessarily the case with potential challengers to De Beers, which could take advantage of changing market dynamics. Ultimately, De Beers had to buy up much of the illicit trade that was taking place in Africa or lose its ability to set global prices. As the international community started to pay more attention to the global diamond trade, the former became a more difficult policy to maintain.

The problems in Angola, for De Beers, soon became an opportunity for other actors to break into the market for African diamonds. In 1997 Lev Leviev, an Israeli billionaire who became wealthy from the Russian diamond trade, signed a contract with the MPLA. This contract made him the leading exporter of Angola's diamonds until 2004 (Gordon and Ngolo 2004). Leviev is the man who "cracked" the De Beers cartel according to Forbes Magazine (2003), and it has often been apparent from Leviev's business choices that he has intended to challenge De Beers in Southern Africa.[7]

In 2000 the Angolan government and Lev Leviev set up a monopsony on the diamond trade, called the Angolan Selling Cooperation (Hodges 2008). This put Leviev in control of roughly 10 percent of the global "legal" diamond trade and was viewed as being a major blow to De Beers. By this time De Beers had left Angola and filed a lawsuit over mining concessions that were given to Leviev in 1997 (Hodges 2004). In 2000 De Beers was able to get a successful court order in Belgium to seize two shipments of diamonds that had originated in Angola, claiming that since De Beers had a contract to be the only legal buyer from where the diamonds originated, technically it was the rightful owner of the diamonds (IRIN 2000).

The monopsony over the diamond trade created by Leviev and the MPLA government was challenging to maintain. Ultimately, there were

[7] During the same period Leviev started buying diamond mines in Namibia, which had been a De Beers stronghold. See Chapter 4 on Namibia.

few guarantees that diamonds that originated in UNITA-controlled areas were not being traded or mixed with diamonds from other sources. Ironically, UNITA likely bypassed selling diamonds to the government-run monopsony for the same reason those other unlicensed smugglers did: the monopsony paid meager prices (Smillie 2014).

Angola's civil war ended about a year before the Kimberley Process was implemented in 2003. However, the relationship between the MPLA and private diamond companies was far from a "blank slate." Historically Angola had been a challenge to the De Beers cartel, because of the high potential for smuggling diamonds outside of the cartel's control. Furthermore, even while the war was going on, it had been a central location of competition for global market share in the diamond industry. These trends would continue in the coming years and would have widespread implications for how the Kimberley Process was initially implemented in Angola.

Diamonds after Blood? 2003–2005

Unlike other countries that had just emerged from diamond-related civil wars, Angola was initially indifferent toward the Kimberley Process, and while it was an original member, it did not play a prominent role in its creation.[8] Despite widespread smuggling, Angolan authorities cooperated little with attempts by the Kimberley Process to strengthen the state's administrative capacity, arguing that they could certify the diamonds without assistance from the Kimberley Process (Grant 2012). This is problematic in a regime where uncertified diamonds that either enter or leave a country constitute a violation of compliance and was different to the strategy pursued by other post-conflict states in sub-Saharan Africa. Until 2005, the Angolan delegation participated little at Kimberley Process meetings, outside of disputing reports of smuggling from Angola (Grant 2012).

When the Kimberley Process was implemented in 2003, De Beers was challenging the Angolan government for the right to mine diamonds based on an agreement signed in 1991. On the other hand, Lev Leviev had become the only legal buyer of diamonds through a joint agreement with the Angolan selling corporation's monopsony. De Beers continued to argue that according to the 1991 contract with

[8] This can be contrasted with Sierra Leone.

the MPLA government, the company was the only legal buyer of diamonds from the Cuango province, at this time representing 80 percent of total production in Angola (Gordon and Ngolo 2004). Furthermore, De Beers had allegedly loaned the MPLA government $50 million to further expand diamond mining, to be repaid by the profits that De Beers made.

Other companies got in on the Angolan diamond market as well, including Lazare Kaplan International, which bought diamonds in Angola until 2008 (Wall Street Journal 2010). This company, owned by American millionaire Maurice Tempelsman, has long been one of the few direct buyers of rough diamonds from De Beers and was an original party to the Kimberley Process (Tempelsman 2008). After Lazare Kaplan International left Angola, Lev Leviev attempted to fill the void by opening local diamond-buying stores (Wall Street Journal 2010). While this trend had already been well underway before the end of the civil war, after the war ended thousands of unlicensed miners came to the diamond fields. According to Gordon and Ngolo (2004), roughly 270,000 to 400,000 miners had descended on Angola's diamond fields, mostly from the Democratic Republic of Congo. This mass migration, and attempts by the Angolan government to expel the miners, would have longstanding implications for how the state has responded to the Kimberley Process.

The end of the civil war in Angola did not bring about an absence of violence in the diamond trade. From 2003 to 2005 the Angolan government expelled roughly 256,400 miners who originated from other countries, often using brutal methods to do so (Blore and Letourneau 2007). Miners had long immigrated to wealthy diamond regions in western Angola from the Democratic Republic of the Congo, but after the civil war ended this trend became more common because of the absence of economic opportunities in the region. Studies have established that numerous undocumented immigrants were abused and even murdered as the Angolan government tried to clear the area of illegal miners (Marques 2005).

These actions by the Angolan government drew widespread criticism from NGOs and human rights groups (Smillie 2014). This could be viewed as ironic because most of these immigrants were not certifying their diamonds according to Kimberley Process regulations. Deportation of miners may have helped raise the level of compliance with the

Kimberley Process in the following years, as some actors who were unlikely to go through any "legal" process to bring diamonds to market were no longer in the country. When governments have perpetrated human rights abuses against their citizens or immigrants in relation to the diamond industry the Kimberley Process has had little influence on these cases, beyond making recommendations.[9] This has created a paradoxical situation, in which the Kimberley Process has little recourse to prevent state violence against "illegal" miners. States will argue that this is a domestic issue and that they have a right to stop the illegal immigration of miners and subsequent smuggling in the diamond trade. In fact, the Kimberley Process requires these measures if diamonds are to be successfully certified (Smillie 2014).

At the outset, the Kimberley Process was mostly ineffective in Angola. Since many neighboring countries to Angola also had inadequate levels of compliance, they became smuggling routes for Angolan diamonds. Gordon and Ngolo (2004) mention a series of countries through which diamonds were smuggled: Democratic Republic of Congo, Tanzania, Guinea, Central African Republic, and the Republic of Congo. Even neighboring countries with higher levels of commitment to and compliance with the Kimberley Process, such as Namibia and South Africa, were allegedly used as smuggling routes.

The lack of initial cooperation with the Kimberley Process can largely be traced to the monopsony Leviev had set up with the Angolan government, and the court battle that was taking place with De Beers. Unlike De Beers, which had been involved in setting up Kimberley Process regulations and has participated in the regime, Leviev has played no role beyond making statements about how diamonds originating from mines he owns comply with the agreement. However, there are cases where the Leviev group have tried to smuggle diamonds without certifying them according to Kimberley Process regulations (Globes 2011, 2012). Thus it is clear that mines owned by Leviev had little commitment to compliance with the Kimberley Process, and during the first few years of implementation Angolan policy reflected this.

[9] This has often been contested, but the definition of a conflict diamond under the Kimberley Process applies only to diamonds that fund rebel movements against "legitimate" governments.

The Return of De Beers, 2005–2009

Angola's diamond sector would change rapidly, so would the response of the state to the Kimberley Process. In 2004, the Angolan government ended the contract with Lev Leviev and opened up the diamond industry to bidding by other foreign companies. In 2005 De Beers and the Angolan government agreed to treat the $50 million loaned by De Beers in 1991 as an investment and created a new joint agreement in which De Beers would have a 49 percent share and the Angolan government-run company Endiama would have 51 percent (BBC 2005). Thus, the court case that had originated over a contract in 1991 between De Beers and the Angolan government was resolved without ever being ruled on. This contract was good for De Beers in comparison to those signed by other private companies to mine in Angola during this period. Most contracts would give Endiama 35–45 percent, a private company would take an amount within the same range, and a "domestic" Angolan company would take about 15–25 percent (Blore and Letourneau 2007). In the Angolan diamond sector, private companies usually provide the technological experience and capital while the "domestic" Angolan companies take some of the profits as part of the government's overall patronage system. Most owners of these companies have connections to the government but little experience in the mining industry or any ability to contribute to the production process (Blore and Letourneau 2007).[10]

In one of the few assertive moves the Kimberley Process has been able to make, the Republic of Congo was expelled from the process in 2004. This happened after diamond exports outpaced any possible level of domestic diamond production, in a country where few diamonds originate (Global Witness 2004). The Republic of Congo had long been viewed as a smuggling route for Angolan diamonds (Grant 2012). While some observers praised this move, outside of this case the

[10] Through joint agreements with private firms, Angolan elites have become wealthy in the diamond trade. The diamond sector has been particularly attractive for elites because there is a low level of risk in comparison to other economic sectors in Angola (Smillie 2014). This has become a prominent part of Angola's patronage system as elites that are loyal to the MPLA government are often given concessions in the diamond trade.

Kimberley Process has had little coercive power against significant diamond producers during this period and was increasingly viewed as a weak regime (Global Witness 2011b). Thus, changes in Angola's response to the Kimberley Process are primarily due to forces outside of direct institutional pressure.

During 2005 Angola changed its response to the Kimberley Process considerably. In fact, during the annual Kimberley Process meeting in November 2005, Angola joined multiple working groups and attempted to become vice chair of the regime in 2006, a position that would make the country chair in 2007 (Grant 2012). This did not take place because of the high level of controversy surrounding Angola's participation in the Kimberley Process to that point, but it does show that policymakers were viewing the country's participation in the regime differently. Because the Kimberley Process has no annual budget, participating in working groups or in a leadership position is paid for directly by the country involved. Therefore, increases in participation within the Kimberley Process represent a higher level of financial investment. At the annual Kimberley Process meeting in 2006, Angola volunteered to lead the "Working Group on Artisanal Alluvial Production" (Kimberley Process 2006). The goal of creating this group was to cooperate around challenges that alluvial diamond producers face, involving Angola investing further in the process.

The return of De Beers as a significant investor in Angola's diamond trade goes a long way to explaining the change in Kimberley Process participation after 2005. The government of Angola wanted to attract more private investors into the diamond market. Thus, participation in the Kimberley Process became an opportunity for Angola to improve the reputation of its domestic diamond trade, even if this did not represent significant administrative improvements in complying with the Kimberley Process on a local level. Alternatively, participating in the Kimberley Process was a way for the government to signal to diamond companies, especially De Beers, that it was serious about improving the reputation of the diamond sector. While participation in the regime was costly, it was probably far cheaper than making investments in local infrastructure that would raise levels of compliance with the Kimberley Process and discourage diamond smuggling, although the government did spend resources on this to some degree during this period (De Boeck 2012).

Angola Becomes Involved, 2009–2015

In 2009 the Angolan government passed more extensive legislation to govern alluvial diamond mining and comply with the Kimberley Process (Grant 2012). In 2011 Angola tried to attract private diamond companies to the country by lowering the tax rate from 35 to 25 percent and the government was only required to own 10 percent of any joint venture (Bloomberg Business 2013). Increasing diamond mining became a way for the Angolan government to "diversify" beyond the oil sector.[11]

Several companies believe that many of Angola's diamonds have yet to be discovered, with at least 60 percent, and potentially over 90 percent, of potential diamond reserves either going undiscovered or not being used. Therefore, it is probable that the same level of diamond mining that exists presently can be maintained or surpassed in the future. Since 2005, there has been a race to find large deposits of diamonds in Angola. De Beers has spent over $250 million in diamond exploration since 2005 (Nyaugwa 2013).

Angola's diamond industry has continued to receive criticism from civil society groups and nongovernmental organizations. For instance, the government has pressed charges of defamation against journalist Rafael Marques de Morais for publishing information critical of the diamond industry and has, in turn, accused him of being involved in the illegal diamond trade (Human Rights Watch 2014a; Office of the High Commissioner for Human Rights 2013). Large-scale smuggling continues as well, totaling roughly $400 million a year (IDEX 2014a). However, smuggling across Angola's borders has declined since the Kimberley Process first came into effect. This is primarily because diamond mines along the common border were sold by both Angola and the Democratic Republic of Congo to large private companies

[11] The Angolan government is often seen as being dependent on the oil sector: oil counts for over 90 percent of the state's export revenue with diamonds accounting for most of the rest, at about 2.5 percent of overall GDP in 2015 (Hodges 2008). While a reliance on oil has made the government less dependent on foreign aid than comparable countries (Nino and Le Billon 2014), this has led government revenue to be dependent on volatile oil markets; thus there is an urgent need to diversify.

(De Boeck 2012).[12] It has been easier for the states to prevent smuggling from large companies in comparison to individual miners. Especially since 2009, cooperation with the Democratic Republic of the Congo has been extensive as both countries have devised strategies to limit smuggling across the border through cooperation between law enforcement agencies (Mining Weekly 2014).

Other countries have also contributed to Angola's increasing attempts to comply with the Kimberley Process. The United Kingdom has been particularly active in assisting Angola to bring about a higher level of compliance with the Kimberley Process (Nam News 2014). The World Diamond Council, a collection of diamond companies, has directly assisted Angola with building capacity to comply with the Kimberley Process (Grant 2012). Even the former US Secretary of State John Kerry praised the Angolan government for leadership in the Kimberley Process and cooperation with other countries in the region (US Department of State 2014). Thus, while Angola's compliance with the Kimberley Process improved to some degree, global perceptions of the diamond trade in Angola changed dramatically. The Angolan government has also started to invest in diamond mining abroad. Angola's state-run oil company, Sonangol, has partnered with Chinese firms to invest in controversial diamond-mining projects in Zimbabwe's Marange diamond fields (Weimer and Vines 2012). Angola also supported Mozambique's bid to join the Kimberley Process and advised the country about how to comply with the agreement (Angola Press 2014).

Beyond questions of compliance with the Kimberley Process that surrounded Angola, the country's ability to effectively lead the regime became controversial even before and right after it assumed the presidency. A significant point of contention has been over a lack of consensus, and therefore inability to choose a vice president for 2015. In early 2015 the Angolan delegation worked to gain consensus on this issue but admitted a lack of resolution (Campos 2015).

[12] Allegedly, Angola placed pressure on the Democratic Republic of the Congo to also pursue a strategy of selling diamond mines to easier-to-police private firms (De Boeck 2012).

The inability to gain consensus on a vice president for 2015, and in turn the likely candidate for president in 2016, was due largely to the fact that both the United Arab Emirates and Australia tried to lobby for this position. Most Western countries were in favor of Australia, with African states and China supporting the United Arab Emirates (IDEX 2014b). Of particular controversy is that Western-based non-governmental organizations criticized the United Arab Emirates for a low level of compliance (IDEX 2014c). In mid-September, Angola was able to announce that the United Arab Emirates would be the chair for 2016 (Barnard 2015). During Angola's tenure as president, this issue took precedence, overshadowing other goals Angola may have had.

New Executive = New Policies?

When João Lourenço took over as president of Angola in 2017, he was widely viewed as a hand-picked successor of Dos Santos. However, in many policy areas Lourenço quickly broke with his predecessor, most notably removing Isabel Dos Santos as head of Angola's national oil company Sonangol (Kindinger 2018). Lourenço also implemented policies designed to undo the large informal economy that had existed in Angola. These policies have had mixed results as formal businesses have benefited, but some of the poorest people in Angola's cities have been left with minimal economic opportunity (Pensador and Alfroy 2018).

In 2018 the Angolan state expelled up to 400,000 Congolese citizens, mainly from the wealthy diamond areas of northwestern Angola (Human Rights Watch 2018; Leotaud 2018). This gained widespread negative attention from NGOs and the global media, as allegedly migrants were abused while being deported from Angola (Human Rights Watch 2018). According to the Angolan government this was done to prevent large-scale diamond smuggling, as many "illegal" diamonds were confiscated and locations where illegal diamond trading was taking place were shut down (Leotaud 2018). Ironically, while it is likely that violations of human rights took place, it is also likely that the government's pursuit of migrants lessened diamond smuggling. These developments did not harm Angola's standing in the Kimberley Process, as in late 2018 it became chair of the Kimberley Process Review and Reform Committee (Agencia Angola Press 2018).

Discussion

As president of the Kimberley Process in 2015, Angola was in charge of an agreement that several observers see as being mostly ineffective to coerce states to change their behavior. However, we can see from the example of Angola's participation in the Kimberley Process that changes in domestic political economy have led Angola to invest scarce resources to cooperate and raise its level of compliance with the Kimberley Process. This is notable because scholars often characterize Angola as a "fragile" state that fails in basic areas of governance (Carment, Samy, and Landry 2013; Nino and Le Billon 2014; Stewart and Brown 2009; Vines and Weimer 2011). Furthermore, it is telling that given the nature of the Angolan state it would respond to the Kimberley Process at all; for many of the more "fragile" states in Africa just participating in the agreement at a minimal level can be a significant cost. In a critique of the ineffective nature of the Kimberley Process in dealing with problematic countries, Kimberley Process founder Ian Smillie (2014, 116) points out "why should other countries enforce costly rules and regulations, submit detailed reports, and attend unproductive meetings in faraway places if these have no meaning, and if there are no consequences to ignoring the entire system." Thus it is significant that states choose to participate at all, and this level of engagement can change over time, as the preceding sections show has been the case with Angola.

In line with the first two hypotheses tested in this case study of Angola (Chapter 2), an explanation for changes in state-level responses to the Kimberley Process can primarily be found in a changing domestic political economy. We can see that with Hypotheses 1 and 2, increases in dependence on the diamond industry for government revenue, and variation in the market share between private economic actors in the diamond sector have led to these preferences that ultimately became reflected in policy. In an attempt to diversify the economy, and increase mining output, the government of Angola has increasingly tried to grow the diamond industry and attract foreign firms to mine diamonds. Table 3.1 shows Angola's legal diamond production from the Kimberley Process (2017).

Diamond production is now consistently over a billion dollars a year, and this trend will most likely continue in the future as Angolan diamonds are among the world's highest quality. Thus, given the

Table 3.1 *Diamond production in Angola*

Year	Volume in carats	Value, US$
2004	6,146,360.89	788,138,694.08
2005	7,079,120.65	1,089,170,955.67
2006	9,175,060.73	1,132,514,825.77
2007	9,701,708.71	1,271,955,353.15
2008	8,906,974.26	1,209,789,970.30
2009	9,238,270.96	804,094,820.79
2010	8,362,139.06	976,318,204.86
2011	8,328,518.96	1,162,625,477.64
2012	8,330,995.68	1,110,222,942.13
2013	9,360,469.88	1,277,644,487.07
2014	8,791,340.01	1,317,456,071.65
2015	9,016,342.67	$1,182,128,882.07
2016	9,021,467.07	1,079,411,359.30
2017	9,438,802.06	1,104,622,553.37

Source: Kimberley Process Diamond Statistics (2017).

importance of this sector both for tax revenue and to reward those who are loyal to the MPLA regime, Angola has a clear incentive to pursue policies around the Kimberley Process that are attractive to private diamond companies. Furthermore, it is likely that this sector will continue to receive government attention as a way to "diversify" the government beyond oil.

As De Beers has gained market share in Angola, especially in comparison to the Leviev group, cooperation and compliance with the process has increased. Because of the close relationship that De Beers has had to the Kimberley Process, it is apparent that when it gains market share in a country, it is likely to pressure the state to take the agreement more seriously. Some observers have even argued that De Beers is more influential in Kimberley Process decision-making than states themselves and that the Kimberley Process is mostly a public provision of a private good in which states bear the costs of regulating the diamond trade, but De Beers gets the reputational benefits (Haufler 2009b).

Beyond just reputational benefits, looking at the case of Angola and the history of the diamond trade in sub-Saharan Africa, the Kimberley Process offered De Beers the opportunity to use an international agreement to lock in policy preferences against diamond smuggling. These have long been the policy preferences of De Beers as diamonds outside of cartel control were a threat to its ability to set prices on the global diamond market. Since De Beers could anticipate losing some of the global diamond trade, the Kimberley Process made it more difficult to change policy in the future through international regulation. Thus, if the relative market share of De Beers were to drop in relation to other actors who do not share the same preferences, such as the Leviev group, policies associated with the preferences of De Beers would be locked in through an international agreement. In fact, since the early 2000s De Beers has increased market share in Angola and Namibia, despite the challenge of Lev Leviev, whose investments are worth about a fourth of what they were when the Kimberley Process was implemented (Forbes 2014; Rough and Polished 2013).[13]

Despite extensive cooperation with other countries and overall preferences for compliance with the Kimberley Process in Angola, the geographical location of diamonds remains a challenge, consistent with Hypothesis 3. Many of Angola's diamonds are spread out over a large area in northern Angola and require little if any technological investment to extract. Similar to other countries with comparable distributions of diamonds, such as Sierra Leone, it is unlikely that Angola will ever be able to comply at the level of other states, such as Botswana or Namibia, that have far easier geographic constraints to navigate (Munier 2016b; Wilson 2011). Drawing on Le Billon (2001a), Angola's diamonds are a distant resource, far from the capital and spread out over a large area. These diamonds are also more correlated with civil war funding. These factors make compliance with the Kimberley Process more difficult, even if states wish to comply.

The state that is most similar to Angola in this study is Namibia, which shares a long southern border and was embroiled in the same conflict until the early 1990s. The clear difference between these cases is that De Beers has been more dominant over the diamond trade in Namibia and the geographical location of diamonds makes governance easier. While it is probable that the diamond sector will continue to be relevant to the political economy of Angola, especially

[13] Even if De Beers has a difficult time dominating the global diamond market, given the growth of the Russian diamond industry, which is largely outside its control, it is clear that the firm intends to maintain a dominant role in sub-Saharan Africa and has been successful in doing so.

with falling oil prices and a desire from the government to diversify, the dependence of the Namibian state on the diamond sector is greater. Thus, while Angola's response to the Kimberley Process has been based on a high level of competition for market share since 2003, the most important factor behind Namibia's higher level of compliance is the consistent dominance of De Beers.

Conclusion

In this chapter it is apparent that private actors can influence state behavior within a single regime over time. As the case of Angola illustrates, important political decisions that states make often involve private actors. By placing pressure on states, private actors can impact the decisions made by international agreements as they compete for market share. This case illustrates that as the dependence of the Angolan government increased over time, preferences by domestic political actors became reflected more prominently in policy. With significant political decisions being increasingly decided at the international level, especially decisions that have important consequences for developing countries, the experience of Angola since the Kimberley Process was implemented gives us insight into how international regimes work and develop in specific cases over time. Furthermore, Angola's experience with the Kimberley Process illustrates how resource dependence allows multinational corporations to influence the political process not only at the domestic level but at the international level as well.

4 Diamonds, Dependence, and De Beers

Monopoly Capitalism and Compliance with the Kimberley Process in Namibia

Although many countries in sub-Saharan Africa have had difficulty complying and cooperating with the Kimberley Process, one exception is Namibia, the focus of this chapter.[1] Namibian compliance is surprising because it has several of the same attributes commonly associated with noncompliance, including a weak state structure; a high poverty rate; a reliance on alluvial diamonds, which are more often tied to conflict; and difficulties with postconflict state building.[2] However, what is different about Namibia is a high level of domestic diamond dependence on De Beers that has led to the state complying with the regime at a high level. This case is important to examine because it

[1] Given that the ultimate goal of the Kimberley Process is for every diamond that originates from or is imported into a country to be certified, this is the main focus when examining compliance. Several countries in sub-Saharan Africa have had difficulty complying with the Kimberley Process despite a high level of diamond production and with varying state responses to the process, including Angola, Democratic Republic of Congo, Liberia, Sierra Leone, and Zimbabwe. For instance, Angola's response to the Kimberley Process has varied over time, from initial reluctance to cooperate with the regime to its current status as president, although the state continues to have a low level of compliance. This varying response to the Kimberley Process and continued low level of compliance in Angola are due largely to changes in market share among private actors in the country and the political geography of where diamonds are found (Munier 2014). While many countries in sub-Saharan Africa have made only minimal efforts to comply with the Kimberley Process (Smillie 2010b), low levels of compliance are not always due to lack of political will. Indeed, there are some countries in the Kimberley Process – a good example is Sierra Leone – that have cooperated extensively with the Kimberley Process but are unable to certify many of their diamonds, and thus their compliance rate is low (Grant 2012; Maconachie 2009). Only a few countries in sub-Saharan Africa, particularly Botswana, Namibia and South Africa, have been viewed as complying with the process (Grant 2013a, 2013b).

[2] Major studies on the relationship between alluvial diamonds and conflict are: Le Billon (2008, 2012); Snyder and Bhavnani (2005). Vlassenroot and Van Bockstael (2008) given an overview of how alluvial diamonds present many governance challenges for post-conflict states.

shows how historical dependence on natural resources can influence state responses to international regimes. Ultimately, as this research will illustrate in Namibia, this condition has led to policy outcomes that undermine state sovereignty and the ability of a democratic government to set resource policy on its own. The case of Namibia also shows that while the Kimberley Process may claim that its goal is to make it more difficult for "conflict diamonds" to reach the global market, in practice it has largely been a regime that has benefited De Beers and a small political elite in Namibia, while making it more difficult for other private companies to successfully enter the Namibian diamond market.

In the late 1990s, when the international community became more aware of how diamonds were fueling conflict in Africa, the Namibian government became concerned that this could lead to a consumer boycott and a drop in the market for diamonds. In May 2000 Namibia was one of the first countries to start creating a system that could restore consumer confidence and ensure that diamonds on the global market had not originated in conflict zones. This would become the Kimberley Process certification scheme in 2003 (Grant and Taylor 2004; Wright 2004). Since this time Namibia has been a prominent part of decision-making in the Kimberley Process; it has cooperated with other countries to help them comply, and it is generally regarded as a country in which the origin of diamonds is effectively monitored in most cases.

The History of Namibian Diamond Dependence

To understand the present-day dynamics that led to compliance with the Kimberley Process in Namibia, it is crucial to examine how the present state became dependent on diamond wealth and how this shapes present-day policy choices. After Germany lost World War One Namibia became part of South Africa.[3] With the South African government in power, this led to a joint extraction process in the diamond trade. In the early 1920s, Ernest Oppenheimer bought up several smaller corporations and created the Consolidated Diamond

[3] During German colonialism most of the coercive capacity of the state was concentrated on diamond-wealthy areas (De Juan, Krautwald, and Pierskalla 2017).

Mines, which would later become De Beers (McIntyre 1998). This agreement placed Namibia's southwestern coast under the control of a large private diamond corporation. A system of contract labor developed around the diamond industry in which workers signed a contract through the government, essentially making them the property of their private employers (Cooper 1999).

However, South African rule of Namibia would soon spark domestic opposition and the South West Africa People's Organization was founded in the early 1960s to oppose South African rule in Namibia and replace the apartheid system with majority rule. This would have significant implications for the Namibia-De Beers relationship. SWAPO initially argued that the existing fifty-fifty partnership with De Beers was incompatible with its socialistic goals. However, eight years before Namibia gained independence from South Africa, De Beers Chairman Harry Frederick Oppenheimer argued that no political arrangement in Namibia could survive independently unless the country took advantage of the money that could be made through a partnership with De Beers (Epstein 1982). His prediction appears to have been correct. In 1994 Namibia signed a fifty-fifty partnership with De Beers, to be renewed every five years (Stein 2001). De Beers also changed the name of its diamond-mining operations in Namibia to Namdeb, to reflect the joint agreement between De Beers and the Namibian state. It is unclear when De Beers started to influence SWAPO. Maurice Temelsman, an influential American diamond trader with close ties to De Beers, allegedly has had ties to SWAPO since the 1960s (Amupadhi 2001), although the first president of Namibia Sam Nujoma (2001) says that talks between SWAPO and De Beers did not start till the late 1980s, when independence was inevitable. During the talks that took place after Namibian independence, Maurice Temelsman served as an advisor to SWAPO (Cooper 2001).

From early on, after independence, SWAPO sided with De Beers over striking workers in the diamond mines. This happened both in 1992, when intervention by the government stopped a strike within a day, and again in 1993 (Bauer 1998). While having a joint agreement with a quasi-monopoly does not fit well with the "socialistic" outlook that SWAPO has tried to portray, in this case it chose what may perhaps have been a pragmatic approach, but in turn had the result of enriching party elites. Given the power base that the party has, while the arrangement with De Beers might not be politically popular, it does not appear as though the party has ever spent political capital on it. Cooper (2001, 321) characterizes SWAPO as a "subsidiary of De Beers" and goes on to say that "the most telling example of Namdeb's centrality in the life of Namibia is the fact that most Independence Day celebrations held during Namibia's first decade of existence took place at DeBeers headquarters in Oranjemund rather than in the capital city of Windhoek."

De Beers has a clear influence over political decision-making in Namibia, given its centrality to the economy. It is also important to point out that since the beginning of the Kimberley Process, De Beers has been very influential in the agreement. In fact, some observers have argued that De Beers is more influential than the states in the process and that the agreement is a public provision of a private good (Haufler 2009b). The Kimberley Process has allowed De Beers, and by extension Namibia, to argue that the diamond trade is largely conflict-free, thus perhaps creating a high level of consumer confidence. It is clear that diamond dependence was an inescapable dynamic of Namibia's political economy long before the Kimberley Process began, and up to the present. This historical legacy leads to a possible explanation for compliance with the Kimberley Process in that it is clear that diamond dependence has strong historical roots.

Since diamond dependence has been a central feature of Namibia's political and economic development, it important to recognize that the introduction of policies designed to comply with the Kimberley Process originated both as a result of and with the constraints brought about by a high level of historical dependence on the diamond trade. The fact that Namibia is diamond dependent answers on a basic level why it would not want to face sanctions from the Kimberley Process, as this would cut it off from most of the global diamond trade. However, given the weak nature of the Kimberley Process, and the fact that it has never pushed sanctions against a major diamond producer, it only partially explains why Namibia goes far above a basic level when it comes to compliance and commitment to the process.[4] Thus this chapter examines in depth how domestic diamond dependence

[4] For a discussion on the institutional weakness of the Kimberley Process see Gooch (2008); Grant (2013b); Maconachie (2009); Smillie (2010b).

facilitates compliance through the ability of De Beers to transfer its preferred policy positions into government policy and how the company has used Kimberley Process regulations to gain market advantage.

The Ability for De Beers to Constrain SWAPO Policy

Namibia's dependence on the diamond industry raises the potential for De Beers to be able to transfer its preferences regarding Kimberley Process compliance into Namibian government policy. This is a useful avenue of inquiry for Namibia as SWAPO had long opposed the role of De Beers in Namibia, but signed a fifty-fifty agreement with De Beers in 1994 that ensured the new Namibian government would be heavily dependent on De Beers (Stein 2001). Since De Beers first entered Namibia, the company has had the ability to constrain the potential policy choices of local decision-makers, and this influence continues today. How profits are split between the government and De Beers is not public information and significant aspects of Namdeb's relationship with the state are kept secret (Boer and Sherbourne 2003; Rieckmann 2008). Unlike Botswana, Namibia does not hold direct shares in De Beers; however, there is a representative from the Namibian government on the board of directors (Rieckmann 2008). For Namdeb, the board of directors is also split fifty-fifty, with six being appointed by the government and the other six by De Beers (Mbwale 2010).

Table 4.1 shows that diamond production in Namibia stayed steady during the 1990s, even during the political transition to SWAPO rule in 1994, and that diamond wealth remained an important part of the economy throughout. Also, diamond proceeds represented a big part of overall GDP and are the main export.

Since a large proportion of Namibia's economic activity derives from the diamond trade, it is unlikely that the government could quickly change policy in this area. Some parts of Namibian society would want this industry to be nationalized, but that would likely lead to lower productivity (Boer and Sherbourne 2004). Furthermore, the threat of nationalization or the removal of De Beers from Namibia would not be a credible threat given its reliance on both tax revenue and unknown earnings from its arrangement with De Beers. Therefore, policy in the diamond sector has been and will continue to be constrained by De Beers in the future.

Table 4.1 ***Diamond dependence in Namibia***

Year	Diamond mining as percentage of tax revenue	Diamond mining as percentage of GDP	Diamonds as percentage of merchandise exports
1993	8.8	5.9	37
1994	11.0	7.0	32
1995	7.4	5.5	34
1996	6.0	7.0	38
1997	7.1	6.7	40
1998	13.8	6.6	32
1999	6.6	7.4	38
2000	6.2	7.3	43
2001	9.0	9.5	40
2002	12.9	10.4	39
2003	17.5	7.2	27
2004	5.4	8.2	35
2005	6.6	7.0	31
2006	4.6	8.7	32
2007	4.8	5.9	21
2008	4.3	8.5	19
2009	2.4	3.5	17
2010	3.3	5.7	20
2011	0.0	4.7	20
2012	5.4	7.6	21
2013	4.7	8.7	24
2014	1.9	9.0	28
2015	6.3	8.1	28
2016	6.5	7.3	23
2017	5.2	7.7	No data

Sources: Chamber of Mines of Namibia (2012, 2017); Ministry of Labour and Social Welfare (2012).

Give and Take

The relationship between the government and De Beers is not completely a one-way street. The joint extraction process has led to the government having a stake in decision-making surrounding diamond policy that it might not have had, given other arrangements. This is important because it gives the Namibian government influence over how many diamonds are extracted. The number of diamonds produced only tells part of the story of Namibia's immense diamond wealth. Namibian diamonds are worth more per unit than those of any other country, with Angola coming a rather distant second (Boer and Sherbourne 2004). Increases in marine diamond mining should also allow Namibia to profit from the diamond trade at a comparable level in the future (Boer and Sherbourne 2004). Therefore, even if the number of diamonds that are mined declines over time, diamond wealth is likely to continue its role as an important part of the Namibian economy and in turn the political system.

The government of Namibia, through its fifty-fifty partnership with De Beers, has been able to pursue some policies that the private diamond sector would not pursue on its own. For instance, through Namdeb in 2007 the Namibia Diamond Trading Company was established, although De Beers did not view this as being economically optimal (Mbwale 2010). It is clear that the government of Namibia had an incentive to try to polish more diamonds as this would add to jobs and more revenue for the state, in contrast to sending them to De Beers' polishing centers in London. Polishing diamonds domestically in Namibia has implications for certifying diamonds as well (Oliver 2011). These diamonds are certified not only as originating in Namibia but also as being polished in Namibia (Rieckmann 2008). The government has viewed this as being a way to get the most out of its diamond wealth, since polished diamonds are often worth far more than those still in a rough form.

Despite the ability of the Namibian government to get De Beers to implement some policies that it would not pursue on its own, this does not necessarily downplay the influence of De Beers. It is likely that decision-makers in De Beers view the joint extraction agreement with the Namibian government as lasting far into the future, so it makes sense to make some suboptimal policy choices in the interest of keeping the overall relationship satisfactory for both actors. Also, there is little evidence that the government of Namibia could get De Beers to change policy in a way that would be clearly to the latter's disadvantage or could pursue government policies in the diamond sector that would seriously marginalize De Beers.

The Use of the Kimberley Process as a Way for De Beers to Maintain Monopolistic Policies

Without the Kimberley Process, certifying that diamonds did not originate in conflict zones may have been left up to private companies.[5] Thus the Kimberley Process allowed private diamond companies to pass some of the cost of regulating diamonds on to states. Given the close relationship between De Beers and the Namibian government, this dynamic can be clearly observed as both had a mutual interest in creating a diamond regulation system that is at least perceived as being successful. Overall, it is likely that both De Beers and the Namibian government calculated the costs of implementing the Kimberley Process against the possibility that the diamond market could lose consumer confidence, and concluded that the latter would be far more costly. At the very least, given De Beers' prominent role in the Kimberley Process and the Namibian economy, it appears as though the Namibian government is forced to implement policies that reach a satisfactory level of compliance.

Few other diamond companies have existed in Namibia outside of De Beers. One exception, and possibly the only company ever to challenge De Beers in Namibia, is the Lev Leviev group.[6] As with the activity of any diamond company, its activities have important implications for the success of the Kimberley Process. In the case of Namibia, this also presents an interesting opportunity for understanding how Kimberley Process rules, and the motives of those who seek to implement, them can influence state behavior.

[5] Some private companies have gone beyond just Kimberley Process regulations in trying to assure that their product is not related to conflict (Responsible Jewelry Council 2014).

[6] Lev Leviev became a multibillionaire by polishing diamonds and controlling a large amount of the market, first in Russia, and then in Angola (Goldman 2003). Lev Leviev has had a strategy of being involved in every area of the diamond supply chain and negotiating directly with governments. This has made him a competitor of De Beers worldwide. While De Beers still controls the vast majority of the diamond market, this position does appear less inevitable than in the past. The Lev Leviev group has nowhere near the media visibility that De Beers has, so when De Beers was being criticized for its role in the Angolan diamond trade this allowed the Lev Leviev group to take a larger share of the country's diamond-mining operations. The Lev Leviev group is secretive, even for a diamond-trading company, and has been controversial for building settlements on the West Bank in Israel and building private prisons; and many will argue that local communities have not benefited from mining operations that the company has led (Chafets 2007).

Lev Leviev Group

Lev Leviev entered Namibia in 2001 when he spent $30 million on a marine diamond-mining operation called Namco, which would ultimately go bankrupt (Boer and Sherbourne 2004). The first president of an independent Namibia, Sam Nujoma, was optimistic about Lev Leviev's entry into Namibia's diamond market, allegedly because he saw it as a way to make the diamond industry more beneficial for local communities (Kaure 2011). Lev Leviev's commitment to polishing diamonds in Namibia was an attractive option as this would lead to more revenue staying in the country. There is reason to believe that the Lev Leviev group may have used financial resources to influence government policy. One example is that Sam Nujoma was given a bursary to study at the University of Namibia by the Lev Leviev group in 2005 (Kaure 2011).

The bursary could, therefore, be seen as a way for the Namibian government to leverage more favorable terms with De Beers, as Lev Leviev had challenged De Beers in other regions. Also, allowing Lev Leviev to gain influence was successful in pressuring De Beers to spend more on polishing diamonds inside Namibia (Goldman 2003; Isaacs 2005). In fact, many in the media saw Lev Leviev's entrance into Namibia as a way to challenge De Beers directly and some De Beers officials admitted that it concerned them (The Economist 2004).

In 2011 the Namibian police took 1,825 diamonds from the Lev Leviev group that were not certified and unlikely to be from Namibia (Globes 2012). Namibia also involved Interpol in the investigation. This was a crime that appeared international in nature as the diamonds were most likely being smuggled to Israel (Globes 2011). Some who were found with the diamonds said that they were following orders from the Lev Leviev office in Tel Aviv, Israel, and that the diamonds had been smuggled into Namibia, a clear violation of Kimberley Process rules (Kisting 2012). One worker, Gabi Shitrit, was allegedly sent back to Israel the night of the illicit diamond discovery, possibly because he was going to talk about the company's activity (Kisting 2011). The Namibian Diamond Trading Company decided to no longer sell diamonds to the Lev Leviev Group, allegedly because of the uncertified diamonds. This greatly hurt the company's polishing operation in Namibia and its future prospects in the country have been greatly diminished and remain unclear (Nyaungwa 2012).

The Namibian government, in dealing with Lev Leviev, has shown that it takes the smuggling of uncertified diamonds seriously, especially if that plays to its economic advantage. This case of finding uncertified diamonds in the Lev Leviev group's factory demonstrates that the Namibian police are willing to work with Interpol, even in cases where people are only suspected of crossing state lines (Haufiku 2014). Since it is likely that uncertified diamonds cross the Namibian border frequently, catching Leviev could be interpreted as "tactical policing," especially when the inclusion of Interpol is taken into consideration. Regardless, this no doubt puts De Beers in a more dominant economic position if the Leviev group is no longer a challenger in Namibia, and this incentive may influence the Namibian government to act more forcefully than it otherwise would. With the decline of the Leviev group in Namibia, Kimberley Process violations give the Namibian government the ability to break ties with a company that appears to have lost what minimal influence it once had on decision-making. Unlike De Beers, which was influential in setting up the rules of the Kimberley Process and is usually viewed as a company that encourages compliance, the Lev Leviev group has had little influence on the process and is therefore unlikely to have the same level of commitment to it. In Angola, Lev Leviev has been controversial as there are reports of diamonds being smuggled to escape taxation and an overall lack of interest in complying with the process.[7]

De Beers and Capital Investment in Namibia

Few if any other companies in Namibia have the resources to ensure compliance with the Kimberley Process beyond De Beers. At the very least, compliance is more costly for competitors, thus making the market inherently more difficult to enter. De Beers has been able to make expensive capital investments in Namibia that would be difficult for other companies. For instance, in 2011 the company announced

[7] While Leviev once controlled the entire diamond trade in Angola, it now competes heavily with De Beers for market share. The government of Angola has become increasingly willing to cooperate with the Kimberley Process as the market share of De Beers has steadily increased after the resolution of a court case allowed the company back into the country in 2005.

that it would spend N$5 billion so that diamond mines off Namibia's southern coast could continue after 2015, which is how long they were predicted to stay open without any changes (Cloete 2011). As the future of diamond mining in Namibia continues to be increasingly based on marine mining, this gives De Beers a further advantage over potential competitors. In 2013 De Beers extracted a record 1.6 million carats from the ocean (Brandt 2014a). The success of marine diamond mining has come through high capital investment from De Beers that would be far more difficult for potential competitors. For instance, De Beers has announced it will invest N$100 million in a new ship for marine diamond mining (Brandt 2014b). If diamond mining in Namibia continues to be increasingly offshore, this will make it more costly to enter the market. Given the high level of capital investment De Beers has made in Namibia's diamond industry in recent years, in comparison to potential competitors, De Beers has the most capacity to comply with the Kimberley Process, whereas any competitor entering the market would have a difficult time paying these costs.

If we take the theory of Haufler (2009b) that the Kimberley Process is largely the public provision of a private good, it would appear as though the potential exists for De Beers to set up rules in the Kimberley Process that would favor it in competition with other firms. At the very least, it is unlikely that De Beers would agree to a certification process that would be difficult to follow for its local companies and the states within which it is active. Smaller firms are unlikely to be as concerned with reputational benefits that the Kimberley Process may offer, as to many consumers De Beers and the diamond industry are synonymous. Also, De Beers has the ability to influence states in which it is a major economic player to push for sanctions against companies that fail to comply with Kimberley Process regulations. This could be due both to a desire by De Beers to lessen competition and/or an interest in keeping states where it is the biggest diamond producer above the criticism that could result from an uncertified diamond supply. In Namibia, the experience of the Lev Leviev group, along with De Beers' near monopoly over the domestic diamond trade, would suggest that there is more to a high level of compliance with the Kimberley Process than just ridding the region of diamonds that are related to conflict; it is also a way in which De Beers can leverage its advantage over competitors.

Reputation: International Dynamics and Domestic Concerns

Reputation is another key mechanism through which diamond dependence has led to a higher level of compliance with the Kimberley Process in Namibia.[8] Given De Beers' dominant role in the diamond industry, any negative publicity in this sector could reflect upon it, even in countries where De Beers is not active, or in circumstances that the company does not control directly. Thus, this desire for a global system to reassure the public that diamonds sold in local stores did not originate from a conflict zone is a central reason why the Kimberley Process was created (Bieri 2010a). In 2008 Namibia was vice chair of the Kimberley Process and then chair in 2009, giving the country a level of influence over the process (Iita 2008). In addition, De Beers has spent resources trying to cultivate a positive image of the company among Namibians setting up the Namdeb Social Fund in 1994, which has funded local schools, research, and healthcare (Karamata 2008).

Namibia has been active in building a reputation for clean diamonds and has spent resources to strengthen the Kimberley Process as a whole. For instance, Namibia has partnered with other countries in the Diamond Development Initiative (Taylor and Mokhawa 2003). This group is intertwined with the Kimberley Process as the same actors are involved in both. The goals of the Diamond Development Initiative are to encourage the use of diamond wealth that is found in sub-Saharan African countries to build higher levels of economic prosperity for the continent (Smillie 2012). Similar to the Kimberley

[8] Scholars have theorized that states join international regimes because they lead to more optimal policy outcomes than if the regime did not exist (Keohane 1984; Keohane and Nye 1977; Mitchell 1994; Simmons 2009). Compliance with a specific regime should be understood in the context of a wide range of commitments a state makes (Guzman 2008). In some cases, especially among weak or new states, participation in regimes can be a way to establish state sovereignty and build reputation among the international community (Weinthal 2002). Furthermore, in many cases states have a vested interest in making an international regime work beyond just its borders, and participation in assisting other states with compliance can be a way to gain a good reputation. Reputation explains variation in compliance in multiple ways. States that have a high commitment to a regime may comply if support for the regime will pay off over time. Even if complying is domestically unpopular, elites can use a regime as a way to justify their policies and it can also signal to both domestic and international audiences that the state is pursuing policies that are in accord with global norms (Hillebrecht 2014).

Process, the Diamond Development Initiative is built on reputational concerns, seeking to show how diamond wealth in sub-Saharan Africa is used for positive goals.

Namibia is also a member in both the Southern African Development Community and the South African Customs Union. These economic organizations that have led to common regional standards in mining policy (South African Development Community 1997). De Beers is active in the states that are members in both of these organizations, in most cases dominating the domestic extraction process through a joint agreement with local governments. Given the level of interdependence between South African states and the fact that these governments are based on similar ideologies, it is likely that policy related to the Kimberley Process would be similar among them. Furthermore, the role of De Beers in the region would reinforce this further. Thus, there are layers of reputational concerns that the Namibian state has when choosing policies that relate to Kimberley Process regulations, and by and large these concerns point to compliance.

A Helping Hand

Given that controversy surrounding the diamond market could affect De Beers and in turn the government in Namibia, this has led to the Namibian government to share its technical knowledge about how to certify diamonds effectively with other states in Africa. For example, when Liberia first entered the Kimberley Process in 2007, amid controversy, Namibia was involved in sharing knowledge about how to certify diamonds with the government (Sibeene 2008). The case of Liberia shows that compliance with the Kimberley Process can be costly to states and local actors, in some cases to the point where it is impossible without help from other states (Reuters 2012a). Thus the Kimberley Process is a case where third-party actors or side-payments may be required in order to make the regime successful overall.[9]

Namibia has also been a major decision-maker in attempts by the Kimberley Process to help Zimbabwe comply with the regulations. The case of Zimbabwe has proven difficult for the Kimberley Process, as allegedly 200 miners were killed in the Marange region in 2008 (Smille 2010b). This led to a crisis for the Kimberley Process, as its inability to

[9] See Weinthal (2002).

pursue sanctions against Zimbabwe led many to believe that the agreement was too weak.[10] Since decision-making in the Kimberley Process is based on consensus, Zimbabwe's regional allies, including Namibia, were able to block sanctions from being pressed. However, at the same time the Namibian government saw the controversy over Zimbabwe as having negative repercussions for its domestic diamond trade (Shejavali 2009).

It is one thing for Namibia to spend scarce resources to certify its own diamonds but why spend resources to help other states certify their diamonds? This shows how in an era of increasing globalization states such as Namibia have to worry about dynamics that exist in other countries, even if this does not immediately implicate them. In fact, what consumers in countries such as the United States or China think about the diamond trade could have clear implications for the Namibian market. Thus, Namibian assistance to other states in Africa to comply with the Kimberley Process has the potential to benefit the Namibian economy. The Namibian government's commitment to the overall reputation of the Kimberley Process is illustrative of the extent to which the state is dependent on diamond wealth.

Diamond Beneficiation in Namibia

This situation has not only undermined our ability to industrialize our economy, but it has also placed our country and the rest of the African continent in a state of dependency.

Namibian President Hifikepunye Pohamba quoted in Hamutumwa (2012)

The diamond beneficiation sector in Namibia has historically been small. In 2017 there were about a thousand workers in eleven small companies that beneficiated diamonds (Brandt 2017). This is up from around 970 workers in 2013, but down from roughly 1,500 in 2008 (De Beers 2014). However, this places Namibia consistently ahead of South Africa in both the relative and absolute size of its diamond beneficiation sector and is ahead of both Angola and Zimbabwe.

[10] Many human rights groups and nongovernmental organizations began to question whether the Kimberley Process had any meaningful influence over state behavior or if it was just a cover for exploitative mining practices (Global Witness 2011a).

The only state in Southern Africa that has had more success in the diamond beneficiation sector is Botswana.

Much of Botswana's success in the diamond sector relative to Namibia's is the ability the government has had to strategize over a long period, since some economic sectors in Namibia, similar to other states in Southern Africa, lacked a clear long-term strategy (Fessehaie and Rustomjee 2018; Lange 2004). While Namibia has a fifty-fifty ownership agreement with De Beers, this is not nearly as strong as Botswana's and is similar to the deal that Namibia had with De Beers when South Africa occupied the country before 1990. Namibia has had a difficult time significantly changing the status quo in the diamond trade post-independence in many areas. For instance, during the time apartheid South Africa occupied Namibia, environmental aspects of mining were poorly regulated and undoing this trajectory has been difficult for the government (Littlewood 2015).

In areas in which diamond mining takes place, many Namibians do see diamond beneficiation and the job opportunities that could result from this as an important political issue (Littlewood 2015). Furthermore, many Namibians feel as though the negative side of mining has been overlooked and that local beneficiation could have positive effects on the local economy after mines have been exhausted. Many Namibians likely understand that they are getting a poor deal from mining companies in terms of local beneficiation, but it has been difficult to find an economically viable alternative. Furthermore, while Namibians may see some aspects of the Zimbabwean push for indigenization in the economy as being legitimate, they are hesitant to implement the same policies locally as these are associated with economic collapse. Namibians would like to get more of the value from their diamonds but are hesitant to change the status quo in this policy area. That lack of economic diversity in regions where mining has taken place has led to the decline if not outright abandonment of mining towns in Namibia (Littlewood 2014).

Namibia in Comparison

The state that is most similar to Namibia in terms of responding to the Kimberley Process is Angola. The clear difference between these states is the ability for the Lev Leviev group to get a foothold in Angola based on a monopsony until 2006. While Lev Leviev has consistently lost market share in Angola since, it is still a viable competitor to De Beers. On the other hand, in Namibia the Lev Leviev group tried to make inroads into the market but has been largely unsuccessful in breaking the traditional monopoly that De Beers has held in Namibia. In Angola, Kimberley Process regulations and an increased commitment to the Kimberley Process have placed competitors to De Beers at a disadvantage. However, Namibia is the clearest example of the political nature of the Kimberley Process, as the state used these regulations to pursue Lev Leviev after the syndicate fell out of favor.

When comparing Namibia with Zimbabwe it is clear that the former has had far more political and in turn regulatory stability in the diamond trade. Given the dominance of De Beers in the country, the Namibian state has mostly had its mining policy dictated to it since independence. On the other hand, Zimbabwe was not a significant diamond producer until 2006, leaving the state to formulate a regulatory policy that did not have longstanding precedence.

Conclusion: Namibia's Democratic Deficit and Diamond Certification

The dominant role of De Beers in both the Kimberley Process and in Namibian politics helps explain why Namibia has been more inclined to comply with the Kimberley Process. Since De Beers was influential in setting up the Kimberley Process, it is clear that it formulated rules that the company expected to follow. De Beers has followed Kimberley Process regulations in Namibia by transferring policy preferences and the cost of compliance onto the Namibian government. Other companies that have entered the Namibian diamond market have lacked the will and possibly the resources to certify diamonds, and the Namibian government has been quick to try to eliminate the trade in smuggled diamonds. Some of this may be because a tainted diamond supply in Namibia would appear bad for De Beers in general, even if De Beers had nothing to do with compliance violations. More importantly, this is a way for De Beers to raise the costs of competitors entering the Namibian diamond market, as it is proportionately more costly for them to spend resources on certifying diamonds and paying taxes to the Namibian government than it is for De Beers.

Since De Beers has more influence on the domestic decision-making process in Namibia than any other economic actor, it is clear that its preferences when it comes to the Kimberley Process are reflected in government policy. As long as De Beers remains the dominant economic force in Namibia, it is likely that the government will take compliance with the Kimberley Process seriously. Also, from this study, we can predict that states in which the diamond sector is dominated by companies that have not been influential in both the Kimberley Process and the domestic political decision-making process are unlikely to comply at as high a level. The main reason for this is that companies that do not have an influence on the Kimberley Process are unlikely to have policy preferences to comply that are as strong as those of Namibia; the governments where these firms are dominant will reflect this.

The Kimberley Process has provided the government of Namibia with some benefits, as it has more influence in the decision-making process than in most international agreements (Bieri 2010a; Grant 2013a, 2013b, 2018), and it is a way for the government to portray itself as having a commitment to international regimes, regardless of how strong that commitment actually is. However, the Kimberley Process has also reinforced Namibia's historical dependence on diamond wealth and ensured that De Beers would be able to maintain monopolistic practices in the region. This study shows that the mechanisms that give rise to compliance with international agreements can be of a dismal nature for economic competition and democratic practice. The Kimberley Process has allowed a monopolistic company, De Beers, to implement its policy preferences through an international regime, as opposed to having sovereign states decide what approach to take toward diamond certification. As this chapter has shown, in Namibia a high level of compliance with the Kimberley Process is grounded in historical diamond dependence. Thus the international regime's influence is far from optimal for domestic decision-makers and those who would desire more broad-based economic participation.

5 The One Who Controls the Diamond Wears the Crown

The Politicization of the Kimberley Process in Zimbabwe

Why has Zimbabwe, a state that has been notorious for utter disregard of international agreements, spent resources to implement policies that are in compliance with the Kimberley Process diamond certification scheme? This research explains variation in Zimbabwean regulatory policy in response to the Kimberley Process since 2003. This chapter contends that this variation can be best understood by tracing the political economy of factional rivalries within the ruling Zimbabwe African National Union-Patriotic Front (ZANU-PF) party. This chapter demonstrates that although the behavior of international regimes and private economic actors matters, in Zimbabwe it is government factions within ZANU-PF that are the main decision-makers in relation to Kimberley Process regulations. This explains both why compliance with the Kimberley Process has been lower than other states in Southern Africa and why Zimbabwe has raised its level of compliance with the regulatory regime over time.

The Zimbabwe African National Union-Patriotic Front, has been the ruling party since Zimbabwe gained independence in 1980. This ruling party and former president, Robert Mugabe, have become notorious for often ignoring international agreements.[1] However, factional rivalries within the ZANU-PF party have created the conditions in which Zimbabwe has raised its level of compliance with the Kimberley Process diamond certification scheme since this international agreement was implemented in 2003. This agreement, which has the stated goal of riding the global market of diamonds that are tied to conflict, has become crucial to understanding the political economy of Zimbabwe since the Marange region in eastern Zimbabwe was the site of the largest diamond find in recent times.[2]

[1] For an in-depth account of politics in Zimbabwe, including the state's foreign policy see Alao (2012); Bratton (2014); Southhall (2013).

[2] Descriptions of Zimbabwe's large diamond find are drawn from Bond and Sharife (2012); Martin and Taylor (2010, 2012).

After independence in 1980, two major factions developed within ZANU-PF (Thornycroft and Laing 2014). One of the major factions was led by a former vice president from 2004 to 2014, Joice Mujuru, and until his death in 2011 former general Solomon Mujuru. This faction demonstrated an indifference to the Kimberley Process and has been funded from mining that has taken place outside of legal channels (Ferrett 2009). The other dominant faction, led by the current president of Zimbabwe and longtime military general Emmerson Mnangagwa, has gained significant control over the official diamond trade and has used Kimberley Process regulations to reinforce increases in market share (Martin and Taylor 2010, 2012). Much attention from academics and the international press has focused on the rivalry between ZANU-PF and the MDC (Movement for Democratic Change) for political control of Zimbabwe. However, in terms of mining policy, the MDC had negligible influence except for between 2009 and 2013 when it participated in a power-sharing agreement but was still marginalized politically. Before Mugabe resigned in 2017, both the Mujuru and the Mnangagwa groups gained control over a large portion of the Zimbabwean economy, allegedly with their eyes on succeeding Mugabe (Bratton 2014).

In the last few years of Robert Mugabe's presidency, his wife Grace Mugabe led another faction of ZANU-PF usually referred to as the G40. This faction, made up mainly of younger ZANU-PF members, appears to have gained influence over the president and some areas of the Zimbabwean economy including diamonds (Newsday 2017; Tinhu 2016). Ultimately, this faction would lose out when Mnangagwa was fired as vice president in late 2017, paving the way for Grace Mugabe and the G-40 to succeed Robert Mugabe. However, the military on behalf of Mnangagwa would intervene and force Robert Mugabe out of office, and Grace Mugabe out of ZANU-PF. Mnangagwa then became interim president, won a controversial election in 2018 for a five-year term, and filled the cabinet with allies who had been loyal to his faction.[3]

While there is a vast amount of diamonds in the Marange region, they are of low quality, mostly suitable for industrial use. Furthermore,

[3] Accounts of irregularities, if not outright fraud, before, during, and after Zimbabwe's 2018 election is given by Malunga (2018a, 2018b).

a poor international reputation about how the diamonds are mined has probably reduced their value even further. Diamonds from Marange usually sell for US$20–45 per carat, whereas the average price per carat globally is about US$100 (Zimnisky 2014). However, there is still a profit to be made on these diamonds because many are found on the surface, making them cheap to mine. The average cost of production in the Marange diamond fields is about US$19–30 per carat, compared to about US$65 globally (Zimnisky 2014). While there are many more diamonds beneath the surface, mining for diamonds in the Marange region could become too expensive at a certain point, given their current worth. While mining will probably take place in Marange, into the foreseeable future, the economic reality calls for a sense of urgency in using at least some of the diamond wealth for national development. As can be seen from Table 5.1, official diamond production rose dramatically until its height in 2012, since which it has fallen.

Since the implementation of the Kimberley Process in 2003 there have been five periods of policy changes around the diamond sector in Zimbabwe that are the focus of this study.

Table 5.1 *Zimbabwe official diamond production, 2004–2017*

Year	Volume, carats	Value, $US
2004	44,454.00	7,984,188.50
2005	248,264.00	35,018,235.88
2006	1,046,025.45	33,853,837.81
2007	695,015.99	31,400,903.61
2008	797,198.10	43,825,425.05
2009	963,501.70	20,426,782.44
2010	8,435,224.02	339,751,797.27
2011	8,502,648.07	476,218,677.86
2012	12,060,162.70	644,033,522.30
2013	10,411,817.65	538,484,829.00
2014	4,771,636.82	238,581,841.00
2015	3,490,881.16	174,544,058.00
2016	2,102,873.49	105,143,674.50
2017	2,507,604.31	175,379,664.09

Source: Kimberley Process Diamond Statistics (2017).

(1) Initially, until 2006, Zimbabwe's small diamond sector was dominated by De Beers and African Consolidated Resources with strong ties to the Mujuru faction (Martin and Taylor 2010, 2012). At this point, there were few questions surrounding compliance with the Kimberley Process.
(2) The large diamond finds in the Marange region in 2006 would lead the government to set up a monopsony over the diamond trade and encourage small-scale miners to immigrate to the Marange region. Since the government monopsony offered well under market value for diamonds, there was wide-scale smuggling and the diamond sector started to be criticized by members of the Kimberley Process (Martin and Taylor 2010, 2012).
(3) The military took over the diamond trade in 2008 and drove small-scale miners away from mining diamonds, placing the "legal" diamond trade directly in the hands of the joint officer's command dominated by the Mnangagwa faction. Ironically this may have led to a higher level of "compliance" with the Kimberley Process because with only one legal producer certification became easier. However, alleged human rights abuses led to an outcry from NGOs and civil society that demanded that the Kimberley Process ban diamonds originating from the Marange region (Global Witness 2010, 2011a, 2011b; Smillie 2010a, 2010b).
(4) The Kimberley Process (2011) agreed to lift all sanctions as part of a "joint work plan" with the Zimbabwean government. As part of the agreement, private diamond companies signed a series of contracts with the government to mine diamonds. Both cooperation and compliance with the Kimberley Process improved in Zimbabwe, although this remained far lower than other countries in Southern Africa (Munier 2014, 2016a).
(5) In 2016 the government decided to nationalize the diamond sector and put all diamond mining under the Zimbabwe Consolidated Diamond Company (ZCDC). Allegedly, this was to allow the government to collect revenue from mining directly and make smuggling of diamonds outside of government control less likely. A few companies were allowed to continue mining, but most private diamond companies challenged nationalization in the Zimbabwean court system (Gumbo 2016a).

This chapter draws on two central concepts to examine why a state such as Zimbabwe would invest resources in complying with the

Kimberley Process.[4] First, government actors in resource-wealthy states are often dependent on this revenue and potentially constrained in policymaking (Frank 1966, 1978; Rodney 1974; Smith and Lee 2018; Taylor 2016; Wallerstein 1974, 2004). Second, when making policy those in government are concerned with political survival above all other considerations (Bueno De Mesquita et al. 2005). Government leaders will pursue regulatory policies that may be different to what they would be predisposed to favor if this can enhance their ability to stay in office. Pursuing a favorable regulatory framework is key to gaining market share (Peltzman 1976; Stigler 1971). This is particularly salient for leaders that are dependent on resource revenue to increase support or that operate in political contexts where control of strategic resources is crucial, as is often the case in sub-Saharan Africa (Reno 1995, 1998; Snyder 2006; Snyder and Bhavnani 2005). Furthermore, actors are likely to vary in their calculations toward regulatory policy over time, as they see a particular policy as more or less useful in gaining a competitive advantage.

De Beers and African Consolidated Resources until 2006

Mining has long been a central part of Zimbabwe's economy. While historically under the control of foreign interests, in the 1990s, and especially after 2001, a series of laws have required over half of most companies to be owned by Zimbabweans (Southhall 2013). This has been part of the overall push for "indigenization" of the economy by ZANU-PF. Beyond mining, this has been a prominent goal of ZANU-PF in other areas of the economy, especially large-scale land redistribution. Critics around mining policy argue that this has mostly benefited elites within ZANU-PF or at the very least only those who are

[4] Past research on resource certification schemes has shown that their supposed "intent" is often not achieved and that they have a minimal ability to change behavior on the global market (Childs 2008, 2014a, 2014b; Spiegel 2015). Research on the Kimberley Process has shown that it does not appear have much of an influence on diamond trading at the retail level (Santiago 2014), and Western countries also have difficulty certifying diamonds (Gooch 2008). Thus, it is not necessarily the case that a state's response to the Kimberley Process is based purely on access to the global market. Furthermore, the Kimberley Process is unable, outside of a few cases, to render much coercive power over countries in order to get them to follow regulations (Grant 2012, 2013a; Haufler 2009b).

strong supporters of the party (Bratton 2014; Compagnon 2011; Southhall 2013).

During the Congolese civil war in the late 1990s, the Zimbabwean government decided to send troops to fight in the Democratic Republic of the Congo. Internally, Mugabe argued that this war was to help a longtime ally, Laurent Kabila, defeat the authoritarian rule of Mobutu Sese Seko. Critics said that this was a war for wealth, because of the large amount of mining that went on during the conflict. The Zimbabwean military mined diamonds extensively in the country while supporting the Kabila government (Alao 2012). Emmerson Mnangagwa was directly involved in gaining mining concessions from the Democratic Republic of the Congo, using the wealth to advance politically during this period (Compagnon 2011; Towriss 2013). Since the Mnangagwa faction controlled no domestic diamond production at this time and lacked the capital to compete with De Beers, both within Zimbabwe and abroad, the conflict in the Democratic Republic of the Congo provided them with a prime opportunity to engage in the diamond trade (Southhall 2013).

The River Ranch diamond mine, located near the border with South Africa, was the largest in the country before 2006. This mine was owned by the company African Consolidated Resources, in which Solomon Mujuru, the late army general and husband of Joice Mujuru, controlled a large amount of revenue (Martin and Taylor 2010). This was part of a large, but often inefficient business empire, built by Solomon Mujuru before he died in a house fire under suspicious circumstances in 2011 (Compagnon 2011). After his death, his wife Joice Mujuru, who had been sitting vice president since 2004, took over his former businesses.

The Mujurus long led one of the two major factions in the ruling ZANU-PF party. The other faction was led by Mnangagwa, who held several high-level positions within the military from the early 1980s. While most international media attention has focused on the rivalry between ZANU-PF and the MDC in terms of mining policy and the ability for private actors to acquire market share in Zimbabwe, factional rivalries within ZANU-PF have been more important. Both the Mujuru and the Mnangagwa factions had gained control over a large amount of the Zimbabwean economy, allegedly with their eyes on succeeding Mugabe. The competition between these factions within ZANU-PF was at the expense of the ZANU-PF party structure overall (Bratton 2014).

Besides the river ranch mine owned by African Consolidated Resources, the only other major diamond producer in the country before 2006 was De Beers. During colonialism, De Beers controlled most of the mining that went on in Zimbabwe, but the company started to fall out of favor with the Mugabe government in the mid-1990s. The main reason for the decline of De Beers in Zimbabwe was that the company was pressured to sell off at least half of its shares to "indigenous" buyers for well under market value (Compagnon 2011). In the early 2000s, De Beers' owner Harry Oppenheimer lost most of his large landholdings during the land reform program, although he was able to sell some of them (Mamdani 2009).

It is hard to envision De Beers being treated in a similar way by other countries in Southern Africa, especially Botswana, Namibia, and South Africa, where the firm has maintained considerable political power (Munier 2016c). It is clear that De Beers had very little bargaining power in dealing with the Mugabe regime. Instead of aligning with foreign capitalists, as is often common in African countries, ZANU-PF pursued a strategy of building a coalition around rural voters and the military; many of the latter also controlled much of the economy. It is the case that large landowners and foreign interests never supported the Mugabe regime in the first place. In fact, Mugabe increased his level of popularity among some sections of Zimbabwean society, and in Africa more broadly, by rejecting "Western" interests and taking on large corporations, even as the economy performed poorly (Kavanagh 2014). It was in this political context that the Kimberley Process went into effect in 2003. Since Zimbabwe at the time was a small diamond producer, and diamonds within the country were centrally located, noncompliance with the Kimberley Process was unlikely to receive scrutiny. However, it is notable that Zimbabwe joined the Kimberley Process in the first place since this came about when the Mugabe regime was rejecting outside interference in most other economic sectors.

Government-Run Monopsony, 2006–2008

Exploration rights to the Marange diamond fields belonged to De Beers till March 2006, after which the company ceased operations in the country altogether (Katsaura 2010a; Southhall 2013). It seems odd that an advanced company, in terms of diamond exploration, would allow these diamonds to go unnoticed. Many people in the region claim that De Beers was mining in the area and smuggled the diamonds through its main base in South Africa without reporting this to the state (Nyamunda and Mukwambo 2012).

The Mujuru-owned African Consolidated Resources gained rights to the Marange region from March to June 2006, but the company was forcefully expelled by the military after a large amount of potential diamond wealth emerged (Martin and Taylor 2010). The state claimed that it could take the diamond field back because the contract with African Consolidated Resources had been improperly given out. This has led to multiple, still unresolved court cases in which African Consolidated Resources claims to have the legal right to mine diamonds. Before being evicted, a large number of diamonds were taken from the African Consolidated Resources office in Harare by the Zimbabwean police, who claimed they were mined illegally. In 2010 the Zimbabwean Supreme Court ordered the diamonds to be kept at the Zimbabwean Central Bank until the issue was resolved (Partnership Africa Canada 2010a). In the context of "indigenization" of the economy, which was taking place across the country at this time, leaders of ZANU-PF claimed that African Consolidated Resources was not suitable to mine the diamonds because it was a "British" company. Although the company is traded on the London stock exchange and has some foreign shareholders, it was suspected that this had more to do with Mujuru's control of the company (Martin and Taylor 2010, 2012).

In addition to African Consolidated Resources, residents in the area claimed that they were the rightful owners of the diamond fields. Many appealed to local religious beliefs about how the diamonds had been placed there so they could overcome poverty (Katsaura 2010b; Nyota and Sibanda 2012). Local inhabitants were upset about the many outsiders, including traders from other countries, who came to exploit the area. Beyond this claim, others who came to the diamond-mining region from other areas of Zimbabwe believe that the diamonds should belong to all Zimbabwean citizens, but not foreigners (Katsaura 2010b). Thus, there were many levels of contestation over who had the right to mine the diamonds. After the nature of the diamond find in the Marange region became clear, thousands of miners descended upon the region in 2006 (Southhall 2013). Initially, the government encouraged this migration as it was the only legal buyer of diamonds through the Minerals Marketing Corporation of Zimbabwe. This quickly became a chaotic scene as a region in which there was little government infrastructure saw the population skyrocket. It could be speculated that the government allowed informal mining to take place as a way for ZANU-PF to gain votes in the 2008 election, since it did not remove the miners until afterwards. ZANU-PF has been hesitant to antagonize voters in rural areas as the party has consistently won a majority of votes outside of large cities.[5] The police who were sent to the Marange region were supposed to facilitate, not systematically prevent the miners from digging (Nyamunda and Mukwambo 2012). Given the weakness of the central state and the conflicting goals of those within the ruling party, the police played a more active role in the region than just oversight. With the deep economic problems that the Zimbabwean government was going through from 2006 to 2008, it paid miners well under market share for diamonds, if it had any resources at all (Gumbo 2013). This led to a high level of diamond smuggling, frequently across the Mozambique border, where there was little security and diamond buying shops were set up. This hurt the ability for the government to draw in revenue from either marketing the diamonds or official tax revenue. The police, who were charged with stopping illegal diamond mining in the region, allowed the illegal trade to continue in exchange for some of the proceeds (Martin and Taylor 2010, 2012).

Around the diamond fields, miners developed a culture of their own to deal with the harsh reality of the work (Katsaura 2010b). Several miners had to bribe police to gain access to the fields or mine in the middle of the night to escape detection. Over time miners had to pay higher bribes, with drugs and prostitution serving as acceptable compensation in many cases. Police both on and off duty, along with other criminal gangs, would rob miners of their diamonds (Human Rights Watch 2009). Diamond miners organized into over 500 syndicates, many of which clashed with each other and the police (Nyota and Sibanda 2012). Some of these syndicates had connections to specific police, and diamond traders, who would provide them protection and connections. Furthermore, many of these roles were mixed, as some miners also traded and smuggled diamonds across borders. Police in

[5] Discussion of urban-rural political dynamics in Zimbabwe is offered by Bratton (2014); Kavanagh (2014); LeBas (2011). Generally speaking, ZANU-PF has tended to gain a large amount of support from rural voters, whereas the MDC originated as an urban trade union movement and has had more support from people in urban areas overall.

the region were able to use their coercive authority along with the questionable legal status of the miners to make big profits. Many within the police force wanted to be stationed in the Marange region because of the economic opportunity it presented, and once they were stationed in the region they would often try and stay (Human Rights Watch 2009; Martin and Taylor 2010, 2012). Thus, it is clear that during this period those who were placed in charge of enforcing policies that deal with Kimberley Process regulations were integral to ignoring these policies altogether.

It is easy to see the Marange diamond fields – from discovery until the military takeover in late 2008 – as being "chaotic," but a more appropriate portrayal is what Human Rights Watch (2010) referred to as "deliberate chaos." Many different actors benefited from a lack of regulation. The police in Zimbabwe have a record of being "politicized," generally giving their support to factions within the ruling ZANU-PF party. The informal diamond trade in Marange likely benefited some within the highest levels of government, especially given the rapid decline of the formal economy. One of the major syndicates that mined diamonds called themselves "Mai Mujuru" after the sitting vice president, who presumably funded the organization (Human Rights Watch 2009; Katsaura 2010a, 2010b). This syndicate paid the most and gained police protection against competitors. Although the Mujurus were unable to profit formally through African Consolidated Resources, they benefited from the newfound diamond wealth through the informal economy that resulted.

Similar to what has been observed in Sierra Leone (Reno 1995, 1998) and Ghana (Hilson 2008), some within the government are able to profit from the "illegal" diamond trade. This blurring between the formal and illicit economy often makes the government unable to provide basic services in regions where mining takes place. For instance, the state may provide protection for those who have ties to ruling elites, and some in the same geographical area may benefit from this security as well, but the state fails to provide protection to much of the population. This appears to be what happened in the Marange region during the period 2006–2008, as the "rule of law" – let alone compliance with the Kimberley Process – was extremely low. Few actors had any economic incentive to comply with Kimberley Process regulations, and the monopsony set up by the Minerals Marketing Corporation of Zimbabwe rarely had enough funds to compete.

After the diamond finds in Marange, the Mugabe administration's initial attitude was that the diamonds mined in Marange would not necessarily need to comply with Kimberley Process regulations. The administration saw this as a "European" scheme enforcing its desired policies on Zimbabwe (Nyamunda and Mukwambo 2012). In time, dynamics within the ruling party would change the calculations of ZANU-PF concerning the regime.

Military Takeover, 2008–2010

Only the government will mine diamonds.

Robert Mugabe (Human Rights Watch 2009)

In 2008 the Zimbabwean government attempted to clear the diamond fields of miners, to take over production directly. This gained international attention from nongovernmental organizations and civil society groups, which portrayed the human rights abuses that resulted from the militarization policy as some of the worst in Zimbabwean history (Global Witness 2010, 2011a, 2011b; Smillie 2010a, 2010b). Not only did the military use armed ground troops to clear the diamond fields, but teargas and helicopters were common (Spiegel 2015). This happened in a context in which ZANU-PF, and the Mugabe-led government, was seen by many as having used violence and intimidation during the 2008 election. A settlement resulted in which ZANU-PF and the MDC would "share power." Many argue that, because of its control over the military and police force, ZANU-PF never intended to give up any significant authority (Alao 2012; Bratton 2014; Compagnon 2011).

In the 2008 election, Mugabe finished second in the first round, but since the MDC leader Morgan Tsvangirai did not get over 50 percent in the official count, a runoff was announced. According to observers, Mugabe was willing to allow Tsvangirai to succeed him as president, but the military rejected the idea (Bratton 2014). Mnangagwa was adamant in supporting Mugabe, allegedly because the alternative would have placed him in a weaker position for succession. Furthermore, he promised Mugabe that he could use his faction to deliver the runoff election in his favor. Mnangagwa could deliver on this because he was the leader of the Joint Officers Command, a group of leaders in the state's security departments, which became the most powerful political and economic organization in Zimbabwe after 2008 (Bratton 2014).

It later became apparent through cables from WikiLeaks that Joyce Mujuru had met with multiple Western representatives on the assumption that her faction of ZANU-PF could form a coalition government with the MDC after Mugabe inevitably lost the election in 2008 (The Herald 2014). To many in the West, the Mujuru faction seemed preferable because they were seen as being opposed to Mugabe's continuation as president, their "soft-line" attitude toward the MDC, and their support for business interests in the country. Mugabe had been known to stay in control by playing factions off against each other. However after the 2008 election, especially after the WikiLeaks documents were made public, his actions clearly showed support for the Mnangagwa faction. At the time, many Western governments argued that Mnangagwa was unfit to rule Zimbabwe because of alleged involvement in the Matabeleland killings in the early 1980s (Bratton 2014).

Tsvangirai withdrew from the runoff election, leaving Mugabe as the only candidate, claiming that the election was illegitimate because of widespread intimidation and violence against supporters. Critics would argue that he dropped out because he calculated that he would lose. While ZANU-PF cadres were involved in violent activity, it should be noted that Tsvangirai also relied on "shadow" organizations within the MDC that were known for attacking ZANU-PF supporters. Opposition to this form of organization, and to Tsvangirai's dominance over the MDC, were major reasons for the party's split in 2005 (LeBas 2011). The runoff election, in which Mugabe was the only candidate, brought about a widespread crisis in government. Many in the West called for Mugabe to be removed from power. This led to a "joint" agreement in which ZANU-PF and the MDC would share power, with Mugabe as president and Tsvangirai as prime minister. Since Mugabe held onto the military and police, the power differential became uneven. This also led leaders within ZANU-PF and the military to see the Marange diamond fields as being a source of funds that they would be able to exploit without MDC interference.

The government of Zimbabwe portrayed the takeover of the diamond fields as an attempt enforce governance in the region. The Mugabe regime went as far as to argue that informal diamond mining in the region was funding "international terrorism" and as an opponent of terrorism it had a duty to put an end to the trade through forceful means (Baxter 2008). Nongovernmental actors and civil society argued that the military takeover of the diamond fields was just another part of a militarization of society that took place after the election in 2008.[6] To those in the Kimberley Process, Mugabe argued that criticism surrounding the diamond trade was just part of an overall scheme to delegitimize and overthrow his regime. In addition, he pointed out that policy in the area of diamond mining was likely to draw criticism regardless of the policies chosen, as had been the case before the military acted in 2008 (Saunders 2008). Some outside the Mugabe government pointed out that many nongovernmental organizations operating in Zimbabwe were likely to criticize any policy that resulted from a Mugabe-led government (Kavanagh 2014).[7]

When the military took over the diamond fields after the election in 2008, it was clear that the Joint Officers Command, and more specifically the Mnangagwa faction of ZANU-PF, stood to gain directly (Towriss 2013). They also gained in relative power against the Mujuru faction, which had more of a foothold in the "informal" trade (Human Rights Watch 2009; Katsaura 2010a, 2010b). With the economy in rapid decline, resources from the diamond trade became a way for Mugabe to maintain control through patronage. In the diamond fields, former miners were forced to work for the military without pay, child labor was common, and soldiers looted the area (Human Rights Watch 2009). Given the accessible nature of the diamond fields and their large area, militarization did not stop "informal" mining. Miners who started before 2008 had already accepted a lot of risks, and some were still able to bribe the army to gain access to the diamond fields.

The debate within the Kimberley Process largely mirrored the dynamics over whether Mugabe should be allowed to stay as president after the contested 2008 election. Most African countries, notably

[6] Some reports that make this argument are Human Rights Watch (2009); Martin and Taylor (2010, 2012).

[7] After the land reform program started in the early 2000s, Mugabe portrayed his regime as seeking to indigenize the Zimbabwean economy and as not afraid to stand up to Western countries and organizations seeking to dominate Zimbabwe's resources. This gained him many vocal critics, especially in the Western world. On the other hand, to some Zimbabweans he stood up for their interests against Western attempts at "neocolonialism" and other African countries viewed him as a leader against longstanding patterns of "imperialism."

South Africa and Namibia, which was chair of the Kimberley Process in 2009, voted that the Marange diamonds were not "conflict" diamonds because they were not being used by a rebel group to overthrow the government (Spiegel 2015). Thus, what was at issue here was a "governance" or state capacity problem, not a problem of a "conflict" diamonds in a technical sense. Under intense scrutiny, the Kimberley Process and Zimbabwe agreed to a joint work plan in which Zimbabwe would admit to some problems with Kimberley Process compliance and allow Kimberley Process monitors into the country (Kimberley Process 2009). Many felt that, given the actions of the Zimbabwean government, this response was ineffective. Global Witness, an NGO that had been influential in starting the Kimberley Process, left the process in protest (Global Witness 2011b).

The joint work plan with the Kimberley Process was the first time that Zimbabwe at least pretended to recognize the Kimberley Process as legitimate and actively implemented policies to raise its level of compliance. This is notable because during the same period the state ignored several other treaties and the sanctions placed on it by Western countries. Furthermore, it agreed to cooperate with other African countries to address the lack of "administration" in the Marange region, which according to Zimbabwe's allies was the reason for noncompliance in the first place. Notably, Namibia, which was Kimberley Process president in 2009, cooperated with Zimbabwe extensively throughout the year to raise its level of compliance (Munier 2016c; Shejavali 2009).

While diamonds from Marange were banned from being sold as part of the agreement with the Kimberley Process, the Ministry of Mines would not issue Kimberley Process certification for the Mujuru-owned River Ranch mine. Since this mine had not been the subject of the sanctions and had been perceived as compliant with the Kimberley Process since it started in 2003, this could be interpreted as an attempt to block the ability of the Mujuru faction to profit from it (Martin and Taylor 2010, 2012).

When this time period is examined purely in terms of the ability to certify diamonds in the Marange region, two things are clear. First, a higher percentage of diamonds were certified as a result of the military takeover, in that few if any diamonds were certified before 2008. Second, the number of diamonds certified remained extremely low, certainly lower than any other country in the region. Given that it was "illegal," estimating the percentage of production in Marange that was not certified during this time is difficult, but some experts estimate around 60 percent (Human Rights Watch 2010). Even if it was only half this, it was still a large amount of illicit revenue flowing into a country where other types of economic activity had declined.

Joint Ventures with Private Companies, 2011–2016

We are trying to play it their own way, that is following the KP but we can do it otherwise and we can sell our own diamonds elsewhere.

Robert Mugabe (Zimbabwe Daily 2010)

When the Democratic Republic of the Congo took over as Kimberley Process president in 2011, the ZANU-PF government had another longtime ally at the head of the Kimberley Process. In November 2011 the Kimberley Process voted to remove all sanctions from Zimbabwe (Kimberley Process 2011). This further angered several nongovernmental organizations, some of which removed themselves as observers from the Kimberley Process in protest (Global Witness 2011a, 2011b; Smillie 2010a, 2010b). Many critics argued that if Zimbabwe did not have to pay a price for low compliance and state-sponsored violence in the diamond fields then the Kimberley Process had shown itself to have little purpose. They argued that Zimbabwe's reacceptance as a certified diamond exporter was about politics, especially alliances with neighboring African countries (Global Witness 2011a, 2011b; Smillie 2011a, 2011b). Mugabe, by turning the debate about Kimberley Process compliance into a discourse about Zimbabwe's right to sovereignty versus Western interference in internal affairs, as the Mugabe regime had done in other issue areas, was able to gain allies in Zimbabwe's bid to trade diamonds without interference. The Mugabe administration, through the Minerals Marketing Corporation of Zimbabwe, began entering into joint agreements with private companies in 2011, an action which was heavily endorsed by the Kimberley Process (Gumbo 2013).

While Western countries continued to push economic sanctions against Zimbabwe, the Chinese built economic ties with the government and many Chinese citizens immigrated to Zimbabwe (French 2014). In the diamond sector, this led to two joint agreements with diamond companies, the larger Anjin and the smaller Jinan, which may have operated as essentially the same company (Global Witness 2017a). Despite Anjin and Jinan's lack of transparency, the Kimberley Process approved them to export diamonds in 2012 (Martin and Taylor 2012). Initially, there was great enthusiasm for Anjin, as some connected with the company even referred to it as the largest diamond producer in the world and the "next De Beers" (Global Witness 2012a). While these claims were probably far too optimistic, it is indicative of the private mining potential that many believed existed at the time.

Anjin was a joint venture between the Chinese-owned Anhui Foreign Economic Construction Group (AFEC) and the Zimbabwean-owned Matt Bronze (Pvt) Ltd. It is hard to determine the nature of this agreement; some observers have speculated that Matt Bronze (Pvt) Ltd was a front for the Zimbabwean Ministry of Defense and that Emmerson Mnangagwa approved the arrangement when he was temporarily the active minister of mines (Global Witness 2012a). Going even further, Global Witness (2012a) argued that the diamond company may be funding a "parallel state" for factions within ZANU-PF, as it did not appear as though the company was paying taxes through official channels and much of its ownership structure was veiled in secrecy. In 2012 the MDC-controlled Ministry of Finance allegedly received no tax revenue from Anjin, although it did receive revenue from other far smaller companies (Global Witness 2012b). This lends further support to the idea that a "parallel state" may have existed for factions within ZANU-PF during this period. It further brings up the possibility that larger companies may have been involved in widespread smuggling during this period. This can also be viewed in a wider context in which ZANU-PF often tried to minimize the influence of the coalition agreement with the MDC. Global Witness (2017a) also reported that 40 percent of Anjin appeared to be owned by Zimbabwe Defense Industries, a firm that was long sanctioned by Western states.

While having a different name, Jinan has been viewed as an extension of Anjin and is also half-owned by AFEC (Global Witness 2017a). Furthermore, Jinan has been known to share equipment and personnel, and even transfer wealthy diamond areas to Anjin (Global Witness 2017a). On AFEC's website, the two companies are presented as both being owned by the company and intertwined in a successful venture in Zimbabwe (AFEC 2018). One possible difference, at least formally, is that Anjin appears to have always been half-owned by the ZMDC, making the influence of the military less clear (Global Witness 2017a).

Of the private mining companies in Zimbabwe, Mbada was probably the largest at its height. Mbada was one of the first companies to get a license to mine in the Marange diamond fields in 2009 and obtained rights to mine in an area six times larger than the original concession in April 2011 (Global Witness 2012b). This made Mbada one of the larger mines in the region and raised questions about possible political connections within ZANU-PF as it appears that the company had gained political favor. Furthermore, Mugabe ally Rovert Mhlanga was believed to own part of the mine and was allegedly involved in exporting diamonds outside of Kimberley Process regulations from 2009 to 2011 (Martin and Taylor 2012).

Mbada holdings was particularly secretive about its ownership structure. Officially, half of the company was owned by the ZMDC and the other half by Mauritius-based Grandwell Holdings. According to Global Witness (2017a), the following companies also have a stake in Grandwell Holdings and in turn the Mbada mines: Windfall 92 Properties PTY (ZA), Reclamation Holdings Pty Ltd (ZA), Transfrontier Minking (HK), Quorum, Leisure Star Ltd (BVI), Golden Universe, Mehta Nominees, Express Agents Ltd (BVI), and Billy LI Sze Kuen. The extensive use of tax havens and the global nature of these companies make it difficult if not impossible to trace where these investments are coming from and where revenue is going (Global Witness 2017a). Furthermore, it is likely that many of the stated owners or investors in these companies are there for legal reasons, while the actual sources of investment remain unknown.

Of the joint agreements between the ZMDC and private investors, probably the strangest turn of events took place with the Gye Nyame mines. Gye Nyame opened in 2011 as a joint venture between the ZMDC and Ghanaian-owned Bill Minerals (Newsday 2014). Allegedly, the owner of Bill minerals, William Ato Essien, was scammed out of US$10 million by officials in the ZMDC (Muronzi 2013). The officials used his investment in the company to pay themselves large salaries, kept most of the profit and diamonds in what amounted to a "looting" of the company (Muronzi 2013). According to the Zimbabwean government, Bill Minerals was removed from ownership in 2014 for lack of funds and breaking environmental regulations (Newsday 2014). Another factor was that Mugabe was reportedly upset about William Ato Essien "misleading" the government about being forced to pay bribes to officials in the ZMDC (Newsday 2014). While some of the specifics of Bill Minerals' partial ownership of Gye Nyame are unclear, it appears Essian lacked political connections that other private investors in Zimbabwe had. Furthermore, regardless of the exact circumstances, by 2014 the ZMDC no longer saw a continued partnership as being profitable.

The most overtly controversial joint agreement would be the Diamond Marketing Corporation (DMC). The DMC began in 2010 as a joint agreement between the ZMDC and the Dubai-listed company Pure Diam, owned by Imad Ahmad (Global Witness 2017a). While the ownership of the DMC is clearer than most other companies that have mined in Zimbabwe, it appears Imad Ahmad led a diamond smuggling syndicate in Zimbabwe from 2007 to 2010 and then continued to smuggle diamonds around the Kimberley Process ban from 2010 to 2012 (Global Witness 2017a). In fact, the "Ahmad Diamond Corporation," with Imad Ahmad as head, was one of the original companies investigated for allegedly trading in diamonds that originated from conflict zones in Angola and the Democratic Republic of Congo (Global Witness 2017a). Given the unclear ownership of other companies that have mined diamonds in the Marange region, it is a puzzle why the government and Pure Diam were open about the ownership of the DMC, especially given the reputation of the ownership.

There are a few other smaller private mining companies that have operated in the Marange region but had little success. Canadile Miners (Pvt) Ltd was one of the first companies to receive a legal license from the Zimbabwean government to mine for diamonds after the takeover of diamond fields in 2008 (Global Witness 2012b). This company soon imploded and was taken over by Marange Resources, which was fully government owned. There appears to have been some ties between Zimbabwe Defense Industries and Marange Diamonds (Global Witness 2017a). Another company with alleged ties to the Zimbabwean government was Kusena, which was officially owned by the ZMDC, but there is speculation that it was controlled by the Central Intelligence Organization (CIO) (Global Witness 2017a). It is also unclear to what extent Kusena mined for diamonds before 2016, as there is a possibility it was a front organization for CIO purposes in which little diamond mining took place (Mambo 2017b).

Political Competition and the Privatization of the Diamond Trade, 2011–2016

With the "unity" government starting in 2009, it was the goal of the MDC to win back some of the international recognition through international agreements that the country had lost. Not surprisingly, the MDC wanted to disband the Joint Officers Command, led by Mnangagwa, and fully audit the diamond industry to prevent the revenue from going to ZANU-PF opponents (Bratton 2014). The MDC also tried and was somewhat successful in limiting military spending. This, however, made proceeds from the diamond industry even more attractive to military leaders as it was a way to keep them in the ZANU-PF coalition (Towriss 2013). Leaders of ZANU-PF within the "unity" government claimed that Zimbabwe lacked the resources to enforce diamond certification, leading the MDC to claim that this was an excuse by members of ZANU-PF to profit from the uncertified diamond trade for the 2014 election campaign (Smillie 2014). Mugabe won big in the 2014 election, with over 60 percent of the vote, sending the MDC into the political wilderness. In addition, he was elected as the chairperson of the African Union.[8]

In late 2014 Mugabe fired Joice Mujuru as vice president and forced members of the Zimbabwean government associated with her out of office. Mugabe had become more suspicious of the Mujuru faction after finding out about their plans in 2008 from WikiLeaks, although it would appear as though he waited until a decisive election victory to act on this (The Herald 2014). Emmerson Mnangagwa was appointed in her place and then appeared to be in the strongest position to take over as president after Mugabe.

Before Joice Mujuru was removed from the vice presidency, Grace Mugabe campaigned for her removal at ZANU-PF party events. She attacked African Consolidated Resources, portraying it as a company that was set up by the Mujuru faction to pillage the country's mining wealth for their own benefit, and eventually gain enough resources to

[8] To some degree Western countries realized after 2014 that they may have no choice but to accept Mugabe's rule for the time being. It was also clear that Mugabe's eventual successor would likely come from within ZANU-PF. With Mugabe's power consolidated in 2014, he brought about some changes to the ZANU-PF party structure and oversaw a relative rebound in Zimbabwe's economy.

replace Robert Mugabe. Furthermore, Grace Mugabe claimed that Joice Mujuru was continuing to benefit from the "illegal" diamond trade (New Zimbabwe 2014).

It is difficult to determine how the joint agreements between the government and private companies should be interpreted in terms of Kimberley Process compliance in Zimbabwe. At the very least, private companies would want to both avoid scrutiny from the Kimberley Process and not be cut off from the world's global diamond trade. While still controlled by elites, it does appear as though Zimbabwe has moved in a direction in which more Zimbabwean citizens have benefited from the diamond trade and this has contributed to the economic growth the country has seen since 2008 (Southhall 2013).

Since 2011 Zimbabwe's compliance with the Kimberley Process has improved, although it is still well below neighboring countries. In addition, Zimbabwe has participated more within Kimberley Process decision-making and is now a member of the "Working Group on Artisanal and Alluvial," which was created to deal with issues around small-scale mining (Kimberley Process 2015b). Thus, gone are the days in which the Zimbabwean state tried to portray the Kimberley Process as just another example of Western imperialism; decision-makers have decided that embracing the process is in their interests. One explanation is that to attract foreign investment it was necessary to comply at a basic level. Having the military mine diamonds from 2008 to 2010 was probably inefficient in that they lacked expertise, equipment, and possibly the desire to dig long hours for diamonds. In turn, it seems as though the Kimberley Process encouraged privatization as a way to increase compliance. Also, with fewer separate actors mining diamonds, especially in comparison to the many "syndicates" that emerged after 2006, having a few companies control most of the trade is easier administratively. Thus, the Kimberley Process had an influence on policy in Zimbabwe by changing the calculations of decision-makers, making privatization more attractive and a monopsony or a military-run system increasingly untenable.

Government Nationalization, 2016–Present

On February 23, 2016, the Zimbabwean government gave diamond companies ninety days to remove their equipment from the diamond mines after stopping their operations. All diamond mining operations would be placed in one nationalized company, the Zimbabwe Consolidated Diamond Company (Gumbo 2016a). During a press conference to explain the nationalization strategy, Mines and Mining Development Minister Walter Chidhakwa said that for seven months before the mines were taken over by the government, private companies were engaged regarding participation in the new arrangement, but most opposed this strategy (Gumbo 2016a).

In an interview with ZBC TV, Mugabe said that Zimbabwe's nationalization strategy was necessary because the Zimbabwean government had only received US$2 billion in comparison to an overall US$15 billion in revenues from the diamond trade. He went on to say that Zimbabweans who worked in this sector should have been more aware of the practices of the foreign-owned companies they worked for (BBC News 2016). Some observers, such as Centre for Natural Resources Governance Director Farai Maguwu, argue that Zimbabwe has lost far more diamond wealth than Mugabe estimates, possibly "More than 30 or 50 Billion" (Mighty Movies Online 2018). Ironically, others question whether the government has even received the estimated $2 billion in revenue.[9]

When nationalization was announced, many informal miners descended on the diamond mines. Mining equipment was allegedly stolen from the mines as the companies were made to leave abruptly without leaving any security (Gumbo 2016b). About fifty informal miners were arrested after nationalization went into effect. The Zimbabwean government sent military personnel to the region to protect the mines and mining equipment it had seized (Now Daily 2016a). Anjin Investments and Mbada Diamonds sued at Zimbabwe's high court to regain control over the mines. Despite winning the suit and sending the legal aspects of the Zimbabwean government's nationalization strategy into disarray, new licenses were not issued for the companies (Reuters 2016).

The Chinese government was angered at the nationalization process (Now Daily 2016a). This came about in a context in which China had wanted Mugabe to name a successor in 2014, as a condition for loans and investment. Mugabe's wife Grace was seen as unacceptable by the Chinese, but allegedly Mugabe agreed to make Mnangagwa his vice

[9] Manenji (2017) estimates that the government received US$971 million to US$1.6 billion between 2006 and 2013.

president and successor to appease the Chinese government in exchange for investment. Mnangagwa had long economic and political ties to the Chinese and was influential in getting contracts for the Chinese in the diamond sector (Now Daily 2016a). Given these dynamics, nationalization within the diamond trade can be seen as a loss of influence by the Chinese in the country and their allies within the government.

After nationalization began in 2016, Mugabe claimed that he spoke to Chinese President Xi Jinping about how Zimbabwe was not benefiting from Chinese companies in the diamond sector and claimed that nationalization of the Marange mines would not cause diplomatic tension between the countries (BBC News 2016). During the nationalization process from 2016, it appeared as though Anjin and other private Chinese firms would be allowed a 50 percent ownership in the single entity ZCDC, however what fraction if any Anjin has received has been unclear (Global Witness 2017a). Jinan became the subject of the most extensive investigation by the Zimbabwean government into diamond mining companies that had operated in the Marange region. Allegedly, the company had smuggled out US$585 million between 2012 and 2014 to an account located in China which then closed (Mambo 2017a). Clearly, Anjin had fallen out of political favor, and the government's pursuit of the company shows it is likely that some within the ownership structure had been temporarily on the losing end of factional rivalries within ZANU-PF.

The experiences of specific private diamond companies differed considerably after nationalization in 2016, from being allowed to continue mining to having their resources confiscated and subject to investigation. After nationalization in 2016, the DMC was the first company to return to mining and make a deal with the government to stay independent from the ZCDC (Global Witness 2017a). However, this may have been because Pure Diam was no longer a partner, with some sources saying that the company had become fully government owned (Matimaire 2017). Marange resources was the only active diamond mining company to support diamond nationalization in 2016 and was allowed to continue operations during this period (Gumbo 2016a). Gye Nyame is believed to have been owned by the ZMDC after 2014, and in turn was directly nationalized in 2016 into the ZCDC without negotiation (Global Witness 2017a). Kusena was nationalized in 2016, in what may be seen as a loss for the CIO or as an avenue through which the CIO will continue to get some revenue from the diamond trade (Global Witness 2017a). Mbada Diamonds had to sell many of its assets and challenge the Zimbabwean government to return the diamond field. These court actions failed, and the company collapsed in 2017 (Manayiti and Mambo 2017; The Financial Gazette 2017).

Many top army officials lost out in the 2016 nationalization of diamonds, as in effect Mugabe placed the sector under his direct control. Allegedly, Mnangagwa and allies within the military, such as longtime Commander of the Zimbabwe National Army Constantino Chiwenga, lost a key funding source through the nationalization process (Now Daily 2016b). After 2016, Mugabe became involved in the day-to-day operations of the ZCDC. While the company is shrouded in secrecy and it is unclear who exactly has been involved in running it, many believe it was a direct source of funding for the pro-Mugabe faction within ZANU-PF (Now Daily 2016b).

Despite the political nature of nationalization, the strategy had supporters who pointed to the inability of the government to control the diamond companies when they were partially owned by private investors (Manenji 2017).[10] Thinking of these changes in terms of Kimberley Process compliance, having a single cohesive entity to mine diamonds would at least on the surface appear to be more effective. Kimberley Process compliance did improve after 2011, but some of this is because it was previously nearly nonexistent, and some private companies do appear to have at least given some attention to Kimberley Process regulations. However, having many different private companies with unclear ownership structures and a fundamental lack of transparency limited Zimbabwe's ability to comply at a high level during this period. It is unlikely, given these arrangements, that Zimbabwe could ever have come close to complying with the Kimberley

[10] Some in the Marange region believe that the pre-2008 period in which small-scale miners could operate openly was better for the surrounding community than allowing foreign companies to mine diamonds in the region. While foreign companies and the government have made many promises about building infrastructure and raising the living standards of people in the Marange region, many people believe they are actually worse off because of diamond mining (Global Witness 2017a).

Process at the level of states in Southern Africa that have a far more cohesive ownership structure in the diamond trade, such as Botswana or Namibia.

There have been constant questions about the apparent lack of official tax revenue from the Marange fields. There are many possible reasons for this, and it is probably a mix of many factors. A common strategy in the diamond trade is to undervalue diamonds and then send them to a state with little or no export tax. In the case of Zimbabwe, this may happen with many shipments of diamonds going to Dubai (Global Witness 2017a). In Zimbabwe, there are officially a series of taxes that need to be paid on diamonds. There is a "resource depletion fee of 2.5%, marketing commission of .875%, marketing commission of 2.5% and then private companies have to pay 25% on all profits" (Global Witness 2017a). To get around these fees, private companies are likely to underreport along this chain of fees or in some cases they may choose that it is better to smuggle some diamonds out of the country altogether, potentially avoiding all taxes and lessening the amount of profit they have to share with the ZMDC. It is challenging to get an idea of how much tax revenue the Zimbabwean government has received in comparison to how much has been made in the mining sector.[11] This lack of transparency and government oversight has clear implications for Kimberley Process regulations. It appears as though a large portion of the diamond trade in Zimbabwe has not been officially taxed, and in turn is unlikely to have complied with the Kimberley Process.

Despite significant questions about the ability for the Zimbabwean state to tax the diamond sector, in 2018 Zimbabwe sent a government delegation of over thirty members to the annual Kimberley Process meeting in Brussels, thus raising controversy over government priorities (Karombo 2018). While this is a sign of increasing acceptance of the Kimberley Process by the Zimbabwean government, it also raises the question of how much of a priority this should be in a state that has had extreme economic difficulty. While some thought that the election in 2018 would bring about stability, some observers have labeled the postelection period as an "economic crisis" (Ntali 2018).

[11] The ZMDC has only published two annual reports and private diamond companies in Zimbabwe never published any (Global Witness 2017a).

Diamond Beneficiation in Zimbabwe

After the collapse of the formal economy in Zimbabwe during the 2007–2008 period, mining became one of the few active economic sectors. The Zimbabwean government, consistent with its overall "indigenization" rhetoric, has always argued that more diamond beneficiation should take place within the country. However, very little diamond beneficiation has taken place in Zimbabwe since the large diamond finds in 2006, leading to questions over whether this is a government priority. Nevertheless, given a large number of diamonds that have been mined in Zimbabwe, diamond beneficiation could, in theory, have a significant positive economic effect (Zikiti 2016). Similar to South Africa, in 2010 Zimbabwe tried to place 10 percent of diamond production aside for local beneficiation (Zikiti 2016). Government actors in Zimbabwe who own shares in mining companies have been reluctant to encourage legislation for more beneficiation as this may lead to lower exports and profits overall (Zikiti 2016). This has led to a paradoxical situation where the government vocally encourages beneficiation, but government actors with investments in the mining sector discourage a change in practice.

Many Zimbabweans have seen diamond wealth as having the potential to raise living standards, but in reality few changes have taken place. While the diamond sector has provided some with jobs, much diamond mining is currently done by small Chinese companies that bring their own workers. When they do hire Zimbabweans, the wages are often not very high, and payment can be unpredictable. The Zimbabwean state has been unable to use diamond wealth to improve infrastructure, mainly because the state lacks a coherent strategy to do so (Fessehaie and Rustomjee 2018).

Ironically, the absence of De Beers from Zimbabwe may be a partial explanation for why very little diamond beneficiation has taken place within the country. While De Beers long opposed diamond beneficiation in Southern Africa, the firm may well be more open to local beneficiation in recent years than many other companies. Furthermore, De Beers is far more capable of providing the capital investment necessary to create a diamond beneficiation sector than the many small Chinese companies that have mined in Zimbabwe.

A further reason for the lack of local diamond beneficiation is that many Zimbabwean diamonds are smuggled outside of formal government or Kimberley Process controls. Much of this is due to the alluvial nature of diamond mining in the Marange region and the sheer size of the region, making it hard to police. Diamonds that are smuggled out of the state are another example of the inability of the Zimbabwean government to capitalize on its diamond wealth, and this adds to the overall level of diamonds originating in the country that are not beneficiated locally. All states in Southern Africa have issues with diamond smuggling, but Zimbabwe probably has the highest level. In fact, there are estimates that during some periods 60 percent of diamond production was being smuggled out of the country (Human Rights Watch 2010). This has probably changed somewhat as the government has decided to abide by Kimberley Process controls, and neighboring states have been willing to help Zimbabwe comply with the Kimberley Process at a higher level. However, the problem continues as some of the local law enforcement may also be complacent or actively involved in diamond smuggling.

Conclusion

If we examine diamond policy in Zimbabwe, particularly since 2008, it benefited the Mnangagwa faction of ZANU-PF to the detriment of the Mujurus. To some degree changing attitudes toward the Kimberley Process reflect this dynamic. The change from diamond mining by the military in 2008–2010 to joint agreements with private corporations was largely facilitated by the Kimberley Process. In both periods the Mnangagwa faction gained power as the military stood to profit the most. On the other hand, the Mujuru faction has largely been left out of the diamond proceeds, beginning with the revocation of their company, African Consolidated Resources. Then the military takeover of the diamond fields in 2008 hurt the illicit trade that the Mujurus were allegedly benefiting from, although it may have continued. Finally, the River Ranch Mine was perhaps the only mining site in Zimbabwe that was effectively banned from trading diamonds from 2008 to 2011 by the Kimberley Process. Although this was not the intention of the sanctions, it was a useful political tool for the Mnangagwa faction. These power dynamics, which both shaped and were in turn shaped by the Zimbabwean response to the Kimberley Process, show that the diamond certification scheme has had little to do with any of its stated goals and in Zimbabwe it has become a terrain in which elites can compete for power.

These findings regarding the Kimberley Process in Zimbabwe could be portrayed as the process being above all else a political tool for powerful political actors to justify policy preferences that they would have had anyway. This is partially true, but also simplistic, as this research shows that the Kimberley Process has also shaped the policies readily available to decision-makers, thus changing their calculations and the feasibility of certain policies in the diamond trade. Certification through the Kimberley Process, especially after the state decided to allow private companies to mine, became important in ensuring that these companies had access to the global market. It is also notable that this increasing responsiveness has not necessarily resulted in policies that many would see as desirable and the state's relationship to the Kimberley Process, in reality, has not had much to do with conflict diamonds or for that matter human rights protection. In fact, the push to get Zimbabwe to gain control over the widespread smuggling that was taking place after the initial rush to the diamond field in 2006 raised the potential for the country to comply with the Kimberley Process, but in turn brought about widespread human rights abuses. This reaction is contrary to what many consumers believe the Kimberley Process is supposed to play a role in protecting. Furthermore, it is easier in terms of compliance with the Kimberley Process to bring foreign-owned private companies into the country, thus placing the average small-scale miner at a disadvantage.

Unlike other states in Southern Africa, such as Botswana, Namibia, and Angola, where large diamond companies control the diamond sector (Munier 2014, 2016b, 2016c), in Zimbabwe it is government actors that have had the upper hand in getting their preferences reflected in policy. This reality has led to policies that reflect the distribution of power among ZANU-PF factions at different periods. Private diamond companies have only been able to operate if they are viewed favorably by the faction within ZANU-PF that has had the upper hand at the time. Given that the Zimbabwean government has not hesitated to take on powerful companies – even taking on De Beers before 2006 – private companies operate in an arena where they have little influence on what policies are pursued.

Resource politics in several "weak" states such as Zimbabwe are often viewed as being driven by powerful private economic interests, and in many instances this is the case. However, in Zimbabwe the preferences of political and military elites competing for power take precedence over the interests of private economic actors. In the case of Marange, private economic actors have only been allowed in because political leaders saw this as being in their interest. The Zimbabwean government has a record of changing the access that private companies have to the diamond fields, even going back on signed contracts when the power differential between ZANU-PF party factions no longer views private economic activity as being in their interests. This dynamic, in which the power of ZANU-PF factions easily dwarfs that of private actors, is the strongest explanation for the state's low level of compliance and cooperation with the Kimberley Process. This is especially the case when we compare neighboring countries in which private companies have far more power, such as Botswana or Namibia.

Looking toward the future of Zimbabwe, diamond revenue will be central to Mnangagwa's presidency and the continuation of the military's dominance over the political process in the country. The inability of the MDC to profit from any of the diamond revenue, despite attempts to weaken ZANU-PF control, has undoubtedly placed it at a disadvantage both electorally and in terms of being able to buy support. The Mujuru faction has become irrelevant after Joyce Mujuru left ZANU-PF and ran for president as part of the People's Rainbow Coalition in 2018, receiving just 0.3 percent of the vote (ZBC 2018).[12] Mnangagwa, who has benefited the most from diamond sector policy, and is now the president of Zimbabwe, would appear to have political control for the time being. However, some have already started to speculate about who will succeed Mnangagwa as president.[13] Regardless of how events play out, future policies within the diamond sector in Zimbabwe, and what this means for the future of the Kimberley Process itself, remain highly uncertain; they are also interrelated.

[12] Many former supporters of the Mujuru faction now favor other factions within ZANU-PF or have even left the party to support the MDC.

[13] The most likely successor is longtime general and current vice president and defense minister of Zimbabwe, Constantino Chiwenga, who could become president of Zimbabwe as early as 2023 (Mhaka 2018).

6 *The Limits of Cooperation after Conflict?*

The Case of the Kimberley Process in Sierra Leone

The diamond trade in Sierra Leone has had a defining influence on the political and economic trajectory of the country. Scholars have and will continue to debate the extent to which diamonds, or mismanagement of the diamond trade, caused the onset of conflict in Sierra Leone.[1] However, there is a consensus that diamonds played a central role in the conflict as diamond fields were often fought over and the trade was a significant source of rebel funding for the Revolutionary United Front (RUF) at approximately $25–75 million a year from 1991 to 2000 (Le Billon 2008, 2012).

Given the history of the diamond sector in Sierra Leone, it is crucial for understanding the Kimberley Process. The case of the Kimberley Process in Sierra Leone is particularly important because the stated goal of the agreement is to prevent conflicts, such as the one that took place in Sierra Leone during the 1990s, being fueled by diamond wealth. Furthermore, the weak state that emerged in Sierra Leone after the conflict in the 1990s has been a constant challenge to the overall viability of the Kimberley Process. Cooperation and compliance with international agreements such as the Kimberley Process has been part of the overall state-building strategy in Sierra Leone. However, despite the willingness of government actors to comply with the Kimberley Process, and some success in lessening the number of diamonds that are smuggled outside of Kimberley Process regulations, Sierra Leone remains a state that has one of the highest levels of diamond smuggling in sub-Saharan Africa.[2]

[1] Given the importance of diamonds in Sierra Leone's political economy, many studies on the relationship between diamonds and conflict or regime type include Sierra Leone as a central part of their analysis Le Billon (2008, 2012); Ross (2004a, 2004b, 2006); Snyder (2006); Snyder and Bhavnani (2005).

[2] Several miners in Sierra Leone operate permanently outside of legal channels without any documentation. In 2006 this was estimated at around 50,000 to

While Sierra Leone has cooperated extensively with the Kimberley Process, in contrast to several other states, its level of compliance remains low. This chapter asks why the postconflict regime in Sierra Leone has been willing to cooperate with the Kimberley Process but has nevertheless been unable to prevent diamonds from being traded without certification. It argues that the domestic political economy of Sierra Leone explains the regime's willingness to comply with the Kimberley Process. However, this research finds that low state capacity in regions where diamond mining takes place leads to widespread smuggling. Furthermore, the "alluvial" nature of most diamond deposits in Sierra Leone, in which diamonds can be mined with little capital investment, makes certification difficult.

Sierra Leone remains one of the most impoverished countries – if not the most impoverished country – in the world.[3] Beyond the geographical challenges that the state of Sierra Leone has faced post-conflict, is a problem of governance. While governance has gradually improved, political elites in postconflict Sierra Leone have reverted to the same ethnic and party-based divisions that divided the country before the conflict. The two dominant parties in Sierra Leone are the All People's Congress and the Sierra Leone People's Party. The power distribution between these parties has defined the national political system since the 1960s (Harris 2014; Kargbo 2014). Traditional chiefs and royal families often compete over the diamond fields, thus adding another layer of political competition in Sierra Leone at the local level (Acemoglu, Reed, and Robinson 2014). There is a tendency to view a postconflict state such as Sierra Leone as having the ability to "start over" and build new institutions. However, the political and administrative challenges that existed before the war remain salient.

This chapter argues that Sierra Leone's low level of compliance with the Kimberley Process is linked to three interrelated dynamics. First, while states can learn from cooperation to raise their level of technology and knowledge about how to prevent diamond smuggling, the same dynamic is at work for those who would want to trade diamonds outside of Kimberley Process controls. In the case of Sierra Leone

100,000 miners, most of them located in the weak eastern region (Gberie and Letourneau 2006).

3 In just about every indicator, such as education, healthcare, human development, GDP per capita, and lifespan, Sierra Leone ranks among the lowest (Kargbo 2014).

smugglers have been able to draw on experience and knowledge of the Kimberley Process to trade outside of these regulations and, in turn, have avoided the costs of dealing through legal channels. Second, the desperation of the postconflict government to attract any foreign investment has made it dependent on the preferences of private companies that are indifferent toward the Kimberley Process. These private companies have often ignored issues surrounding human rights and the government has lacked the capacity to regulate them effectively (Human Rights Watch 2014b). Finally, Sierra Leone has a difficult political geography that has been a challenge for every government since diamonds were discovered and has continued to make Kimberley Process regulations challenging to implement. While the postconflict government of Sierra Leone has to some degree supported the prevention of smuggling and in turn complying with the Kimberley Process, it has lacked the level of state administration in diamond-wealthy areas to do so (Gberie and Letourneau 2006).

Sierra Leone as a Recurring Problem for the De Beers Cartel

The ability to smuggle diamonds from the territory of Sierra Leone has long posed a challenge to the dominance of De Beers over the global diamond trade. Diamonds were first discovered in 1927, and by 1935 the British colony had given De Beers the sole legal authority to mine diamonds (Frost 2012; Reno 1995). This changed the nature of the colonial government as it now needed to prevent locals from smuggling diamonds in regions of the country where it had little influence and usually deferred to local chiefs. Since the state government was unable to prevent smuggling, it allowed De Beers to use armed security to do so, a move opposed by many people who lived in the wealthy diamond areas (Reno 1995; Smillie 2014).

Smuggling was a persistent problem. In the 1950s the government of Sierra Leone set up a monopsony with De Beers to undermine local chiefs and diamond traders who had become more powerful through diamond smuggling (Reno 1995). Nevertheless, diamond smuggling continued, and after independence it became a significant source of funding for rival parties. In 1971 authoritarian president Shiaka Stevens came to power and profited off both legal and illegal diamond traders until he stepped down in 1985. This led to a nightmare for De Beers as many diamonds from the country were released onto the global market outside of the cartel's control. Despite the weakening of the state, researchers have argued that Stevens's ability to coopt illegal mining led to a level of political stability in the country that would gradually erode after he was succeeded by Joseph Momoh in 1985 (Snyder 2006; Snyder and Bhavnani 2005). Momoh was generally unable to coopt illegal diamond mining, and he inherited a state that was increasingly weak in terms of its ability to provide security or public goods to most of the population (Snyder 2006). The inability for the formal state to take advantage of the diamond trade led to wide-scale smuggling and nonstate actors gained wealth through plunder. This untimely led to the complete collapse of the state and "warlord politics" filled the power vacuum (Reno 1998).

By the early 1990s the longstanding joint extraction agreement between the government and De Beers, now referred to as DIMINCO, was in utter disarray as profits had declined and the high level of smuggling made this agreement increasingly untenable (Frost 2012). The longstanding conflict in the 1990s flooded the market with diamonds outside of De Beers' control and created a significant challenge for the cartel. This led De Beers to leave Sierra Leone permanently.[4] While the company has and for the foreseeable future will maintain a dominant position in the diamond trade, the ability for De Beers to price-fix the global market has been greatly diminished. Since the early 2000s, the strategy of De Beers has been to hold onto its large share of the diamond trade in Southern Africa and focus less on West Africa, where its relationship to most governments was more tenuous.[5]

On some level, the Kimberley Process locks in the preferences, in terms of diamond smuggling, that De Beers has long held. Sierra Leone is a good example of this as De Beers tried to set up a monopoly in the country since diamonds were first found. Compared to most countries in Africa, this has been both politically difficult as leaders have often been open to coopting "illegal mining" and administratively difficult as

[4] This strategy by De Beers in Sierra Leone can be contrasted with Angola, another war-torn diamond-wealthy country that De Beers would eventually reenter in 2005 (Munier 2014).

[5] Maintaining a near-monopoly over the diamond trade in Southern Africa has been a difficult task for De Beers. The Lev Leviev group controls a significant portion of the diamond trade in Angola. Zimbabwe has become a major producer of diamonds since 2006 and in the same year forced De Beers out of the country. However, in Botswana, Namibia, and South Africa De Beers has maintained a near-monopoly on the diamond trade (Munier 2016c).

the state has been unable to prevent a high level of diamond smuggling, regardless of its desire to do so. When Sierra Leone emerged from conflict in the early 2000s, the Kimberley Process was a vehicle that had the potential to undo both of these problems, or at the very least create an agreement by which other states would pressure the government of Sierra Leone to make diamond smuggling less common. Nevertheless, most likely due to the continuation of large amounts of diamond smuggling and a need to focus on other regions in Africa, De Beers has not returned.

Understanding the role of De Beers is essential in understanding the nature of how diamond mining developed in the country and how the choices that the government of Sierra Leone has made since the early 2000s are influenced by a history in which the cartel was the prominent actor. Some observers in the early 2000s argued that Sierra Leone might benefit from a joint extraction agreement with De Beers, in contrast to other strategies in the diamond sector (Hart 2001). If De Beers had reentered Sierra Leone after the conflict it is likely that implementing Kimberley Process regulations would have been easier, as having a wealthy private company with vast resources, committed to implementing them, would have helped. However, it is also notable that the historical dynamics that made Sierra Leone a recurring problem for De Beers remain. Thus, while compliance with the Kimberley Process would likely be higher if De Beers was involved in the domestic diamond trade, the absence of the company does not alone explain Sierra Leone's difficulty in implementing the Kimberley Process, as the political geography that makes compliance difficult would still exist.

Diamond Dependence

The upward trend in Sierra Leones official diamond production since the 2008–2011 period does potentially mirror a reduction in smuggling, as illustrated in Table 6.1 (Kimberley Process Diamond Statistics 2017). Observers have estimated that diamond smuggling had dropped by half from the period immediately following the conflict when the Kimberley Process was implemented. These estimates have placed the overall level of diamond smuggling from about 40–60 percent of the overall trade initially to about 20–30 percent by 2009 (Gberie and Letourneau 2006; Smillie and Letourneau 2009; Wilson 2011). This trend is probably correct, in that in 2003 Sierra Leone had almost no

Table 6.1 *Sierra Leone official diamond production, 2004–2017*

Year	Volume, carats	Value, US$
2004	691,756.92	126,652,634.26
2005	668,709.57	141,940,243.85
2006	603,566.07	125,304,842.46
2007	603,623.04	141,565,685.21
2008	371,260.95	98,772,170.78
2009	400,842.98	78,423,595.09
2010	437,516.09	106,062,932.98
2011	357,160.97	124,150,581.01
2012	541,165.66	163,196,193.41
2013	608,955.35	184,482,656.63
2014	620,181.11	221,713,243.46
2015	500,000.13	154,253,128.68
2016	549,086.26	158,872,778.11
2017	289,141.18	122,316,627.92

Source: Kimberley Process Diamond Statistics (2017).

capacity to prevent smuggling, so compliance could only improve. However, when making an estimate about illegal activity, in which data collection is impossible, it is an important caveat that estimates are only useful at uncovering broad trends. Nonetheless, it is likely that the percentage of diamonds that are smuggled from Sierra Leone outside of Kimberley Process regulations is higher than most states.[6] While cooperation and the desire of government leaders to comply with the Kimberley Process has led to higher levels of compliance with the Kimberley Process across sub-Saharan Africa, and to some degree this is true in Sierra Leone, the government and the Kimberley Process agreement continue to fight an uphill battle in Sierra Leone.

It is notable from Table 6.1 that in the period from 2014 to 2016 the diamond sector stayed stable as the Ebola crisis hurt many other types

[6] Other West African states may have comparable levels of smuggling, such as Liberia and Guinea, but these states have far lower domestic production, so they are not as crucial to the Kimberley Process. When the Kimberley Process was first implemented, up to roughly 2009, almost all of Zimbabwean diamonds were smuggled out of the country. However, through cooperation with the Kimberley Process since 2011, while the number of diamonds being smuggled outside of Kimberley Process regulations in Zimbabwe remains high for a state in Southern Africa, it has lowered significantly.

of economic activity. This is due to what Maconachie and Hilson (2018) describe as the "resilience" of miners, who faced tough socio-economic conditions both before and after the crisis. Also, during this period many farm workers used diamond mining as a way to get by, because agriculture was harder hit by the crisis. However, the government has had difficulty harnessing diamond mining into a thriving economic sector since the crisis, as many of the areas most damaged by Ebola have not seen infrastructure and economic activity improve significantly.

To attract foreign investment, the Ministry of Mineral Resources has often pursued a strategy of giving exceptionally favorable tax deals to companies looking to invest. Some diamond companies in Sierra Leone pay as little as 3 percent of their revenue in taxes, causing conflict with other branches of government that could benefit from a higher level of tax revenue (Dieckmann 2011; Gberie and Letourneau 2006). This has created a problematic situation where the government needs a low tax rate to attract foreign investors, given that even a low level of tax collection is better than the absence of any tax revenue that the government gets when diamonds are smuggled illegally. However, the low tax rate makes it difficult for the government, and in turn citizens of Sierra Leone, to benefit directly from diamond wealth. Diamond mining companies in Sierra Leone have further minimized their tax rate by using tax havens and systematically undervaluing their diamond production, so as to pay very little to the central government (Dieckmann 2011). Thus, while the government has been dependent on the sector for revenue, it has been ineffective in setting up an effective tax system.

A primary goal for the government of Sierra Leone is to get a better understanding of how much diamond wealth is in the country.[7] Sierra Leone has received funding from both England and the World Bank to take on this endeavor (Gberie and Letourneau 2006). It is also believed that Sierra Leone has offshore oil reserves, but state weakness has made it difficult to govern or take advantage of maritime resources (Nyokabi, Ikpe, and Alao 2017). If there is oil, this has the potential to change the trajectory of the state significantly but could serve to

[7] As Collier (2010) argues at length, the ability for resource-wealthy countries to get a better understanding of their resource endowments can prevent corruption, allow governments to strategize far better about the future, and lower the level of risk to private investors.

reinforce past patterns of dependence that have been historically present in other resource sectors.

With the election in 2018 of Julius Maada Bio, who has a background in the diamond trade, there has been increasing interest in bringing diamond beneficiation to Sierra Leone as a strategy for the country to get more revenue and employment (Thomas 2018). Bio also promised to revisit past mining policy and review contracts with private mining companies (Nyaungwa 2018). In the same year, the government canceled forty licenses to mine diamonds that may have been connected to smuggling (Gooding 2018).

Learning to Smuggle

Official diamond production dropped off significantly from 2008 to 2011 in Sierra Leone (Kimberley Process Diamond Statistics 2017). While global economic problems were partially to blame, according to Smillie and Letourneau (2009), it also appears as though smugglers in this period had learned better tactics to avoid official channels. Since the Kimberley Process had been in place for four years, it is an interesting phenomenon that while the Sierra Leonean government may have gained from cooperation with other countries, technology, and experience in implementing Kimberley Process regulations, these dynamics appear to be present for those who wish to work around the process as well. Furthermore, the overall decline in global diamond markets during this period made any cost associated with legal diamond channels, including those associated with the Kimberley Process, more difficult for miners to afford. Paradoxically, while illegal mining and buying of diamonds are seen as socially acceptable to many in Sierra Leone, smuggling is frowned upon because it deprives the state of revenue (Engwicht 2016). Furthermore, legal diamond traders are often involved in smuggling to avoid paying taxes (Engwicht 2016). This illustrates the complex interdependence between the legal and illegal diamond trade, often blurring the legality of the entire process. The implementation of laws in Sierra Leone has changed continuously, making it unclear what constitutes an illegal or legal activity (Vorrath 2018).

Since diamonds are worth more per carat in Sierra Leone than in most other African countries, there are also reports of smuggling from other states in West Africa into Sierra Leone (Smillie and Letourneau

2009). These diamonds are then sold to outside official channels for the higher prices that diamonds originating in Sierra Leone generally receive. Many diamond smugglers watch the diamond markets in Western Africa and move their diamonds to where they can get the highest price (Engwicht 2016). Smuggling diamonds and gold from Liberia into Sierra Leone, to avoid higher export taxes, has become particularly pervasive (Genoway 2018). There have also been cases where diamonds that likely originated in Sierra Leone have been smuggled using counterfeit Kimberley Process certificates (Shishlo 2016).

Some mines monitoring officers have admitted that they take bribes or at times have allowed smuggling to take place because they can relate to the lack of economic opportunities faced by the miners (Smillie and Letourneau 2009). Many law enforcement officers may have grown up with people involved in the “illegal” diamond trade or may develop a cooperative relationship in order to get them to follow some regulations while overlooking others. Often illegal mining is tolerated, if not seen as a legitimate form of economic activity, by many groups in Sierra Leone. If illegally mined diamonds are sold to a legal buyer, this is frequently viewed as socially acceptable because the state still collects revenue (Engwicht 2016). Illegal diamond traders often have independent agreements and codes of conduct that do not involve any formal state actors. In some cases, foreign nationals will pay above market value for diamonds as a strategy to launder money (Engwicht 2016).

While smuggling diamonds in and out of Sierra Leone’s porous borders may not be particularly difficult, given weak controls, there is also evidence that smugglers have become more sophisticated on where they transfer their diamonds to. European cities, especially Antwerp and London that have traditionally been centers of the global diamond trade, are avoided because they tend to require more paperwork and certification of where diamonds originated (Smillie and Letourneau 2009). In its place, Dubai and Tel Aviv have become major routes for uncertified diamonds from sub-Saharan Africa because noncertified diamonds receive less, if any, scrutiny.

This reality made the September 2015 appointment of the United Arab Emirates as vice chair of the Kimberley Process controversial.[8]

[8] Some of the controversy surrounding the UAE becoming the vice chair of the Kimberley Process in 2015 was due to alleged smuggling. However, many Western states and nongovernmental organizations were also worried that this

Most Western countries and nongovernmental organizations involved in the process had opposed the United Arab Emirates becoming vice chair and instead preferred Australia (IDEX 2014b, 2014c). While the vice chair is appointed along with the chair before the calendar year starts, the fierce disagreement led to a vice chair not being appointed for over a year.[9]

Preferences of Private Actors

In a manner that left so much to be desired.

Sierra Leone's minister of mineral resources, Alhaji Jalloh, responding to a question about the government's ability to negotiate mining contracts (Smillie and Letourneau 2008, 15)

The government of Sierra Leone has been adamant that when agreeing to contracts with private companies, it has tried to tie this to local development and economic diversification. The reality is that given the state's impoverishment and lack of development in other sectors, it often lacks bargaining power when it comes to negotiating with private companies, as the country is desperate to attract investment. It is common for government actors in Sierra Leone to argue that they have little influence over what takes place in diamond-wealthy areas (Smillie and Letourneau 2009). There is evidence that multinational private companies smuggle some of their more expensive diamonds to avoid government taxes (Engwicht 2016).

The largest diamond producer and employer in Sierra Leone is a London-based company called African Minerals Limited (Human Rights Watch 2014b). This company has been controversial as its production has moved people from diamond-wealthy areas with little compensation. Furthermore, there have been several questions about the treatment of miners in these areas (Human Rights Watch 2014b). Official tax revenue from this company has also been far lower than

would make the United Arab Emirates the chair of the process in 2016 (Barnard 2015).

9 The issue of succession to vice chair of the Kimberley Process overshadowed Angola's tenure as chair, which is notable because, similar to Sierra Leone, Angola emerged from a conflict in which diamonds had played a prominent role and Angola initially had a low level of compliance with the Kimberley Process, but has improved over time (Munier 2014).

expected as the firm's ownership structure has made it difficult to tax and it has not been transparent in its expenses (Dieckmann 2011).

Another major company in Sierra Leone has been Koidu Holdings, which drew widespread scrutiny in 2007 when police killed two protesters at a mine owned by the company (Smillie and Letourneau 2009). This led to its short-term suspension, thus demonstrating that at times the government can have bargaining power with diamond companies. However, this case also shows the paradox of enforcement of human rights in diamond-wealth areas: the government lifted the suspension about five months later and allegedly had lost $12 million in tax revenue (Smillie and Letourneau 2009). The Sierra Leonean government's relationship with Koidu Holdings has been viewed as an example of the desperation and weak negotiation skills that government has had (Engwicht 2018). Koidu Holdings has also extensively used tax havens to pay a lower rate to the Sierra Leonean government (Dieckmann 2011). In turn, Koidu Holdings and other private companies that have had especially favorable deals in Sierra Leone can be viewed as taking advantage of a dire situation. Given the history of these companies, it is unlikely that their preferences are aligned with Kimberley Process regulations, despite the interest they have in stopping diamond smuggling in areas in which they mine.

Much diamond mining in Sierra Leone has continued to go on under conditions that some observers compare to slavery (Smillie and Letourneau 2008). It is common for miners to get only a fraction of what the diamonds they find are worth and to be paid meager wages. However, given the lack of economic opportunities in the region, private enterprises are nevertheless able to employ workers under these conditions. Child labor continues to be a big issue in the mining sector and the country overall, although legislation has been passed that would set the minimum legal age to begin mining at eighteen (Kargbo 2014).

Geography

The location of diamonds in Sierra Leone has made for difficult political geography. If we use Le Billon's (2001a) theory, for how the location of resources can influence the nature of civil wars, the same political geography that has made Sierra Leone prone to conflict also makes implementing Kimberley Process regulations difficult. Most diamond wealth is located far from the capital in the eastern part of the country, making this a "distant" resource profile according to Le Billon (2001). Furthermore, these diamonds are spread across a wide region, possibly up to a fourth of the country, making them "diffuse" (Le Billon 2001a). This makes the state especially prone to difficulties in resource management. Most notably, if we use research on how resources contribute to conflict (Le Billon 2008, 2012; Ross 2004a, 2004b, 2006; Snyder 2006; Snyder and Bhavnani 2005), the "lootability" of most of the "alluvial" diamonds found in Sierra Leone has made the country particularly susceptible to conflict, and in turn has made implementing Kimberley Process regulations far more difficult than in most states, even other weak states. Given that these "alluvial" diamonds are found on the earth's surface and require few startup costs to begin mining, without extensive efforts to secure diamond mining areas preventing smuggling is near impossible.[10] Moreover, given that diamonds are located over a vast area and that Sierra Leone is one of the world's poorest states, building the extensive security that would be needed to prevent diamond smuggling is difficult if not virtually impossible. The political geography of Sierra Leone makes the reality of complying with Kimberley Process regulations so difficult that even states with good infrastructure and funding face many challenges when it comes to Kimberley Process compliance.

A contributing factor to the government of Sierra Leone's inability to prevent diamond smuggling is that the Ministry of Mineral Resources is headquartered in the capital city of Freetown, far from where most diamonds are located. Even in the headquarters this ministry has often lacked resources and has been severely understaffed (Gberie and Letourneau 2006). Most workers for the Ministry of Mineral Resources avoid going to the most diamond wealthy areas in the eastern part of the country, where officials have been assaulted by miners (Gberie and Letourneau 2006). Government monitors often lack the resources to even reach the diamond-wealthy areas of Sierra Leone, such as vehicles or mobile phones (Engwicht 2018). Moreover, while some officers were trained in South Africa to prevent illicit smuggling in Sierra Leone, many lack any training (Gberie and Letourneau 2006). An inconsistent pay schedule, in which

[10] Namibia has diamonds found over a large area. However, given extensive capital investment from De Beers, and the fact that these diamonds are located near a large desert, Namibia has not had the same governance challenges as Sierra Leone (Munier 2016c).

government monitors sometimes go without pay for over a year, makes them even more accepting of smuggling and leads to an overall willingness to overlook illegal mining if they get some of the proceeds (Engwicht 2018).

In Sierra Leone, many local chiefs and royal families view the diamond trade as part of their patronage system, adding another level of governance that is likely to be inadequate at the local level (Acemoglu, Reed, and Robinson 2014). Local chiefs are known for either ignoring, or in some cases overtly supporting, illegal activities in the diamond trade that they benefit from monetarily (Engwicht 2018). Arbitrary taxation, or enforcement of laws, is another obstacle that miners in Sierra Leone often must navigate. Ultimately, what constitutes illegal activity in the mining sector is often shifting and "renegotiable" between actors on the local level (Vorrath 2018).

There have also been questions about the level of security at Lungi International, the largest airport in Sierra Leone. In the early 2000s this was allegedly a significant source of smuggling as few people moving through the airport were searched for diamonds (Gberie and Letourneau 2006). In recent years the Sierra Leonean government has invested resources in lessening the amount of diamond smuggling in the airport, although monitors remain undertrained (Engwicht 2018).

On top of the lack of infrastructure in Sierra Leone's diamond-rich regions, the situation is made worse by the porous borders and lack of governance that exist in Guinea and Liberia, the two states that border Sierra Leone. Liberia did not become a member of the Kimberley Process until 2007 when a United Nations ban on the diamond trade was lifted (European Commission 2007). Liberia has long been a smuggling route for diamonds that originate in Sierra Leone. Since 2007, Liberia has faced challenges similar to Sierra Leone in implementing Kimberley Process regulations. Despite a desire to cooperate with the Kimberley Process from the central government in Liberia, it is common for local law enforcement agents to take bribes in exchange for looking the other way when diamonds are being smuggled (Hilson and Van Bockstael 2011). The only advantage that Liberia has when it comes to Kimberley Process implementation is that it has far fewer diamonds than Sierra Leone. Guinea has also been known as a significant diamond-smuggling channel and, given the long border that it shares with Sierra Leone, it is most likely the leading state that diamonds are smuggled into (International Alert 2006). The borders are so open in some places along the border with Sierra Leone that smugglers can safely cross on a motorbike or car as there is no checking of passports or searches for illicit goods (IRIN 2009). Furthermore, local law enforcement in Sierra Leone is likely to turn a blind eye to smuggling diamonds into the country if they then enter legal channels, because this adds to state revenue (Engwicht 2018).

A Governance Problem

Ideally, the implementation of Kimberley Process regulations in 2003 was a way to assist the state-building process in Sierra Leone. The reality of attempts to implement this agreement has been far different, as it is now apparent that the inability of Sierra Leone to implement Kimberley Process regulations is one of the clearest examples of how slow state building can be. This is especially the case when an international agreement tries to homogenize policy across a wide variety of circumstances. While states in sub-Saharan Africa are often characterized as being weak or virtually nonexistent outside of major cities, this varies considerably, and the experience of the states examined in this study in implementing Kimberley Process regulations is an excellent example of this variation.

Even for a sub-Saharan country in West Africa, Sierra Leone is an exceptionally weak state. Given its lack of government resources, one must wonder if implementing the Kimberley Process is the best strategy for Sierra Leone to take. Resources that Sierra Leone spends on compliance with the Kimberley Process have the potential to be used on other government programs, some of which may address more urgent problems. This is especially the case in a state where pressing issues, such as child labor and rampant corruption, remain salient (Kargbo 2014). Furthermore, the Kimberley Process has contributed to a regulatory system in Sierra Leone's diamond sector that is often opaque. In some cases, miners are justifiably unclear as to whether their activities are legal or not (Engwicht 2016). The illegal and legal trade in Sierra Leonean diamonds has become so intertwined that it is hard to distinguish, especially given the arbitrary nature of law enforcement.

Kimberley Process regulations may be ill-suited to the socioeconomic reality that exists in Sierra Leone. This is because Kimberley Process regulations have tended to place small diamond companies and impoverished miners at a disadvantage in comparison to large companies, as it is far harder for them to pay the costs associated with complying. Since most private diamond companies in Sierra Leone are relatively small and miners in rural areas lack the resources to pay any of the costs associated with legal mining, criminalizing small-scale mining may be ill suited to the state's reality. Police may be mainly motivated to turn a blind eye toward diamond smuggling because of bribes or overall corruption. However, in Sierra Leone there is reason to believe that some police officers or officials turn a blind eye to diamond smuggling because they understand that the miners are often treated unfairly and only receive a fraction of what their diamonds are worth (Smillie and Letourneau 2009). Moreover, since women or people of small ethnic groups are more likely to work within Sierra Leon's ill-defined black market, regulation of the diamond trade may disproportionately hurt them without offering viable alternatives (Kargbo 2014).[11]

The goal of homogenizing diamond policy on a global level inherently overlooks local factors, especially when local conditions differ wildly and the impoverished countries that are most influenced by these agreements also lack the resources to participate fully in them. This study uncovers some interesting dynamics about how the process has influenced miners and diamond-wealthy areas on a local level. It inherently raises the question of how much of a priority should be placed on Kimberley Process regulations in a state that fails to deliver essential services and suffers from a lack of infrastructure.

[11] Siegel's (2009) contention that the Kimberley Process was largely designed by NGOs, De Beers and Western governments that had little understanding of the local reality of diamond mining in Africa would seem particularly salient in the case of Sierra Leone.

7 No Private Companies = No Compliance

The Crisis of the Kimberley Process in the Central African Republic

Understanding the ongoing conflict in the Central African Republic is essential to understanding the Kimberley Process. Unlike other cases examined in this book, given any plausible definition diamonds have contributed to conflict in the Central African Republic since the Kimberley Process was implemented.[1] Thus, examining the influence of the Kimberley Process on the conflict in the Central African Republic is crucial to understanding whether the agreement is useful in its original goal of preventing diamonds that are tied to conflict from entering the global market, Furthermore, even when compared to other weak states such as Sierra Leone or Zimbabwe, why has compliance with the Kimberley Process been so low in the Central African Republic?

With years of political instability and ineffective government, there may be a tendency to see the Central African Republic as not having a government in any real sense. However, when examining the Central African Republic, it is more useful to view it as a state. As Lombard (2016) argues, the Central African Republic has many of the same attributes as other states but is an extreme case of state weakness. Many of the characteristics most ascribed to the Central African Republic, such as a weak, unresponsive, and distant government, are present on some level in most states, including many examined in this study. Thus, the Central African Republic is a "predatory" or "phantom" state but nonetheless an entity where having the legitimacy

[1] Even given the narrow definition of conflict diamonds as diamonds that contribute to a rebel group's funding in overthrowing a legitimate government, the Central African Republic would qualify (Kimberley Process 2018). The Central African Republic is also a country in which multiple rebel groups have later become the government, at least in the sense of holding the capital city, so this case is particularly challenging for any classification that tries to define what exactly is a conflict diamond and what is not.

of holding the central government matters, although this has changed hands many times.[2]

Examining the conflict in the Central African Republic forces us to question how we think about civil wars more generally. Usually, most economic activity is seen as being depressed by conflict, or as Collier (2007) calls it, "development in reverse." However, in most civil wars some economic sectors are not harmed by conflict or may even become more profitable (Fearon 2004; Mitchell and Thies 2012; Regan and Norton 2005). Thus the traditional view that different groups fight each other to "win" a war might not work when actors find that perpetual conflict is economically profitable (Keen 2008). It is in this context that the domestic political economy of the Kimberley Process in the Central African Republic should be viewed. Like other states discussed in this study, diamond dependence and the power differentiation between government actors matters for understanding the role that the Kimberley Process has played in the agreement. However, more so than in any other case the preferences of government and private actors toward the Kimberley Process is challenging to define as these roles are often blurred. However, understanding these preferences is as essential to understanding the attempt by the Kimberley Process to certify the diamond trade in the Central African Republic as it is anywhere else.

The political geography of the Central African Republic makes it one of the most difficult, if not the most difficult, to govern of any state. All diamonds in the Central African Republic are believed to be alluvial (de Wit et al. 2016). Throughout the history of the Central African Republic over 80 percent of diamond production has been done by small-scale miners, the participation of large companies and industrial-scale mining has been rare (Matthysen and Clarkson 2013). In fact, the only multinational mining company active in the Central African Republic is a Canadian-owned gold-mining firm called AXMIN

[2] For instance, Bierschenk and Sardan (1997) refer to the Central African Republic as a "phantom" state in which the central government is only occasionally able to extend beyond the capital. Beyond simply not providing public good or security to most of the population, the state in the Central African Republic is an example of a "predatory" state in which the central government has often interacted with rural areas just to extract resources. In some periods of the Central African Republic's history one could even go as far as to argue that the central state had become essentially a criminal enterprise or what Bayart, Ellis, and Hibou (1999) refer to as the "criminalization" of the state.

(Matthysen and Clarkson 2013). Thus, unlike most states in Africa, the influence of large diamond-mining companies on the state's political economy has been minimal. Instead, it has been common for government leaders to use the diamond trade as part of their direct patronage system or a source to be exploited for personal, private wealth. While in many states it has been common for multinational companies to have a direct influence over local policy, the Central African Republic has been too unstable and geographically isolated for outside companies to gain a firm foothold. Thus, on the surface, it would appear as though government leaders could get their policy preferences implemented without worrying about the private sector. However, in the Central African Republic the public and private sector, if not criminal activity, are blurred to the extent that these categories make little sense in this context. Often government officials have extensive private economic interests, and they see their position in office as a way to leverage their economic benefit. In many cases, government officials were once rebels themselves, and most transitions of political power have not taken place through democratic elections. Thus, when gaining political power through a rebellion or coup, the new leaders have often seen the state apparatus as a "prize" to be exploited by a narrow group of actors.[3]

Most of the diamonds in the Central African Republic are located in two regions, in the west near the border with Cameroon and in the central east over a large area (de Wit et al. 2016). While these diamond deposits are similar, including in scale and distribution, the political geography of the central-eastern region has made governing this area more difficult (Malpeli and Chirico 2014). Both regions where diamonds are found in the Central African Republic are relatively far from the capital city of Bangui, the only city in the country. The Central African Republic has continuously been a state that rarely interacted with rural areas except to coerce the local populations (Bierschenk and Sardan 1997). Throughout most periods since colonization the state has provided little in social programs. If the central government does interact with any of the diverse local tribes, it is usually negative. This creates a power vacuum throughout much of

[3] The idea that the diamond trade exists to be exploited by political elites is commonly accepted in Central African Republic's political culture. For example, high political officials have been known to wear very expensive diamonds as a sign of their status (Dalby 2015).

the country, and local tribal leaders, religious groups, and trade or farmers' organizations have filled the void. Often these localized forms of government have had the same sort of chaotic nature that has characterized the central government, with local rivalries or power struggles. In the Central African Republic, both formal and informal institutions have taken on a "predatory form." Elites, rebel groups, or just outright criminality have often been intertwined to the point where it is hard to distinguish one from another. Despite many crises in the history of the Central African Republic, the predatory nature of government institutions has stayed remarkably consistent, despite a large range of actors holding formal political office (Glawion and De Vries 2018).

The predatory nature of the government has long shaped and been shaped by the dominant economic sector in the country: the diamond trade. No government in the Central African Republic has ever had success certifying or taxing the diamond trade formally. At least half of the Central African Republic's diamond production has been smuggled out of the country in most periods (de Wit et al. 2016). In the post-2016 period, some estimates place the amount smuggled, outside of Kimberley Process regulations, at around 80 percent of overall production (International Peace Information Service 2018). Thus, the Central African Republic has one of the lowest levels of compliance with the Kimberley Process of any state that is part of the agreement. Diamond mining has also been a major source of income, as during most years about 50,000–100,000 miners have been active in the country (Chirico, Barthélémy, and Ngbokoto 2010). There is likely to be a vast amount of diamond wealth still located in the Central African Republic, as estimates state that only about a third has been mined (Chirico, Barthélémy, and Ngbokoto 2010). While the diamond distribution and level of diamond smuggling makes the Central African Republic an extreme case, it shares many attributes with other states in this study, such as a wide distribution of alluvial diamonds far from the capital city, a region with other weak states, porous borders with ineffective policing, and a sparse population outside of the capital.

This study of the Kimberley Process in the Central African Republic will proceed as follows. First, the historical development of predatory institutions in the Central African Republic, and the role that diamond wealth played in reinforcing this institutional arrangement will be examined. Next, the implementation of the Kimberley Process in 2003, and the paradoxical nature of the agreement in addressing the coup during that year in the Central African Republic will be observed. The ongoing difficulty in implementing Kimberley Process regulations will be discussed, as at times both rebel groups and the central government have had incentives to deny the existence of conflict diamonds. The suspension of the Central African Republic by the Kimberley Process, after the Seleka rebel coalition took power in early 2013, will then be studied, along with attempts by the Kimberley Process to allow some regions of the country back into the legal diamond trade after 2016.

Decolonization, Diamonds, and Dependence

Diamonds were first found in the Central African Republic in 1914 (Dietrich 2002). Before independence, there were about ten French mining companies that owned most of the diamond production. These companies passed a few of the potential benefits on to the people of the Central African Republic, but it did become a significant sector of the economy. During French rule, the Central African Republic was viewed as not being an important colony, and only one city developed, the longtime capital of Bangui (Lombard 2016).

The end of official French rule gave rise to a predatory state and continued dependence on the diamond trade. David Dacko became president in 1961 but was overthrown by Jean Bokassa in 1966. Bokassa would become one of the most brutal and erratic dictators in postcolonial Africa, ruling the Central African Republic as though it was his fiefdom (Titley 1997). In 1969 Bokassa expelled the larger French diamond companies and took control of diamond production directly (Dietrich 2002). Some foreign companies were allowed to continue mining, but they had to pay the government mostly through bribes; therefore most of them left. This also marked the end of the involvement of large mining companies in the Central African Republic as since the French companies left no large foreign company has been operating in the country. While there have been smaller mining companies that have been active in the Central African Republic, there has never been a large company that controls a significant share of the production, as there are in many African countries. Thus, early on this placed the Central African Republic on a different trajectory outside of De Beers' control.

Bokassa's policies resulted in a significant decline in the diamond trade as official diamond production fell from 600,000 carats in 1968 to 314,000 carats in 1979 (Dietrich 2002). Government earnings overall also dropped at about the same rate, by half, but diamonds continued to be about a third of all exports. Because of the extreme corruption that went on during this period, it is hard to come to any reliable conclusions, as government control over most of the official diamond trade led to a high level of diamond smuggling that has persisted. What can be said about this period is that Bokassa's thirteen years in power, which ended in a coup that restored Dacko in 1979, created weak and predatory government institutions (Titley 1997). Successive governments would see the diamond trade as a private "prize" for controlling the central government, and not as a means to build the state or provide government services.

One of the primary reasons for the historically weak development of institutions in the Central African Republic is the dependence on the French government for aid and investment that has persisted since the state gained formal independence. As was the case with Bokassa being overthrown, rarely has a political change taken place in the Central African Republic without the French being directly involved (BBC News 2011). Therefore, most leaders in the Central African Republic have cared more about their relationship with the French than their domestic popularity among the average citizen or responsiveness to local issues. Many of the institutions and the overall political culture in the Central African Republic have been shaped by French influence, and this has continued long after formal colonization ended.

Dacko would be overthrown in a coup in 1981 that brought about a military government led by Andre Kolingba (Kalck 2004). Official diamond wealth had fallen off considerably in this period, as smuggling became common. For instance, in 1983 the discrepancy between official production and the official amount of diamonds imported by neighboring countries was 495,000 carats (International Crisis Group 2010). The World Bank would gain more of an influence over the Central African Republic under Kolingba, and it made one of the first attempts to control diamond smuggling by creating a certification system. This system probably lowered the number of smuggled diamonds somewhat, but it was mostly ineffective.

Diamond Production and Conflict Increase

Eventually, Kolingba's government came under pressure to hold elections and did so in 1993. Felix Patasse became the first "democratically" elected president. Patasse had become wealthy from the diamond trade and used these resources to win the presidency. After his administration took over, he used his political power to accelerate his diamond production (International Crisis Group 2010). Patasse directly owned one of the larger mining companies and had people buy diamonds from other local miners as well. He would gain a grip on much of the diamond trade by making many companies exempt from regulation or taxes in exchange for part of the wealth. While there was some enthusiasm over Patasse because he was "democratically" elected, his rule became one of the most overtly predatory in the Central African Republic's history and led to collapse.

Under pressure from the World Bank, Patasse decided to do something about the smuggling of diamonds (International Crisis Group 2010). He instituted a quota system in the country that failed to work. To make matters even more complicated, diamonds directly tied to conflict from the Democratic Republic of Congo were being brought into the Central African Republic. In 1996 and 1997 many soldiers mutinied, and there was widespread chaos in the Central African Republic (BBC News 2011). With help from the French and other African countries, stability was restored, and Patasse won a controversial election over former presidents Kolingba and Dacko in 1999 (BBC News 2011). It is notable that just a few actors have constantly dominated politics in the Central African Republic as political influence is relegated to a tiny group of people representing narrow economic interests. The narrow focus and intertwined nature of power in the Central African Republic led to continued instability as many people in the Central African Republic lived in extreme poverty and had little to lose by joining rebel groups.

Diamond production grew to become the major export resource in the Central African Republic; according to the United States Department of State (2010) diamonds were around 50 percent of export earnings in 2002. The instability and unpredictability of the government have often kept foreign investment out. In the 1990s there were a few examples of foreign diamond companies from South Africa and Canada that tried to start extracting diamonds from the Central African Republic, but the ongoing instability and infrastructure made these enterprises too risky (Dietrich 2002).

Much of the Central African Republic's connection to conflict diamonds in the early 2000s had to do with its location as a landlocked country in one of the most unstable "neighborhoods" in the world. This made regulating the diamond trade in the country impossible. As Zoellner (2006, 10) points out, the capital city of the Central African Republic, Bangui, has "six buying agencies and a direct pipeline to Antwerp is a ten-minute canoe ride from the edge of the Congo." According to his analysis, the mines in the Central African Republic probably produce around 500,000 carats a year but at least twice that shows up in foreign markets. Therefore, it seems evident that some of the diamonds were coming from the Democratic Republic of the Congo in the early 2000s. The Central African Republic officially exported 461,000 carats in 2000, whereas imports to the Central African Republic numbered at 1.3 million (Smillie 2010a).

The First Crisis for the Kimberley Process

Right after the Kimberley Process came into effect, the Central African Republic became a controversial case when rebels led by Francois Bozize overthrew Patassé in 2003 (Global Witness 2003a, 2003b). The rebels now controlled the state apparatus and were able to use diamond wealth to consolidate their overthrow of what many viewed as a legitimate government, thus potentially placing them in violation of the Kimberley Process. This raised the question of whether the Kimberley Process should become involved or suspend the Central African Republic because of the apparent role that diamonds had played in funding both sides. Much of the world condemned the rebels, including the United Nations (UN News Centre 2003).

In reaction, Corinna Gilfillan from Global Witness (2003a) summed up the view of many nongovernmental organizations that were initial partners to the Kimberley Process by saying "Since rebels have seized power and overthrown a legitimate government, the Central African Republic is now in violation of the Kimberley Process and should be banned from trading in diamonds until constitutional rule is re-established." The problem was that the Kimberley Process had at this time rules in place for reacting to rebel groups that were involved in the diamond trade, but not for dealing with a situation in which rebels had taken over the state and had become the government, thus leading to a paradoxical situation that has since occurred multiple times in the Central African Republic.

The Central African Republic was initially removed from the Kimberley Process for about two months following the coup but was let back in when the new government insisted that it could implement the goals of the Kimberley Process and prevent conflict diamonds from going to market (Global Witness 2003a, 2003b). This led to an internal review of the Central African Republic in which representatives from the Kimberley Process inspected mines and trading sites and discussed the Kimberley Process with relevant government officials. As the first review of a member country undertaken by participants in the Kimberley Process, this was a sort of test about the potential effectiveness of the agreement (Global Witness 2003a, 2003b).

The Report of the Review Mission of the Kimberley Process to the Central African Republic (2003, 2) stated the following in its report: "After reviewing the various elements of the Kimberley Process and their implementation in the Central African Republic, the mission concluded that the process was being implemented satisfactorily overall. However, the mission noted that specific legislation implementing the Kimberley Process Certification Scheme was still in the process of being drafted." The report goes on to say that their inspection of diamond sites shows that they usually comply with the regulations of the Kimberley Process, but there is much room for improvement. The report outlines smuggling as a significant problem, though it also says that the landlocked geography of the Central African Republic makes controlling its borders nearly impossible. However, the Kimberley Process was making it more challenging to market smuggled diamonds.

It appears the Bozize government did initially take participation in the Kimberley Process seriously, as it was a way to reinforce and legitimize his rule, leading to a higher level of compliance and formalization in the sector than had existed in the past (International Peace Information Service 2018). Much of this was because reform in the mining sector was a precondition for assistance from the World Bank (Matthysen and Clarkson 2013). United States Agency for International Development (USAID) set up a program called Property Rights and Artisanal Diamond Development Project (PRADD) to assist in raising the Central African Republic's compliance with the Kimberley Process. The Bozize regime's cooperation with the project was selective and only halfhearted from the beginning (Matthysen and Clarkson 2013). Given the weakness of the state in the Central African Republic, outside assistance is particularly essential in raising the state's compliance with the Kimberley Process. However, since the central government in most periods only controls some of the overall territory of the country, even if it does cooperate with well-funded aid programs there are clear limitations to this approach.

The role of the Kimberley Process in the Central African Republic, after the coup in 2003, highlights early on some of its limitations. Even if the Kimberley Process was successful to some extent in preventing rebels from trading diamonds, if former rebels become the new government or the government itself becomes exploitative there is little in the agreement to address these issues. Thus, the Kimberley Process showed itself to be a limited and paradoxical agreement, even if it did have some influence in changing state behavior in this case. However, due to changing dynamics in which the regime faced multiple rebel groups, complying with Kimberley Process regulations ceased to be a priority, although the government continued to go through the motions of cooperating with the agreement. This illustrates how compliance with Kimberley Process regulations can often be useful to reinforce specific strategies that leaders have in the diamond sector but can also be discarded by the same leaders when these regulations are no longer to their advantage.

Diamond Extracting "Militias" and the Disincentive to Disarm during the Bozize Regime

Diamonds have consistently funded conflict in the northeast region of the Central African Republic more than anywhere else. Some of the reasons are that this area has never been integrated economically, the central government has ignored it, there is much extreme poverty and diamonds are the only significant source of economic opportunity (Berg 2008). These factors led to the creation of a group that is ironically called the Union of Democratic Forces for Unity. This group was able to take advantage of the poor living conditions of many miners and encourage them to rebel.

Initially, in 2004, the stated goal of the Union of Democratic Forces for Unity was to force more government investment and economic distribution into the northeast part of the country (International Crisis Group 2010). However, diamond wealth seems to have been a motivation, as they took over diamond mines and robbed diamond traders. In 2007 the military of the Central African Republic, along with French troops, were able to stop the rebellion by fighting the rebels to a deadlock and getting them to sign a treaty to disarm. In many areas, however, they did not disarm and continued to demand new conditions to the ceasefire. Continuing the conflict allowed them to profit through mining, thus disincentivizing an end to the conflict. Many rebels were directly involved in the diamond trade, selling their diamonds to both legal and illegal middlemen. These rebels have also benefited from people who formally worked for the government defecting to their side (Berg 2008).

In early 2010 the Ugandan army entered the northeast region of the Central African Republic to pursue the Lord's Resistance Army, a rebel group that was hiding in the region (International Crisis Group 2010). They put an end to some of the Union of Democratic Forces for Unity's ability to profit from diamonds but at the same time gave the group a further disincentive to disarm. When the Ugandan army left later that year, the diamond trade returned to what it was before. None of these groups had ever been invited into the Central African Republic by the government, but there is little to stop armed groups from using the Central African Republic at will, as security on many parts of the border was nonexistent and the Bozize regime never had firm control of large amounts of territory.

The Union of Democratic Forces for Unity represents another paradoxical problem for the Kimberley Process. Technically, since they signed a treaty to disarm in 2007, they were no longer officially at war. Thus, their diamonds do not qualify as conflict diamonds, although it was clear that they were still operating. The central government had an incentive to deny the existence of conflict diamonds, because it could lead to a potential suspension from the Kimberley Process and hurt their ability to profit from diamonds. If the Kimberley Process suspended the whole country, as it did in 2003, this would cut off the Bozize regime's primary source of revenue as well. Thus, all parties had an incentive to downplay the existence of conflict diamonds in the country and continue a low-scale conflict over the diamond trade. In this situation, it is hard to see what would be different if the Kimberley Process was absent. The potential for diamond wealth, along with other security concerns, gave the rebels a clear disincentive to disarm and the Bozize regime had an incentive to pretend that this is what had happened. The Bozize regime's continuation of predatory patterns in the diamond trade led to a situation where rural areas of the country were ignored, and most people lacked necessary economic opportunities. Thus, the opportunity to join a rebel group or participate in illegal economic activity became attractive for many.

To make matters more complicated, in the late 2000s another rebel group that had fought both the Union of Democratic Forces for Unity and the official government – the Convention of Patriots for Justice and Peace – gained in popularity (International Crisis Group 2010). The relationship between these rebels and the diamond trade was less certain, but some of their leaders had ties to diamond wealth, and they have operated in areas where they likely mined for diamonds. On top of these rebel groups, many purely criminal elements operated in much of the Central African Republic and the line between them, the rebel groups, and even the official government became blurred. These dynamics led to the fall of the Bozize regime.

The 2012–2013 Crisis for the Kimberley Process

In December 2012 a coalition of rebel groups called Seleka controlled part of the northeastern Central African Republic where diamonds are found and threatened the central government (Reuters 2012b). For a few months, a ceasefire was in effect, and some of the rebels entered a power-sharing agreement with the government. However, the Seleka rebels started to move on Bangui, and on March 25 the new president, Michel Djotodia, announced his rule after taking control of the capital (Chothia 2013). While the new government pursued the rhetoric of reform in the diamond sector, ultimately past patterns of predation prevailed (International Crisis Group 2014).

Similar to the events in 2003, the Kimberley Process was caught in a quagmire because a former rebel group had become the government, but in this case, the process moved to suspend all diamond exports from the country and legal diamond production halted for the next three years (Kimberley Process Diamond Statistics 2017). The new leaders moved quickly to control the diamond trade, often coercing or coopting local miners and traders. Many who joined the Seleka coalition saw control over the diamond trade as a potential business opportunity (International Crisis Group 2014). After taking power, Seleka leaders created a sort of "parallel" government in which they allowed mining in exchange for bribes or local taxes (Global Witness 2017b). According to a report by the United Nations Security Council (2014, 3): "Since the suspension of the Central African Republic from the Kimberley Process in May 2013, an additional 140,000 carats of diamonds, valued at $24 million, are estimated to have been smuggled out of the country." Despite extreme instability and the ban on diamonds from the Kimberley Process, the Seleka-controlled government was able to get interest from international companies in future diamond-mining ventures (Global Witness 2017b).

Militias opposed to Seleka's rule, often called anti-balaka, often fought over wealthy diamond areas and used this as a source of funding (International Crisis Group 2014). These groups have also been known to set up protection rackets or illegal taxation for miners in regions under their control and some leaders have been involved in the diamond trade directly (Global Witness 2017b). To make matters even more complicated, it appears as though members of the same armed group fought directly over resources in some cases (United Nations Security Council 2014). In other cases, it also appears as though "competing" armed groups colluded in order to mutually gain from mining wealth (International Peace Information Service 2018). Thus, the primary motivation of many actors in the conflict seems to have been economic.

Throughout the conflict in the Central African Republic most major armed groups claimed to be protecting local miners, along with local "militias" or criminal gangs. Often this "protection" was in exchange for some of the profits or outright extortion. This dynamic has been present in all types of economic activity in the Central African Republic, but because of the increased potential for economic gain in the mining sector and the stationary nature of mining production, competition for mining wealth has been particularly pervasive and has led to some of the deadliest events of the conflict (International Peace Information Service 2018).

Despite fierce opposition, it was the Seleka coalition itself that imploded and splintered into many factions. This led to the resignation of Djotodia in late 2014 and the acting presidency of Catherine Samba-Panza, the first women to lead the country. Ex-Seleka fighters remained active, retreating to the northern and eastern parts of the Central African Republic. The extreme predation, conflicting motivations, and economic mismanagement that characterized the Djotodia regime was likely a significant reason for the splintering of Seleka and eventual collapse of the government (International Crisis Group 2014).

The conflict and Kimberley Process sanctions did lessen diamond production in the Central African Republic and raise the costs associated with diamond smuggling when the ban initially went into effect

(International Crisis Group 2014). However, in some regions diamond mining went on unaffected, and now all diamonds that left the country were outside of Kimberley Process control.[4] In response to lower initial demand for diamonds and the Kimberley Process ban, many diamond miners started to branch out into gold mining, which was even less regulated. In fact, in the gold-mining sector, 95 percent has been exported out of the Central African Republic in most years (International Peace Information Service 2018). However, within a few years it appeared as though the diamond sector in the Central African Republic had reached past levels of production, or even higher levels (International Peace Information Service 2018). Actors learned how to work around Kimberley Process regulations and the extreme instability and poverty that existed in the country at this time drove many workers into the mining sector to get by economically.[5]

The Kimberley Process Allowed Some Regions Back in 2016

In 2016 the Kimberley Process removed restrictions on some regions of the Central African Republic that complied with the agreement (Kimberley Process 2015c). Most areas in which the ban was lifted were in the western part of the country, where some government control had been established (Global Witness 2017b). The idea was that in these regions a legal diamond trade could contribute to stabilizing the country, as until this point all diamonds originating in the country could not be exported legally. However, this added another layer of complexity as now the government of the Central African Republic was supposed to prevent diamonds originating in "complicit" regions from being transferred into "non-complicit regions." Since monitoring the cross-border trade has proven very difficult, the expectation to effectively police the intrastate trade is impossible. This would probably be nearly impossible for even very capable states.

As shown in Table 7.1, the Central African Republic did begin legal diamond production again in 2016. However, in 2016 and 2017 official diamond production did not return to anywhere near the level

[4] Illegal smuggling was not just limited to diamonds in this period, as poaching and car theft also became common (International Crisis Group 2014).

[5] While local political stability is likely to have a clear influence on diamond production, so do other factors such as weather or the ability for workers to find employment in other sectors on a local level.

Table 7.1 *Central African Republic official diamond production, 2004–2017*

Year	Volume, carats	Value, US$
2004	348,205.16	51,709,404.00
2005	382,756.00	60,572,404.80
2006	419,528.35	59,066,866.49
2007	467,710.53	59,857,870.53
2008	377,209.12	47,752,281.70
2009	311,779.42	47,086,829.60
2010	301,557.62	48,892,376.57
2011	323,575.50	60,893,286.76
2012	365,916.63	62,129,596.66
2013	81,628.85	14,816,692.37
2014	0.00	0.00
2015	0.00	0.00
2016	10,653.63	1,688,143.00
2017	47,636.70	6,505,304.82

Source: Kimberley Process Diamond Statistics (2017).

of 2004–2012. Furthermore, as actual diamond production may have dropped initially because of the conflict and Kimberley Process sanctions, it also appears to have recovered to pre-2013 levels, if not grown as a consequence of sociopolitical factors (International Peace Information Service 2018). Thus, the official diamond production (Table 7.1) is also illustrative of a large number of diamonds that entered the market during this period outside of Kimberley Process controls. Furthermore, Table 7.1 demonstrates that while the overall volume of diamonds from the Central African Republic produced yearly is not particularly high, many of these diamonds are of very high value.

The new regulations put in place by the Kimberley Process in 2016 led to widespread confusion. Some diamond traders appeared to believe that the lifting of the Kimberley Process ban for some regions meant that the trade was now legal across the whole country (Global Witness 2017b). There are few examples of diamonds being suspected of originating in the Central African Republic once they make their way off the African continent (Global Witness 2017b). This demonstrates the difficulty of having any certainty regarding where diamonds originate; once the diamonds make it to certain points they are no longer scrutinized, an incentive to reach those points. Social media has made coordination in global diamond smuggling easier, as participants can coordinate over large geographical areas that would have been difficult in the past (Global Witness 2017b). Furthermore, it is likely that over time smugglers have learned more effective techniques to move their diamonds to countries where they will no longer be suspect.

While Kimberley Process regulations banned the export of diamonds from 2013 to 2016, it did not ban their purchase. Thus, some trading houses purchased diamonds that may have been tied to conflict but did not export them (Global Witness 2017b). This allowed the potential for rebel groups to continue profiting from the diamond trade. The existence of this legal loophole raises the question of what to do with these diamonds now that some restrictions have been lifted. Some of these diamonds were sourced from regions where conflict was not as prevalent and were the first to be allowed back into the legal trade. Furthermore, some of these trading houses tried to play by Kimberley Process rules, and it may seem unfair to penalize them when other actors were exporting banned diamonds without trying to stay in compliance.[6]

Widescale smuggling of diamonds around the Kimberley Process continued in both "compliant" and "noncompliant" zones of the Central African Republic. It is likely that close to two thirds of the yearly production in 2017, from compliant zones, was smuggled outside of Kimberley Process and central government control (International Peace Information Service 2018). Thus, lifting the ban only provided minimal help to the central government's ability to gain revenue from the diamond trade. However, in a sense, compliance was higher in 2017 because in the 2013–2016 period all diamonds were traded outside of Kimberley Process regulations and official government control. In 2018 it appears as though compliance with the Kimberley Process dropped even lower than 2017, as official diamond production was reportedly at around 10,000 carats, suggesting widescale smuggling during this year (Political Analysis South Africa 2018).

A significant reason for diamond smuggling outside of Kimberley Process regulations is that complying is too costly for many actors. If

[6] It does seem as though the Kimberley Process may have made it more difficult for buying houses in the Central African Republic to maintain a consistent flow of diamonds, although many found ways around this (Global Witness 2017b).

one were to try and export diamonds "legally" they would often encounter a layer of "illegality" from government actors through corruption or outright extortion. Even international peacekeepers have been implicated in the illegal diamond trade (International Peace Information Service 2018). Thus, the process to comply with the Kimberley Process on a local level is often too complicated and unprofitable for miners at best, at worst controlled by criminals. Furthermore, even if miners wanted to comply with the Kimberley Process, the government of the Central African Republic has lacked basic resources and staffing to produce proper Kimberley Process certification in most regions (Matthysen and Clarkson 2013).

The Porous Borders of the Central African Region

Another dynamic of the diamond trade in the Central African Republic is widescale smuggling across the Cameroonian border. At times the conflict in the Central African Republic has spilled across the border, prompting Cameroon to become more actively involved (Vircoulon 2015). Cameroon was late to join the Kimberley Process, only becoming a participant in 2012 (Kimberley Process 2012). Cameroon is often used as a transit point for smuggling as export taxes are extremely high on diamonds, about 25 percent (Obale 2016). Thus, it is likely that many of the diamonds smuggled through Cameroon end up being exported in West Africa, where it is more difficult to trace their origin from the Central African Republic. When local officials in Cameroon do enforce Kimberley Process regulations, often they document where diamonds are purchased, not where they originate, which violates the agreement (Obale 2016). There have been many instances of fake Kimberley Process certificates being used in Cameroon (Locka 2016).

Some involved in the illegal diamond trade in Cameroon are refugees from the civil war in the Central African Republic (Obale 2016). This adds a dimension to this issue in which some people are just trying to participate in the trade to ensure a minimal existence until they can return to the Central African Republic. A significant reason why the Cameroonian border is an attractive option to smugglers from the Central African Republic is that local diamond mining in Cameroon is not organized through the official government on the local level. Very few miners have licenses, many miners have never heard of the Kimberley Process or have any understanding of its regulations, and diamond mining often takes place as an agreement with local chiefs and not the central government (Obale 2016).

Beyond Cameroon, other states that border the Central African Republic – notably Chad, Sudan, and South Sudan – are also routes for diamond smuggling. While there may be undocumented diamonds in these states, none are known to have any domestic production (International Peace Information Service 2018).[7] None of these states are members of the Kimberley Process; thus any member state is forbidden to export or import diamonds from them. However, diamonds from these states can be smuggled into a country that is a member of the Kimberley Process, gaining access to most of the global market. Furthermore, it is not necessarily "illegal" for non-Kimberley Process members to trade diamonds with other nonmembers if domestic laws allow it. This provides another loophole through which diamonds can be traded outside of Kimberley Process control, although this is probably a small proportion of the overall global diamond trade.

Globally, outside of the "Kony 2012" phenomenon, the Central African region is usually overlooked (Invisible Children 2012). The Lord's Resistance Army, led by Joseph Kony, is often thought to be in the border area between the Central African Republic, Democratic Republic of Congo, and South Sudan. While it is unclear if the group has been involved with diamond production in the Central African Republic, they have looted mining areas (International Peace Information Service 2018). Troops from Uganda and advisors from the United States were involved in the eastern Central African Republic to defeat the Lord's Resistance Army, but they left in 2017 (Allison 2017). This made it more difficult to contain the Lord's Resistance Army. Although the group is no longer large enough to challenge any government in the region directly, it nonetheless adds another dimension of instability to the region.

Conclusion

What is apparent from looking at these periods is that the Kimberley Process has often been weak and ineffective in dealing with a series of crises in the Central African Republic. However, while this is an

[7] Sudan is a large gold producer but is not known to have any diamond production.

extreme case, it is similar in the way the Kimberley Processes has raised the costs and benefits to certain actors, giving some an upper hand in relation to others. While both government and private actors are more indifferent to the Kimberley Process than in other cases, and the division between these two groups is particularly blurred as some have found themselves rebels one day and government officials the next, their preferences regarding the Kimberley Process do matter for cooperation and compliance with the agreement. Ultimately, though, it is clear from looking at the political geography of the Central African Republic that Kimberley Process regulations are a futile exercise that is not suited to the complexity of the conflict in the country.

In the Central African Republic, the absence of any private companies with a preference for compliance and cooperation with the Kimberley Process has led to a situation where there is little political will to spend scarce resources to comply. One must suspect that in other cases, even where the government is more capable, the absence of any large diamond companies with a preference to support the Kimberley Process would also lead to lower levels of compliance and cooperation, as has been the case with Sierra Leone. Thus, the Central African Republic reinforces a central argument of this study, that state-level compliance and cooperation with the Kimberley Process is driven by large diamond companies that have preferences for compliance. All other cases in this study have at least some private interests that prefer to support the Kimberley Process or at least avoid overt scrutiny from the agreement. These dynamics are not present in the Central African Republic; thus, the domestic political economy of the country is particularly unconducive to compliance.

Even if government actors in the Central African Republic support the Kimberley Process, this can only go so far and may have little influence over how the regulations brought about by the agreement play out on a local level. Furthermore, in the context of the Central African Republic, government leaders who vocalize support for the Kimberley Process are likely to do so as part of a strategy to appease the global community or Western states. Support for the Kimberley Process is unlikely to reflect a strong personal commitment to a regulatory framework that is ill suited and unrealistic given the political geography of the Central African Republic. This is also problematic because government officials in the country often put more effort into gaining the support of outside groups in order to perpetuate their time in power than building a support base among the broader domestic population. When government officials have appealed to domestic interests, these have usually been narrow economic interests intertwined with military support. Thus, institutions in the Central African Republic have developed historically to be particularly predatory, and the diamond trade has played a central part in this reality. In turn, private multinational companies, which have led to higher levels of compliance and cooperation with the Kimberley Process in other contexts, have stayed away from the Central African Republic because of political instability and the tendency for government officials to see the trade as part of their patronage network. As a result, the Central African Republic may have the lowest level of compliance with the Kimberley Process of any state and is likely to prove a continuous problem for the agreement.

8 Understanding the Nature of the Kimberley Process and International Agreements

It is clear from this study that the Kimberley Process is a weak regime. The "consensus" nature of decision-making within the Kimberley Process and in turn the level of pressure that the agreement can impose on states has generally been constant since the agreement was implemented in 2003.[1] However, when we look at each case in depth, the Kimberley Process does have enforcement potential that operates independently of the agreement itself. As the domestic political economies of states change over time, so do their responses to the Kimberley Process. As private actors that have preferences in line with Kimberley Process regulations gain market share, this dynamic leads to higher levels of cooperation and compliance with the Kimberley Process.[2] This chapter looks at what we can learn from examining the role of the Kimberley Process in Angola, Central African Republic, Namibia, Sierra Leone, and Zimbabwe and what this can tell us about resource politics and international agreements more generally.

Within-Case Variation

A significant finding of this study is that since the Kimberley Process went into effect in 2003, some countries have changed their response to the Kimberley Process. Whereas initially this study was set up to compare across cases, this research uncovers interesting variation within specific cases over time. Below is a discussion on the trajectory of state responses in each case and what this means for understanding state responses to the Kimberley Process overall.

1 Thus, researchers need to look elsewhere to understand the changing response of states to the agreement, as this study does in depth.

2 This stands in contrast to some of the original goals of major actors within the Kimberley Process, especially NGOs, which saw this agreement as a way to deal more assertively with states in which human rights abuses surround the diamond sector (Global Witness 2011b).

Angola presents the most apparent case of within-state variation as the state was mostly indifferent to the Kimberley Process until De Beers reentered the country after the resolution of a court case in 2006 (Grant 2012; Munier 2014). As De Beers has grown in market share since 2006, the Angolan state, in turn, has become more active in the Kimberley Process at every level. With the recent drop in oil prices on the global market, it is probable that the diamond trade will matter more to Angola's domestic political economy and this, in turn, will make Kimberley Process regulations more consequential.

The case of Namibia is notable in this study because its response to the Kimberley Process has not varied since it was implemented in 2003. This is principally because of the virtual monopoly that De Beers has held in the country, both historically and since the Kimberley Process was implemented (Munier 2016c). For a state that has little influence over most international agreements, Namibia has been a major actor in Kimberley Process decision-making throughout the history of the regime. This is also primarily a function of the influence that De Beers has over the Namibian state, and the Kimberley Process more broadly. As with any state, Namibia has not been able to stop all noncertified diamonds originating or entering its territory from being smuggled, but for a significant producer of alluvial diamonds, it has probably come the closest.

Sierra Leone has raised its level of compliance with the Kimberley Process since 2003, mainly through cooperation. Nevertheless, Sierra Leone remains a state with one of the highest percentages of uncertified diamonds (Gberie and Letourneau 2006; Smillie and Letourneau 2009; Wilson 2011). This case presents a clear example of cooperation being a necessary but not sufficient condition to bring about compliance. In negotiating with private diamond-mining companies, the state of Sierra Leone has often needed to accept whatever deal they could get (Smillie and Letourneau 2008). If we are to think about Sierra Leone counterfactually, had De Beers reentered the country after 2003, it is almost certain that the state would take the Kimberley Process more seriously and the overall level of compliance would be higher.[3]

[3] While private companies in Sierra Leone today have little incentive to follow Kimberley Process regulations if the costs of this are too high, at the same time they want to avoid negative scrutiny in general.

Ironically, in the Central African Republic cooperation and compliance with the Kimberley Process has been relatively stable, although at a very low level. The predatory nature of the Central African Republic's institutions persists, despite extreme political instability and a wide range of actors that have competed for power in the country. Since the Central African Republic has not had any production from private diamond companies since 2003, it has been stable in lacking the domestic political economy that would make compliance and cooperation more likely. Thus, no government or rebel group is likely to spend scarce resources in response to the Kimberley Process, and this holds constant across a wide range of actors with otherwise different motivations.

Zimbabwe is the state with the most in-country variation in response to the Kimberley Process. This is mostly a reflection of politics, specifically different political arrangements resulting in five different government strategies toward the growing diamond trade: small-scale mining before 2006, a government monopsony from 2006 to 2008, military control from 2008 to 2011, the introduction of joint agreements with private companies from 2011 to 2016 and government nationalization after 2016 (Munier 2016a). This is an interesting example of political arrangements, and variation within them is a driving force behind variation in response to an international agreement. Whereas much of the international media tends to focus on the dominance of ZANU-PF over the political system and the challenge posed by the MDC in elections, this study shows that to understand Zimbabwe's response to the Kimberley Process it is factions within the ruling ZANU-PF party that are largely responsible for changes in policy.

When we examine the trajectory of these five cases in response to the Kimberley Process, it becomes clear that despite the agreement itself having little enforcement power, cooperation and compliance can diverge within a single state over time. The principal mechanism for this is the variation in market share among private actors and the influence that the diamond trade has on state policy overall. It is also plausible that in the future all five states will gain in state capacity and this should lead to a higher level of compliance as well.

Comparing the Cases

In all five cases that are examined in this study, clear patterns emerge. Diamonds have and will continue to play a central role in the domestic political economy of these states. In fact, in all five states examined in this study, an easy argument could be made that diamonds will become more important, especially with other commodities such as oil losing value on the global market. This presents a sort of paradox in which NGOs and civil society actors argue that the Kimberley Process is increasingly irrelevant in terms of its original intent, but the regulatory framework brought about by the process has increasing influence over the regulatory policies readily available to policymakers.

Most important is the evident influence that private economic actors have on the policymaking process. This is exceptionally clear in the case of Namibia, where a high level of compliance and cooperation with the Kimberley Process can largely be viewed as a condition of historical dependence on De Beers. Furthermore, as De Beers has gained market share in Angola, the state has responded far more to the Kimberley Process. In the three states where De Beers has less influence – the Central African Republic, Sierra Leone, and Zimbabwe – compliance and cooperation with the Kimberley Process has been lower and has been less of a priority for these governments. If we think about this counterfactually, had De Beers controlled more market share in these countries it is all but certain that their response to the Kimberley Process would have been more favorable. On the other hand, had companies with different preferences toward the Kimberley Process than De Beers controlled more market share in Angola and Namibia the trajectory of these cases would have been different as well. Therefore, by comparing these cases, it is clear that compliance and cooperation with the Kimberley Process is mostly a function of the competition for market share. A domestic political economy in which the diamond trade is dominated by De Beers is a necessary although not always sufficient condition to bring about a high level of compliance and cooperation with the Kimberley Process when examining the specific cases in this study.

The Zimbabwe case is notable because government actors have often had the upper hand when deciding the response of the state to the Kimberley Process, instead of private actors. This finding gives some insight into the often fractured nature of Zimbabwean politics in which the president remains the most powerful actor, but other factional leaders within ZANU-PF maintain significant influence over specific policies that can differ from the preferences of the president. This provides an interesting contrast with Angola, as most economic policy is under the direct control of the president (Hodges 2004, 2008). Namibia is notable for having the most stable policies in the diamond sector. This reflects a higher level of political stability in comparison to either Angola or Zimbabwe, but it too has had only one party in power since independence.[4] The Central African Republic demonstrates further that private actors with policy preferences that support the Kimberley Process are a necessary condition for a high level of compliance or cooperation. The absence of any private actors in the state's diamond trade demonstrates that, in the absence of a domestic political economy that supports compliance and cooperation with the Kimberley Process, the agreement will have little influence on state behavior.

Cooperation

A contribution of this study is that it is the first to explain variation in state cooperation with the prevention of an illicit good. Studies have compared cooperation across different illicit goods, although this literature remains small (Andreas 2015), but have not compared state-level cooperation to prevent an illicit good from reaching the global market, as this study does with uncertified diamonds. Given the increasing importance of understanding state cooperation to prevent the trade in illicit goods, this research provides a framework for future studies in this area.

While research to this point has argued that state cooperation to prevent the trade of illicit goods is based on Western dominance (Andreas and Nadelmann 2006), or a "cost-benefit" analysis to explain why states cooperate around the prevention of illicit goods (Efrat 2012), this study has gone beyond these to find some contradictory evidence. While powerful Western states have played a role in the Kimberley Process, it is notable that weaker states that are large diamond producers have had significant influence as well (Grant 2013b, 2018). It may be the case that without the participation of powerful Western states the Kimberley Process may not exist, but this does not explain the trajectory the regime has taken or the response that different states have had to the agreement. As this study

[4] Melber (2015) portrays Namibia as being run by "crony capitalists" who go through the motions of supporting multiparty democracy but are unlikely to give up power.

demonstrates, it is often the competition for market share between private actors that is a driving force behind state responses to the Kimberley Process, not pressure from Western governments.

In liberal regime theory, it is often argued that states will create international agreements when the benefits of having an international agreement outweigh the costs of not having one. In the same vein, after an agreement is created, states will cooperate with it if the benefits of doing so outweigh the costs (Efrat 2012; Guzman 2005, 2008; Keohane 1984; Keohane and Nye 1977). This study of the Kimberley Process shows that the focus on states as the major actor in creating and responding to an international agreement is outdated, as private economic actors continue to gain a level of influence that can rival if not replace that of states, especially those that are resource dependent. Furthermore, liberal regime theory tends to view state preferences to international agreements as being monolithic, but as this research has shown, actors both within and outside of government have differing preferences, and specific policies that are chosen in response to international agreements can have clear winners and losers.

Public/Private Partnerships?

This study would suggest that the portrayal of diamond companies as "socialized agents" (Kantz 2007), or of the Kimberley Process as part of a global push for "corporate social responsibility" (Haufler 2013; Scherer and Palazzo 2011; Scherer, Palazzo, and Baumann 2006), tends to overlook some important dynamics of the global diamond trade. While the "discourse" surrounding the diamond trade has differed over time, the Kimberley Process has served to reinforce previous modes of exchange in the global diamond trade. In fact, the Kimberley Process and the desire of major diamond companies to be viewed in a different light by global civil society has reinforced the dominance of De Beers in Southern Africa against competitors that emerged in the late 1990s but have since lost market share. This reality raises important questions about the role of "corporate social responsibility" in legitimizing private economic actors. In the diamond trade, it appears these "legitimizing" appeals of "responsibility" have served to uphold long-existing policies and have changed little about how the trade operates.

These findings on the Kimberley Process complement literature that examines how private and public actors often work together to lower the cost of providing necessary private goods that would be difficult for either actor to deliver independently (Knill and Lehmkuhl 2002). While much of the literature on "corporate social responsibility" focuses on the conditions under which private firms agree to regulatory frameworks independent of direct state involvement (Haufler 2013; Scherer and Palazzo 2011; Scherer, Palazzo, and Baumann 2006), the Kimberley Process is a case where private firms, particularly De Beers, pushed for a particular regulatory framework to be accepted not just at the domestic level in particular countries but globally. Not only did major diamond companies have a role in creating the global certification system set up by the Kimberley Process, but they were the pivotal rule-makers in setting up these global regulations (Haufler 2009a, 2009b). This shows a level of influence by private economic actors on global policymaking that goes beyond what several scholars of "corporate social responsibly" would envision. Furthermore, the Kimberley Process is a case where private actors were able to get governments to take more of the cost of regulating the diamond trade compared to what had usually been the case before a global certification scheme was created.

This study supports a significant finding of the "fair trade" literature, in that local mining conditions are often far different to what is being portrayed by these marketing strategies (Childs 2008, 2014a, 2014b; Hilson 2008, 2014). The production process and the reality of how local miners are compensated in these schemes may have little to do with what people commonly associate with "fair trade." The same can be said about the Kimberley Process, because the motivations of decision-makers that led to the implementation of Kimberley Process regulations may have little to do with "conflict diamonds" and even less to do with human rights concerns that consumers may associate with the regime.

Dependency Theory, Survival Theory, and the Global Diamond Trade

This study shows that the variant of dependency theory developed by Frank (1966, 1978) and Wallerstein (1974, 2004) has substantial explanatory power when examining the global diamond trade.[5] African states remain at the bottom of the production process, despite efforts to change this (Grynberg 2015). In simple terms, rough diamonds are produced in African countries, which are usually considered part of the global "periphery." Then they are shipped to the "semiperiphery," such as India and Israel, to gain value through polishing, to be sold for far more in the global "core," for instance in the European Union or the United States. World systems theory provides a "bird's eye view" of the global economy, and if one were to take a "bird's eye view" of the global diamond trade, this would align surprisingly well with the prediction of world systems theory (Sterling-Folker 2013). Furthermore, the prediction that governments in the global periphery will be heavily constrained by their place at the bottom of the production process, in terms of pursuing specific policies in response to international agreements, clearly holds when state responses to the Kimberley Process are examined in this study.[6]

An approach that has a high level of explanatory usefulness in the five cases examined here is that of "political survival" theory (Bueno De Mesquita et al. 2005). All the cases are post-conflict countries in which government actors have had to pursue policies that are ideologically inconsistent and almost certainly different than what they would prefer. Three of the cases – Angola, Namibia, and Zimbabwe – gained independence in the same interrelated conflict. In all three cases, the left-wing liberation movements that came to power promised to pursue nationalization in the diamond sector, in contrast to the private control of diamond mining that had long existed in the region. All these governments pursued different policies than their rhetoric would have predicted. This can be explained by the weakness of these states at independence. For the very survival of the ruling coalition, if not the state itself, revenue was necessary, and the mining sector was one of the only options to gain revenue. The same has been the case in Sierra Leone, where the state has been desperate for any foreign investment, thus constraining the ability of government actors in placing

[5] Although in the early 1990s dependency theory fell out of fashion, this study demonstrates how it is relevant today when looking at states where resource extraction influences every level of society.

[6] A major finding that holds across all four cases, although to different levels, is that government actors are constrained in their ability to get their preferences reflected in policy and thus defer to private actors in the decision-making process.

conditions on these foreign actors. Even more directly, in the Central African Republic government officials have often tried to bring the diamond trade under their control as a survival strategy. Political geography that has made it difficult for the diamond trade to be dominated by one entity is an essential factor in understanding why the Central African Republic has often experienced extreme political instability.

The Public Provision of a Private Good

The Kimberley Process has allowed the policy preferences that have historically been pursued by De Beers in individual states to become part of an international agreement. This is notable because it was inherently more difficult for De Beers to get its preferences reflected in policy on a domestic level and to persuade these states to enforce the policies consistently over time. This is in line with a prediction made by neoclassical economics, in which private firms press for a public regulatory policy that will be to their advantage (Peltzman 1976; Stigler 1971). Nonmarket strategies have long been pursued by De Beers, given its historical ability to fix prices in the global diamond market. Historically, the global diamond market has been one of the least competitive economic sectors, although De Beers does face more challenges in maintaining its dominance now than in the past (Forbes 2014). This explains a significant factor behind the impetus for the Kimberley Process: the goal of De Beers to lock in policy preferences with an international agreement while still maintaining a dominant market share, in anticipation of declining market share over time.

In the two cases that this study examines where De Beers is most active, Angola and Namibia, enforcement of the Kimberley Process has helped De Beers gain market share over competitors that do not share these preferences. In Namibia, the high level of dependence that the government has had on the diamond trade has led to De Beers having a near monopoly over the diamond trade, and Kimberley Process regulations have reinforced this. In Angola, as De Beers has gained in the diamond trade the Angolan government has taken the agreement more seriously. To think about this counterfactually, if De Beers did not have a high level of influence on policy in these states, their level of cooperation and compliance with the Kimberley Process would be lower. Furthermore, when we look at Sierra Leone, where De Beers has not been active since the early 1990s, this is also the state that has the lowest level of compliance among the countries in this study. Also, while Zimbabwe has raised its level of compliance with the Kimberley Process over time, the absence of De Beers, or for that matter any private actors in the diamond sector till 2011, undoubtedly led to less compliance during this period.

There is much literature on how the decline of the state in providing public goods has led to a more significant role for private economic actors in public goods provision (Haufler 2013; Scherer and Palazzo 2011; Scherer, Palazzo, and Baumann 2006). This research suggests that the Kimberley Process is not just about creating a global regulatory framework in the diamond trade, but in fact has allowed private economic actors a key role in global decision-making that goes beyond what existed in the past. The Kimberley Process is an example of how the growing influence of private economic actors led to a higher level of regulation in the diamond industry. Private actors in the diamond industry did not try and minimize the state's ability to regulate the diamond trade, but instead used an increase in influence to give the state a more prominent role in regulation but also pass the cost of regulation on to the state (Knill and Lehmkuhl 2002; Scherer and Palazzo 2011; Scherer, Palazzo, and Baumann 2006). This suggests that with the Kimberley Process an increase in power by private actors led not to an undermining of state influence, but instead shaped the nature of influence the state could have.

Wither the State and the Rise of the Private Economy

This research demonstrates that approaches to examining state responses to international agreements are often overly state-centric. Much of the variation in how states respond to international agreements, especially those that have a large economic dimension, can primarily be explained by the level of influence that private actors have on state policy. This is an important but often overlooked dimension in the study of international regimes. Some of these dynamics have been briefly examined when explaining the trajectory of international environmental regimes (Falkner 2008; Young 2010) but has been unnoticed when explaining variation within a single regime and substate variation over time.

This study contends that some of the unusual amount of influence that weak states such as Botswana, Namibia or South Africa (Grant 2013a, 2018) have on the Kimberley Process in comparison to most international agreements is primarily due to their policy preferences being heavily influenced by the monopolistic nature of De Beers in these states. This goes against realist "power predictions," but also those of constructivists, who would be inclined to argue that these Southern African states have been able to gain influence over the Kimberley Process because they are motivated by security concerns around the issue of "conflict diamonds" or because they are effective "agenda setters" in the global "discourse" on the diamond trade. While there may be some truth to the latter claim, the results from this research would point to that explanation as being incomplete. While states in Southern Africa are some of the largest diamond producers in the world, these states have a comparatively low level of market power because the diamonds produced gain in value dramatically after they leave these countries. Despite recent efforts to change this (Grynberg 2015), the clearest explanation for the influence these states have had on Kimberley Process decision-making is that because of their condition of dependence on De Beers domestically, they have preferences that most reflect those of De Beers and, in turn, have influence through this mechanism.

Geography Matters

In line with the civil war literature that has found alluvial diamonds and certain geographical distributions of diamonds to be a contributing factor in making a state more at risk for conflict (Buhaug and Gates 2002; Buhaug and Lujala 2005; Buhaug and Rod 2006; Le Billon 2008; Snyder and Bhavnani 2005; Vlassenroot and Bockstael 2008), the results of this study show that these factors also explain variation in compliance with the Kimberley Process. The nature of alluvial diamond mining makes compliance with the Kimberley Process inherently more difficult for states. Among the states examined in this study, the variation in political geography is a further factor impacting variation in compliance levels.

State-level noncompliance with the Kimberley Process is often due to an overall lack of "public administration" in diamond-wealthy areas.[7]

[7] This finding is in line with the "managerial school" of international regimes (Chayes and Chayes 1993, 1998). This school argues that most states enter into

Given the cross-border nature of the diamond trade, cooperation is a necessary but not sufficient condition for a state to comply with the Kimberley Process at a high level. A significant reason why Namibia has a higher level of compliance with the Kimberley Process than any other state in this study, despite several similarities, is that the political geography of the state inherently makes compliance easier. On the other hand, states such as the Central African Republic, Sierra Leone, and Zimbabwe are unable to comply with the Kimberley Process at the level of Namibia, regardless of their desire to do so, given that their diamonds are located over vast regions far from where the state is strongest.

It is important to note that the political nature of the resource distribution in a state varies over time, even if the territory stays the same. The clearest example of this is the large diamond find in the Marange region of Zimbabwe in 2006. While the Zimbabwean state had long controlled the region, the discovery of diamonds and the geographical distribution of these diamonds dramatically changed the political landscape in Marange (Munier 2016a). This is also the case in Namibia, in which a large number of high-quality diamonds are likely to be mined offshore in the future, thus changing the nature of diamond mining in a state where most mining has previously taken place on the coast (Munier 2016c). These new diamond finds ensure that the resource sector will continue to have a considerable influence on the domestic political economy of these states. Furthermore, as Collier (2010) suggests, most developing states have no idea how much resource wealth is found within their territorial borders. Thus, there is reason to believe that the geographical distribution of resources and the governance challenges that this leads to will become an increasingly salient issue in the future.

Political geography is not as strong a factor in explaining variation in compliance with the Kimberley Process as a state's willingness to take compliance seriously on a basic level. Zimbabwe is an excellent example of this, as until 2008 the state's unwillingness to enforce compliance with the Kimberley Process led to almost no compliance

international agreements intending to comply, thus noncompliance by states with international regimes usually involves a lack of administrative capacity in those states.

in any state. However, once a state's primary preference to comply is established, then political geography becomes an important variable.

The cases looked at in this study show that there will, for the foreseeable future, be states, if not regions, in which compliance with the Kimberley Process will be difficult. This raises the question of how much priority should be given to compliance with the Kimberley Process. In some states, such as Sierra Leone, Kimberley Process regulations represent a sort of paradox. For instance, as an initial member of the Kimberley Process in 2003, Sierra Leone had agreed to a series of regulations in the diamond trade before comprehensive legislation protecting children or women existed (Kargbo 2014). Should complying with the Kimberley Process be a priority in this context, or does it have the potential to undermine fundamental socioeconomic issues that need to be urgently addressed?

Modes of Exchange and Conflict Diamonds

This study shows that the Kimberley Process may not have much to do with "conflict diamonds." On the other hand, it does demonstrate how the Kimberley Process has created a regulatory environment in which there are clear winners and losers. De Beers is a winner in that its preferences surrounding the diamond trade now exist in an enforceable international agreement that will be hard to change, even if De Beers loses market share over time. This regulatory environment has helped De Beers in specific cases, as demonstrated in the case studies of Angola and Namibia. It is also safe to say that, as with any series of regulations in which there are costs, larger private firms are generally going to have an easier time paying them compared to smaller firms.

The Kimberley Process could be viewed as a way to bring corporate "responsibility" to the diamond trade in a new and innovative way. The findings from this study contend that the Kimberley Process is more about reinforcing already existing "modes of exchange" in the diamond industry than about changing them. It is true, as it is in any economic sector, that change is inevitable, and the dominance of De Beers may not be what it once was. On the other hand, it is remarkable how in the twenty-first century one multinational firm has such a level of dominance over an economic sector. It may be inevitable that more diamonds will be produced outside of De Beers' control, but in Southern Africa the regulatory environment brought about by Kimberley

Process regulations has reinforced the firm's historical dominance of the diamond trade. In turn, the Kimberley Process has reinforced a "mode of exchange" in which Southern African countries, and their citizens, are only able to get a fraction of what their diamonds are worth.

Several actors that favored implementation of the Kimberley Process probably had the best of intentions, and most people would agree that it is desirable to keep diamonds away from criminal armies or syndicates. It may be that in a select few cases the Kimberley Process has raised the costs for "bad actors" to use diamond wealth. However, the actors most affected by the attempts to certify the global diamond trade are small-scale miners who lack the capacity to comply with the Kimberley Process. Given high levels of unemployment and poverty in sub-Saharan Africa, it is hard to see these miners as having the "nefarious" motivations that the Kimberley Process is allegedly supposed to prevent, as countless workers are forced into the black market just to get by. In fact, there is evidence that in some situations local police have understood the difficulties that drive miners into "informal" mining and have chosen not to pursue these violations, considering other coexisting problems (Smillie and Letourneau 2009).

As more international agreements influence the domestic policy of states, if not, in this case, their economic trajectory, what does this mean for "democracy" or citizenship in an increasingly globalized world? Many of the people most influenced by the Kimberley Process have no say in how the agreement was set up or has developed over time. While every case looked at in this study is at least "nominally" democratic, the Kimberley Process set up an agreement where major questions about resource regulation are not decided within the "democratic" state but are instead decided by actors that are not selected by the citizenry. This is a significant factor as to why Kimberley Process regulations appear to be better suited to some country contexts than others.

The Kimberley Process inherently raises questions about the sovereignty of the state and the role that private economic actors should be allowed to play in it. This study demonstrates that instead of being governed, the growth of international agreements may also include a dimension in which private actors are setting their own rules and doing the governing themselves at the expense of states. Does it enhance the ability of states to pursue good policies to have much of the decision-making process outsourced to international agreements? Or is the regulatory environment when it comes to a state's natural resources best decided within an elected congress or parliament, despite the shortcomings these institutions may have? It is these questions that are as inescapable as ever, and this project has attempted to uncover some of the dynamics that can inform debate on these issues.

Works Cited

Acemoglu, Daron, Simon Johnson, and James Robinson. 2002. "An African Success Story: Botswana." *CEPR Discussion Paper No. 3219*. https://economics.mit.edu/files/284

Acemoglu, Daron, Tristan Reed, and James A. Robinson. 2014. "Chiefs: Economic Development and Elite Control of Civil Society in Sierra Leone." *Journal of Political Economy* 122 (2): 319–368.

Agencia Angola Press. 2018. Angola Takes over Chair of Kimberly Process Review Committee. November 23. www.angop.ao/angola/en_us/noticias/economia/2018/10/47/Angola-takes-over-Chair-Kimberly-Process-Review-Committee,7f5b15c1-50e3-4d1a-9d7e-977379ed223f.html

Anhui Foreign Economic Construction (Group) Co. (AFECC). 2018. AFECC Profile. www.afecc.com/english.php/profile.html

Akerlof, George. 1970. "The Market for 'Lemons': Quality Uncertainty and the Market Mechanism." *Quarterly Journal of Economics* 84 (3): 488–500.

Alao, Abiodun. 2012. *Mugabe and the Politics of Security in Zimbabwe*. Ithaca, NY: McGill-Queen's Press – MQUP.

Allison, Simon. 2017. CAR Spirals Further out of Control. *Mail and Guardian*. July 21. https://mg.co.za/article/2017-07-21-00-car-spirals-further-out-of-control

Alter, Karen J. 2014. *The New Terrain of International Law*. Princeton, NJ: Princeton University Press.

Amupadhi, Tangeni. 2001. Minister "Told UN of American Mine Link." *The Namibian*. Friday, March 9.

Andreas, Peter. 2015. "International Politics and the Illicit Global Economy." *Perspectives on Politics* 13 (3): 782–788.

Andreas, Peter, and Ethan Nadelmann. 2006. *Policing the Globe: Criminalization and Crime Control in International Relations*. Oxford: Oxford University Press.

Angola Press. 2014. Angola: Mozambican Minister of Mining Resources in Luanda for a Work Visit. May 19.

Azzam, Azzeddine M., and Dale G. Anderson. 1996. Assessing Competition in Meatpacking: Economic History, Theory, and Evidence. US

Department of Agriculture, Packers and Stockyards Programs, Grain Inspection, Packers and Stockyards Administration. www.gipsa.usda.gov/psp/publication/con_tech%20report/rr96–6.pdf

Banchirigah, Sadia Mohammed. 2008. "Challenges with Eradicating Illegal Mining in Ghana: A Perspective from the Grassroots." *Resources Policy* 33 (1): 29–38.

Barnard, Lucy. 2015. Dubai to Head up Fight against Trade in Blood Diamonds. *The National.* September 9. www.thenational.ae/business/dubai-to-head-up-fight-against-trade-in-blood-diamonds-1.131366

Barnett, Michael, and Martha Finnemore. 2004. *Rules for the World: International Organizations in Global Politics*. Ithaca, NY: Cornell University Press.

Basedau, Matthias. 2005a. "Resource Politics in Sub-Saharan Africa beyond the Resource Curse: Towards a Future Research Agenda." In *Resource Politics in Sub-Saharan Africa*, ed. Matthias Basedau and Andreas Mehler. 325–348. Hamburg: Institut fur Afrika-Kunde.

2005b. Context Matters – Rethinking the Resource Curse in Sub-Saharan Africa. Global and Area Studies Working Paper 1. http://edoc.vifapol.de/opus/volltexte/2009/1562/pdf/wp01_basedau.pdf

Bates, Robert. 1981. *Markets and States in Tropical Africa: The Political Basis of Agricultural Policies*. California Series on Social Choice and Political Economy. Berkeley, CA: University of California Press.

1987. *Essays on the Political Economy of Rural Africa*. Vol. 38. Berkeley, CA: University of California Press.

1997. *Open-Economy Politics: The Political Economy of the World Coffee Trade*. Princeton, NJ: Princeton University Press.

1998a. "The International Coffee Organization: An International Institution." In *Analytic Narratives*, ed. Robert Bates, Avner Greif, Margaret Levi, Jean-Laurent Rosenthal, and Barry Weingast. 194–231. Princeton, NJ: Princeton University Press.

1998b. *Open-Economy Politics: The Political Economy of the World Coffee Trade*. Princeton, NJ: Princeton University Press.

2017. Another NGO Leaves Kimberley Process. JCK. www.jckonline.com/editorial article/another-ngo-leaves-kimberley-process/

Bauer, Gretchen. 1998. *Labor and Democracy in Namibia 1971–1996*. Athens, OH: Ohio University Press.

Baxter, David. 2008. Zimbabwe Diamonds Could Be Financing International Terror Groups. *The Namibian*. www.namibian.com.na/index.php?id=43398&page=archive-read

Bayart, Jean-Francois, Stephen Ellis, and Beatrice Hibou. 1999. *The Criminalization of the State in Africa*. Bloomington, IN: Indiana University Press.

BBC News. 2005. De Beers in Angolan Diamond Deal. May 27. news.bbc.co.uk/2/hi/business/4587269.stm

2011. Central African Republic Profile: Timeline. www.bbc.co.uk/news/world-africa-13150044

2016. Zimbabwe's Robert Mugabe: Foreign Companies "Stole Diamonds." March 4. www.bbc.com/news/world-africa-35720912

Berg, Patrick. 2008. The Dynamics of Conflict in the Tri-border Region of the Sudan, Chad and the Central African Republic. Friedrich Ebert Foundation. http://library.fes.de/pdf-files/iez/05423.pdf

Bieri, Franziska. 2010a. *From Blood Diamonds to the Kimberley Process: How NGOs Cleaned up the Global Diamond Industry*. Burlington, VT: Ashgate Publishing Company.

2010b. "The Role of NGOs in the Kimberley Process." *Globality Studies Journal: Global History, Society, Civilization* 20. https://gsj.stonybrook.edu/article/the-roles-of-ngos-in-the-kimberley-process/

Bierschenk, Thomas, and Jean-Pierre Olivier De Sardan. 1997. "Local Powers and a Distant State in Rural Central African Republic." *Journal of Modern African Studies* 35 (3): 441–468.

Bloomberg Business. 2013. De Beers Expects to Dig Angola Gem Mine to Recoup Expense. January 18.

Blore, Shawn, and Josee Letourneau, eds. 2007. *Diamond Industry Annual Review: The Republic of Angola*. The Diamonds and Human Security Project. Ottowa: Partnership Africa Canada, June.

Bockstael, Mark Van. 2008. "Economic Dynamics of Artisanal Diamond Mining in Relation to the Kimberley Process." In *Artisanal Diamond Mining: Perspectives and Challenges*, ed. Koen Vlassenroot and Steven Van Bockstael. 56–66. Ghent: Academia Press.

Boer, Martin, and Robin Sherbourne. 2003. *Getting the Most Out of Our Diamonds: Namibia, De Beers and the Arrival of Lev Leviev*. Briefing Paper No. 20. Windhoek: Institute for Public Policy Research.

2004. *Managing Diamond Dependency: Should Namibia Risk More to Gain More?* Research Report No. 6. Windhoek: Institute for Public Policy Research.

Bond, Patrick, and Khadija Sharife. 2012. "Zimbabwe's Clogged Political Drain and Open Diamond Pipe." *Review of African Political Economy* 39 (132): 351–365.

Brandt, Edgar. 2014a. Production Record of 1.16 Million Carats in 2013 for Debmarine. *New Era*. April 8.

2014b. Debmarine to Invest N$100 Million on New Crawler. *New Era*. April 9.

2017. Namibia: Recovering Diamond Market Could Result in More Cutting and Polishing Factories. *New Era*. April 24. https://neweralive

.na/posts/recovering-diamond-market-could-result-in-more-cutting-and-polishing-factories

Bratton, Michael. 2014. *Power Politics in Zimbabwe*. Boulder, CO: Lynne Rienner.

Bueno De Mesquita, Bruce, Alastair Smith, Randolph Silverson, and James Morrow. 2005. *The Logic of Political Survival*. Cambridge, MA: MIT Press.

Buhaug, Halvard, and Scott Gates. 2002. "The Geography of Civil War." *Journal of Peace Research* 49 (4): 417–433.

Buhaug, Halvard, and Paivi Lujala. 2005. "Accounting for Sale: Measuring Geography in Quantitative Studies of Civil War." *Political Geography* 24: 399–418.

Buhaug, Halvard, and Jan Ketil Rod. 2006. "Local Determinants of African Civil Wars: 1970–2001." *Political Geography* 25: 315–335.

Burgis, Tom. 2015. *Corporations, Smugglers, and the Theft of Africa's Wealth*. New York: Public Affairs.

Campbell, Greg. 2002. *Blood Diamonds: Tracing the Deadly Path of the World's Most Precious Stones*. London: Westview Press.

Campos, Bernardo. 2015. Announcement of KP Chairmanship for 2015. *Kimberley Process*. www.kimberleyprocess.com/en/announcement-kp-chairmanship-2015

Cardenas, Sonia. 2007. *Conflict and Compliance: State Responses to International Human Rights Pressure*. Philadelphia, PA: University of Pennsylvania Press.

Carment, David, Yiagadeesen Samy, and Joe Landry. 2013. "Transitioning Fragile States: A Sequencing Approach." *Fletcher Forum of World Affairs* 37 (2): 125–151.

Cater, Charles. 2003. The Political Economy of Conflict and UN Intervention: Rethinking the Critical Cases of Africa. In *The Political Economy of Armed Conflict: Beyond Greed and Grievance*, ed. Karen Ballentine and Jake Sherman. 19–43. Boulder, CO: Lynne Rienner.

Chafets, Zev. 2007. The Missionary Mogul. *New York Times: Magazine*. September 16.

Chamber of Mines of Namibia. 2012. Annual Review 2012. Windhoek Central: Chamber of Mines. www.chamberofmines.org.na/index.php/publications/annual-reviews/

2017. Annual Review. www.chamberofmines.org.na/index.php/publications/annual-reviews/

Chayes, Abram, and Antonia Handler Chayes. 1993. "On Compliance." *International Organization* 47 (2): 175–205.

1998. *The New Sovereignty: Compliance with International Regulatory Agreements*. Cambridge, MA: Harvard University Press.

Childs, John. 2008. "Reforming Small-Scale Mining in Sub-Saharan Africa: Political and Ideological Challenges to a Fair Trade Gold Initiative." *Resources Policy* 33 (4): 203–209.

2014a. "A New Means of Governing Artisanal and Small-Scale Mining? Fairtrade Gold and Development in Tanzania." *Resources Policy* 40 (1): 128–136.

2014b. "From 'Criminals of the Earth' to 'Stewards of the Environment': The Social and Environmental Justice of Fair Trade Gold." *Geoforum* 57: 129–137.

Chirico, Peter G., Francis Barthélémy, and François A. Ngbokoto. 2010. Alluvial Diamond Resource Potential and Production Capacity Assessment of the Central African Republic: US Geological Survey Scientific Investigations Report, 2010–5043. https://pubs.usgs.gov/sir/2010/5043/pdf/sir2010-5043.pdf

Chothia, Farouk. 2013. Michel Djotodia: Central African Republic Rebel Leader. BBC News. www.bbc.co.uk/news/world-africa-21938297

Cilliers, Jakkie, and Christian Dietrich, eds. 2000. "Angola's War Economy." *Institute for Security Studies*. https://issafrica.org/research/books-and-other-publications/angolas-war-economy-the-role-of-oil-and-diamonds

Cleveland, Todd. 2014. *Stones of Contention: A History of Africa's Diamonds*. Athens, OH: Ohio University Press.

2015. *Diamonds in the Rough: Corporate Paternalism and African Professionalism on the Mines of Colonial Angola, 1917–1975*. Athens, OH: Ohio University Press.

Cloete, Luqman. 2011. Namdeb to Invest N$5 Billion to Extend the Mine's Lifespan. *The Namibian*. March 24.

Collier, Paul. 2007. *The Bottom Billion: Why the Poorest Countries Are Failing and What Can Be Done about It*. New York: Oxford University Press.

2010. *The Plundered Planet: Why We Must – and How We Can – Manage Nature for Global Prosperity*. Oxford: Oxford University Press.

Collier, Paul, and Anke Hoeffler. 1998. "On Economic Causes of Civil War." *Oxford Economic Papers* 50: 563–573.

Compagnon, Daniel. 2011. *A Predictable Tragedy: Robert Mugabe and the Collapse of Zimbabwe*. Philadelphia, PA: University of Pennsylvania Press.

Cooper, Allan. 1999. "The Institutionalization of Contract Labour in Namibia." *Journal of African Studies* 25 (2):121–138.

2001. *Ovambo Politics in the Twentieth Century*. New York: University Press of America.

Cox, Robert, and Harold Jacobson, eds. 1973. *The Anatomy of Influence: Decision Making in International Organization*. New Haven, CT: Yale University Press.

Creswell, John. 2013. *Qualitative Inquiry and Research Design: Choosing among Five Approaches*. 3rd edn. Thousand Oaks, CA: Sage.

Dalby, Ned. 2015. "A Multifaceted Business." In *Making Sense of the Central African Republic*, ed. Tatiana Carayannis and Louisa Lombard. 123–141. London: Zed Books.

De Beers. 2014. The Diamond Insight Report. www.debeersgroup.com/~/media/Files/D/De-Beers-Group/documents/reports/library/de-beers-the-diamond-insight-report-2014pdfdownloadasset.pdf

De Boeck, Filip. 2012. "Diamonds and Disputes: Conflict and Local Power on the Border between Congo and Angola (1990–2008)." In *Mining Frontiers in Africa: Anthropological and Historical Perspectives*, ed. Katja Werthmann and Tilo Gratz. 73–96. Koln: Rüdiger Köppe Verlag.

De Juan, Alexander, Fabian Krautwald, and Jan Henryk Pierskalla. 2017. "Constructing the State: Macro Strategies, Micro Incentives, and the Creation of Police Forces in Colonial Namibia." *Politics & Society* 45 (2): 269–299.

De Wit, M. C., Bhebe, Z., Davidson, J., Haggerty, S. E., Hundt, P., Jacob, J., Lynn, M., Marshall, T. R., Skinner, C., Smithson, K., and Stiefenhofer, J. 2016. Overview of Diamond Resources in Africa. https://repository.up.ac.za/handle/2263/58441

Dieckmann, Sarah. 2011. *Not Sharing the Loot: An Investigation of Tax Payments and Corporate Structures in the Mining Industry of Sierra Leone*. DanWatch. Copenhagen: Danish Development Organisation IBIS.

Dietrich, Christian. 2002. Hard Currency: The Criminalized Diamond Economy of the Democratic Republic of Congo and Its Neighbors. Occasional Paper. https://reliefweb.int/report/angola/hard-currency-criminalized-diamond-economy-democratic-republic-congo-and-its

Downs, George, David Rocke, and Peter Barsoom. 1996. "Is the Good News about Compliance Good News about Cooperation?" *International Organization* 50 (3): 376–406.

Dunning, Thad. 2008. *Crude Democracy: Natural Resource Wealth and Political Regimes*. Cambridge: Cambridge University Press.

Easterly, William. 2006. *The White Man's Burden: Why the West's Efforts to Aid the Rest Have Done So Much Ill and So Little Good*. Oxford: Oxford University Press.

2013. *The Tyranny of Experts: Economists, Dictators, and the Forgotten Rights of the Poor*. New York: Basic Books.

The Economist. 2004 The Cartel Isn't Forever. July 15. www.economist.com/node/2921462

Efrat, Asif. 2012. *Governing Guns, Preventing Plunder: International Cooperation against Illicit Trade*. Oxford: Oxford University Press.

Engwicht, Nina. 2016. After Blood Diamonds: The Moral Economy of Illegality in the Sierra Leonean Diamond Market. MPIfG Discussion Paper No. 16/9.

2018. "The Local Translation of Global Norms: The Sierra Leonean Diamond Market." *Conflict, Security & Development* 18 (6): 463–492.

Epstein, Edward Jay. 1982. *The Diamond Invention*. London: Hutchinson.

European Commission. 2007. Kimberley Process: Liberia Enters the Diamond Trade. https://ec.europa.eu/commission/presscorner/detail/en/IP_07_612

Falkner, Robert. 2008. *Business Power and Conflict in International Environmental Politics*. New York: Palgrave Macmillan.

Fanon, Frantz. 1963. *The Wretched of the Earth*. Paris: Presence Africaine.

Fearon, James. 1998. "Bargaining, Enforcement, and International Cooperation." *International Organization* 52 (2): 269–305.

2004. "Why Do Some Civil Wars Last So Much Longer than Others?" *Journal of Peace Research* 41 (3): 275–301.

2005. "Primary Commodity Exports and Civil War." *Journal of Conflict Resolution* 49 (4): 483–507.

Ferrett, Grant. 2009. Zimbabwe "Illegal Gold Sale Bid." *BBC News*. http://news.bbc.co.uk/2/hi/africa/7907177.stm

Fessehaie, Judith, and Zavareh Rustomjee. 2018. "Resource-Based Industrialisation in Southern Africa: Domestic Policies, Corporate Strategies and Regional Dynamics." *Development Southern Africa* 35 (3): 404–418.

The Financial Gazette. 2017. Mbada Diamonds Loses Diamond Case. Staff Reporter. June 22. www.financialgazette.co.zw/mbada-diamonds-losesdiamond-case

Forbes. 2003. Cracked De Beers: Lev Leviev Is Taking on the Most Successful Cartel in the World, 15 September.

2014. The World's Billionaires: Lev Leviev. www.forbes.com/profile/lev-leviev/

Fowler, Robert, 2000. Report of the Panel of Experts on Violations of Security Council Sanctions against UNITA. UN Security Council Committee Established Pursuant to Resolution 864 (1993) concerning the Situation in Angola. www.globalpolicy.org/global-taxes/41606-final-report-of-the-un-panel-of-experts.html

Frank, Andre Gunder. 1966. *The Development of Underdevelopment*. Boston, MA: New England Free Press.

1978. *Dependent Accumulation and Underdevelopment*. London: Macmillan Press.

French, Howard. 2014. *China's Second Continent: How a Million Migrants Are Building a New Empire in Africa*. New York: Random House.

Frost, Diane. 2012. *From the Pit to the Market: Politics and the Diamond Economy in Sierra Leone*. Rochester: James Currey.

Gale, Fred. 1998. *The Tropical Timber Trade Regime*. London: Macmillan Press.

Garcia-Johnson, Ronie. 2000. *Exporting Environmentalism: U.S. Multinational Chemical Corporations in Brazil and Mexico*. Cambridge, MA: Massachusetts Institute of Technology.

Gberie, Lansana, and Josee Letourneau. 2006. *Diamond Industry Annual Review: Sierra Leone*. Ottowa: Partnership Africa Canada.

Geddes, Barbara. 2003. *Paradigms and Sand Castles: Theory Building and Research Design in Comparative Politics*. Ann Arbor, MI: University of Michigan Press.

Genoway, Edwin G. 2018. Liberia Losing Gold, Diamond Revenue to Sierra Leone & Guinea. *Front Page Africa*. May 29. https://frontpageafricaonline.com/business/liberia-losing-gold-diamond-revenue-to-sierra-leone-guinea/

Gerring, John. 2007. *Case Study Research: Principles and Practices*. Cambridge: Cambridge University Press.

Gilmore, Elisabeth, Nils Petter Gleditsch, Paivi Lujala, and Jan Ketil Rod. 2005. "Conflict Diamonds: A New Dataset." *Conflict Management and Peace Science* 22: 257–272.

Glawion, Tim, and Lotje De Vries. 2018. "Ruptures Revoked: Why the Central African Republic's Unprecedented Crisis Has Not Altered Deep-Seated Patterns of Governance." *Journal of Modern African Studies* 56 (3): 421–442.

Global Witness. 1998. A Rough Trade: The Role of Companies and Governments in the Angolan Conflict. December 1. www.globalwitness.org/en/archive/rough-trade/

1999. Is the UN Getting Tough on Sanctions and the Diamond Trade? June 8. www.globalwitness.org/library/un-getting-tough-sanctions-and-diamond-trade

2003a. The First Real Test in the Kimberly Process Is in the Central African Republic. www.globalwitness.org/library/first-real-test-kimberley-process-central-african-republic

2003b. Kimberly Process Undertakes First Review Mission to the Central African Republic. www.globalwitness.org/library/kimberley-process-undertakes-first-review-mission-central-african-republic

2004. The Kimberley Process Gets Some Teeth: The Republic of Congo Is Removed from the Kimberley Process for Failing to Combat the Trade in Conflict Diamonds. July 9. www.globalwitness.org/en/archive/kimberley-process-gets-some-teeth-republic-congo-removed-kimberley-process-failing-combat/

2006. The Truth about Diamonds. November. www.globalwitness.org/sites/default/files/import/the_truth_about_diamonds.pdf

2010. Kimberly Process. www.globalwitness.org/campaigns/conflict/conflict-diamonds/kimberley-process

2011a. Kimberley Process Lets Zimbabwe off the Hook (Again). www.globalwitness.org/en/archive/kimberley-process-lets-zimbabwe-hook-again/

2011b. Global Witness Leaves Kimberley Process, Calls for Diamond Trade to Be Held Accountable. December 5. www.globalwitness.org/library/global-witness-leaves-kimberley-process-calls-diamond-trade-be-held-accountable

2012a. Financing a Parallel Government? June. www.globalwitness.org/en/archive/financing-parallel-government-Zimbabwe/

2012b. Diamonds: A Good Deal for Zimbabwe? February. www.globalwitness.org/en/reports/diamonds-good-deal-zimbabwe/

2017a. An Inside Job: Zimbabwe: The State, the Security Forces, and a Decade of Disappearing Diamonds. September. www.globalwitness.org/en/campaigns/conflict-diamonds/inside-job/

2017b. A Game of Stones. www.globalwitness.org/en/campaigns/central-african-republic-car/

Globes. 2011. Interpol Probes Leviev's Namibian Diamond Factory. August 8.

2012. Leviev Fails Namibian Diamond Cut. June 14.

Goldman, Phyllis. 2003. Cracked De Beers: Lev Leviev Is Taking on the Most Successful Cartel in the World. *Forbes*. www.forbes.com/forbes/2003/0915/108.html

Goldsmith, Jack, and Eric Posner. 2005. *The Limits of International Law*. Oxford: Oxford University Press.

Gooch, Tina Muscarella. 2008. "Conflict Diamonds or Illicit Diamonds: Should the Difference Matter to the Kimberley Process Certification Scheme?" *Natural Resources Journal* 48: 189–195.

Gooding, Ophaniel. 2018. Sierra Leone News: NMA Drives to Sanitize Artisanal Mining. *Awoko*. November 17. https://theccex.com/nma-drives-to-sanitize-artisanal-mining/

Gordon, Christine, and Charaf Ahmimed abd Ngolo, eds. 2004. *Diamond Industry Annual Review: The Republic of Angola*. The Diamonds and Human Security Project. Ottowa: Partnership Africa Canada..

Grant, J. Andrew. 2012. "The Kimberley Process at Ten: Reflections on a Decade of Efforts to End the Trade in Conflict Diamonds." In *High-Value Natural Resources and Post-Conflict Peacebuilding*, ed. Paivi Lujala and Siri Aas Rustad. 159–181. New York: Earthscan.

2013a. "Commonwealth Cousins Combating Conflict Diamonds: An Examination of South African and Canadian Contributions to the Kimberley Process." *Commonwealth and Comparative Politics* 51 (2): 210–233.

2013b. "Consensus Dynamics and Global Governance Frameworks: Insights from the Kimberley Process on Conflict Diamonds." *Canadian Foreign Policy Journal* 19 (3): 323–339.

2018. "Agential Constructivism and Change in World Politics." *International Studies Review* 20 (2): 255–263.

Grant, Andrew, and Ian Taylor. 2004. "Global Governance and Conflict Diamonds: The Kimberley Process and the Quest for Clean Gems." *The Round Table* 93 (375): 385–401.

Green, David. 2017. Who Is Lev Leviev, the Israeli Billionaire with Ties to Jared Kushner and Putin. July 25. www.haaretz.com/us-news/who-is-the-israeli-billionaire-with-ties-to-kushner-and-putin-1.5435007

Grynberg, Roman. 2015. Region Fails to Cut It in Diamonds. *Mail and Guardian.* November 6. http://mg.co.za/article/2015-11-05-region-fails-to-cut-it-in-diamonds

Gumbo, Tynos. 2013. "Public-Private Partnerships (PPPs) and Sustainable Natural Resources Exploitation in Africa: Lessons from Diamond Mining in Chiadzwa, Zimbabwe." *Africa Institute of South Africa* 88.

Gumbo, Lloyd. 2016a. Diamond Firms Get 90 Days to Wind Up. *The Herald.* March 7. www.herald.co.zw/diamond-firms-get-90-days-to-wind-up/

2016b. Looters, Panners Storm Chiadzwa. Sacking of Firms Triggers Chaos. Ministerial Delegation to Visit Fields. *The Herald.* February 24. www.herald.co.zw/looters-panners-storm-chiadzwa%E2%80%A2-sacking-of-firms-triggers-chaos-%E2%80%A2-ministerial-delegation-to-visit-fields/

Guzman, Andrew. 2005. "The Design of International Agreements." *European Journal of International Law* 16 (4): 579–612.

2008. *How International Law Works: A Rational Choice Theory.* Oxford: Oxford University Press.

Haas, E. B. 2008. *Beyond the Nation State: Functionalism and International Organization.* Colchester: ECPR Press.

Hafner-Burton, Emilie. 2013. *Making Human Rights a Reality.* Princeton, NJ: Princeton University Press.

Haggard, Stephan, and Beth A. Simmons. 1987. "Theories of International Regimes." *International Organization* 41 (3): 491–517.

Hamutumwa, Ndeulipula. 2012. In Need of an Action Plan! *The Namibian.* Front Page. February 24. www.namibian.com.na/index.php?id=92147&page=archive-read

Harris, David. 2014. *Sierra Leone: A Political History.* Oxford: Oxford University Press.

Hart, Matthew. 2001. *Diamond: A Journey to the Heart of an Obsession.* London: Walker & Company.

Hasenclever, Andreas, Peter Mayer, and Volker Rittberger. 1997. *Theories of International Regimes*. Cambridge: Cambridge University Press.

Haufiku, Mathias. 2014. Interpol after 5 Most Wanted Namibians. *New Era*. February 5.

Haufler, Virginia. 2009a. "The Kimberley Process Certification Scheme: An Innovation in Global Governance and Conflict Prevention." *Journal of Business Ethics* 89 (4) 403–416.

2009b. "The Kimberley Process, Club Goods, and Public Enforcement of a Private Regime." In *Voluntary Programs: A Club Theory Perspective*, ed. Matthew Potoski and Aseem Prakask. 89–107. Cambridge, MA: MIT Press.

2013. *A Public Role for the Private Sector: Industry Self-Regulation in a Global Economy*. Washington, DC: Carnegie Endowment.

The Herald. 2014. Mujuru Plot, the WikiLeaks Footprint. www.herald.co.zw/mujuru-plot-the-wikileaks-footprint/

Hillebrecht, Courtny. 2014. *Domestic Politics and International Human Rights Tribunals: The Problem of Compliance*. New York: Cambridge University Press.

Hilson, Gavin. 2008. "'Fair Trade Gold': Antecedents, Prospects and Challenges." *Geoforum* 39 (1): 386–400.

2014. "'Constructing' Ethical Mineral Supply Chains in Sub-Saharan Africa: The Case of Malawian Fair Trade Rubies." *Development and Change* 45 (1): 53–78.

Hilson, Gavin, and Martin Clifford. 2010. "A 'Kimberley Protest': Diamond Mining, Export Sanctions, and Poverty in Akwatia, Ghana." *African Affairs* 109 (436): 431–450.

Hilson, Gavin, and Steven Van Bockstael. 2011. "Diamond Mining, Rice Farming and a 'Maggi Cube': A Viable Survival Strategy in Rural Liberia?" *Journal of International Development* 23 (8) 1042–1053.

Hodges, Tony. 2004. *Angola: Anatomy of an Oil State*. Bloomington, IN: Indiana University Press.

2008. The Economic Foundations of the Patrimonial State. In *Angola: The Weight of History*, ed. Patrick Chabal and Nuno Vidal. 175–199. New York: Columbia University Press.

Holm, John. 1987. "Botswana: A Paternalistic Democracy." *World Affairs* 150 (1): 21–30.

Human Rights Watch. 2009. Diamonds in the Rough: Human Rights Abuses in the Marange Diamond Fields of Zimbabwe. https://reliefweb.int/report/zimbabwe/diamonds-rough-human-rights-abuses-marange-diamond-fields-zimbabwe

2010. Deliberate Chaos: Ongoing Human Rights Abuses in the Marange Diamond Fields of Zimbabwe. www.hrw.org/sites/default/files/reports/zimbabwe0610webwcover_0.pdf

2014a. Submission to the Universal Periodic Review: Angola. February. www.hrw.org/sites/default/files/related_material/HRW%20UPR%20Submission%20Angola%20February%202014.pdf

2014b. Whose Development? Human Rights Abuses in Sierra Leon's Mining Boom. www.miningresettlement.org/elibrary/whose-development-human-rights-abuses-in-sierra-leone

2018. Angola: Stop Abusive Expulsions of Migrants. November 15. www.hrw.org/news/2018/11/15/angola-stop-abusive-expulsions-migrants

Humphreys, Macartan. 2005. "Natural Resources, Conflict, and Conflict Resolution: Uncovering the Mechanisms." *Journal of Conflict Resolution* 49 (4): 508–537.

IDEX. 2014a. Angola Sets 10M Carat Output Target in 2014. July 3.

2014b. KP Faces Fractious Battle over 2015 Vice-Chair Vote. November 11.

2014c. UAE Denies Claims of NGOs at Kimberley Process Plenary Meeting. November 11.

Iita, Joseph. 2008. Speech by the Incoming Chair of the Kimberley Process Certification Scheme (KPCS) – Namibia. New Delhi, India. November 6. www.mme.gov.na/files/pdf/speech-incoming-chair.pdf

International Alert. 2006. The Current State of Diamond Mining in the Mano River Basin and the Use of Diamonds as a Tool for Peace Building and Development. www.internationalalert.org/sites/default/files/publications/D4D_Background_report.pdf

International Crisis Group. 2010. Dangerous Little Stones: Diamonds in the Central African Republic. December. www.crisisgroup.org/africa/central-africa/central-african-republic/dangerous-little-stones-diamonds-central-african-republic

2014. The Central African Crisis: From Predation to Stabilisation. Africa Report No. 219. June 17. https://d2071andvip0wj.cloudfront.net/the-central-african-crisis-from-predation-to-stabilisation.pdf

International Peace Information Service. 2018. Central African Republic: A Conflict Mapping. https://ipisresearch.be/wp-content/uploads/2018/09/1809-CAR-conflict-mapping_web.pdf

Invisible Children. 2012. Kony 2012. https://invisiblechildren.com /kony-2012/

IRIN. 2000. ANGOLA: De Beers, Luanda in New Dispute over Diamond Marketing. April 4. www.irinnews.org/report/13366/angola-de-beers-luanda-in-new-dispute-over-diamond-marketing

2009. SIERRA LEONE: Diamond Smuggler, "It Is Worth It to steal." www.irinnews.org/report/85470/sierra-leone-diamond-smuggler-it-is-worth-it-tosteal

Isaacs, Denver. 2005. Gem Factory "a Shining Example." *The Namibian*. October 3.

Kalck, Pierre. 2004. *Historical Dictionary of the Central African Republic*. Lanham, MD: Scarecrow Press.

Kantz, Carola. 2007. "The Power of Socialization: Engaging the Diamond Industry in the Kimberley Process." *Business and Politics* 9 (3): 1–20.

Karamata, H., 2008. *Corporate Social Responsibility at Namdeb Diamond Corporation: An Exploratory Case Study*. MA thesis. University of Stellenbosch.

Karatani, Kojin. 2014. *The Structure of World History: From Modes of Production to Modes of Exchange*. Durham, NC: Duke University Press.

Kargbo, Abubakar Hassan. 2014. *Post-Conflict Governance in Sierra Leone*. Bloomington, MD: Author House.

Karombo, Tony. 2018. Preaching Austerity at Home, Zimbabwe Sends 30 Officials to Belgium Conference. www.zimlive.com/2018/11/preaching-austerity-at-home-zimbabwe-sends-30-officials-to-belgium-conference/

Katsaura, Obvious. 2010a. "Violence and the Political Economy of Informal Diamond Mining Chiadzwa, Zimbabwe." *Journal of Sustainable Development in Africa* 12 (6): 340–353.

2010b. "Socio-cultural Dynamics of Informal Diamond Mining in Chiadzwa, Zimbabwe." *Journal of Sustainable Development in Africa* 12 (6): 101–121.

Kaure, Alexactus. 2011. Nujoma's Conversion to a Capitalistic Agenda. *The Namibian*. November 18.

Kavanagh, Robert. 2014. *Zimbabwe: Challenging the Stereotypes*. Harare: Themba Books.

Keck, Margaret, and Kathryn Sikkink. 1998. *Activists beyond Borders: Advocacy Networks in International Politics*. Ithaca, NY: Cornell University Press.

Keen, David. 2008. *Complex Emergencies*. Cambridge: Polity Press.

Keohane. Robert. 1984. *After Hegemony: Cooperation and Discord in the World Political Economy*. Princeton, NJ: Princeton University Press.

Keohane, Robert, and Joseph Nye. 1977. *Power and Interdependence: World Politics in Transition*. Boston, MA: Little, Brown.

Keohane, Robert, and David Victor. 2011. "The Regime Complex for Climate Change." *Perspectives on Politics* 8 (1): 7–23.

Kimberley Process. 2006. Kimberley Process Plenary. November 6–9, Gaborone, Botswana. www.state.gov/documents/organization/87160.pdf

2009. Administrative Decision Zimbabwe and Work Plan Compendium. www.kimberleyprocess.com/en/2009-administrative-decision-zimbabwe-and-work-plancompendium

2011. Administrative Decision on Marange. www.kimberleyprocess.com/en/2011-administrative-decision-marange

2012. Cameroon Annual Report, September–December. www.kimberley?process.com/fr/system/files/documents/cameroon_annual_report_2012_0.pdf

2013a. KP Basics. www.kimberleyprocess.com/en/about

2013b. History of KP Review Visits. www.kimberleyprocess.com/web/kimberley-process/review-visits

2013c. Administrative Decision on the Central African Republic (Temporary Suspension). www.kimberleyprocess.com/documents/10540/84771/Administrative%20Decision%20CAR%2023%20May%202013.pdf

2015a. Angola Diamond Production. https://kimberleyprocessstatistics.org/public_statistics

2015b. Working Group on Artisanal and Alluvial. www.kimberleyprocess.com/en/artisanal-and-alluvial-wgaap-0

2015c. Operational Framework for Resumption of Exports of Rough Diamonds from the Central African Republic. www.kimberleyprocess.com/en/2015-administrative-decision-central-african-republic-annex

2017. Chair. www.kimberleyprocess.com/en/chair

2018. Annual Report Central African Republic. www.kimberleyprocess.com/en/2018-annual-report-central-african-republic

Kimberley Process Diamond Statistics. 2017. Annual Summary Charts. https://kimberleyprocessstatistics.org/public_statistics

Kimberley Process Statistics. 2014. Annual Summary Charts. https://kimberleyprocessstatistics.org/public_statistics

Kindinger, Matthew. 2018. President Lourenço's Economic Reforms Are Making Angola Attractive. *BusinessDay*. www.businesslive.co.za/bd/opinion/2018-02-16-president-lourenos-economic-reforms-are-making-angola-attractive/

King, Gary, Robert Keohane, and Sidney Verba. 1994. *Designing Social Inquiry: Scientific Inference in Qualitative Research*. Princeton, NJ: Princeton University Press.

Kisting, Denver. 2011. Diamond Man "Deported." *The Namibian*. July 22.

2012. LLD Fails Gem Selection Test. *The Namibian*. June 13.

Knill, Christoph, and Dirk Lehmkuhl. 2002. "Private Actors and the State: Internationalization and Changing Patterns of Governance." *Governance* 15 (1): 41–63.

Lamont, Christopher K. 2016. *International Criminal Justice and the Politics of Compliance*. New York: Routledge.

Landman, Todd. 2003. *Issues and Methods in Comparative Politics: An Introduction*. New York: Routledge.

Lange, G. M. 2004. "Wealth, Natural Capital, and Sustainable Development: Contrasting Examples from Botswana and Namibia." *Environmental and Resource Economics* 29 (3): 257–283.

LeBas, Adrienne. 2011. *From Protest to Parties: Party-Building and Democratization in Africa*. Oxford: Oxford University Press.

Le Billon, Philippe. 2001a. "The Political Ecology of War: Natural Resources and Armed Conflicts." *Political Geography* 20 (5): 561–584.

2001b. "Angola's Political Economy of War: The Role of Oil and Diamonds, 1975–2000." *African Affairs* 100 (398): 55–80.

2008. "Diamond Wars? Conflict Diamonds and the Geographies of Resource Wars." *Annals of the Association of American Geographers* 98 (2): 345–372.

2012. *Wars of Plunder: Conflicts, Profits and the Politics of Resources*. New York: Columbia University Press.

Lee, Levkowitz, Marta Ross, and J. R. Warner. 2009. The 88 Queensway Group: A Case Study in Chinese Investors' Operations in Angola and Beyond. US-China Economic and Security Review Commission. July 10. www.uscc.gov/sites/default/files/Research/The_88_Queensway_Group.pdf

Leotaud, Valentina Ruiz. 2018. Almost 400,000 Migrants Left Angola in Massive Diamond Crackdown. Mining.com. October 21. www.mining.com/almost-400000-migrants-left-angola-massive-diamond-crackdown/

Lie, John. 1992. "The Concept of Mode of Exchange." *American Sociological Review* 57 (4): 508–523.

Littlewood, David. 2014. "'Cursed' Communities? Corporate Social Responsibility (CSR), Company Towns and the Mining Industry in Namibia." *Journal of Business Ethics* 120 (1): 39–63.

2015. "Corporate Social Responsibility, Mining and Sustainable Development in Namibia: Critical Reflections through a Relational Lens." *Development Southern Africa* 32 (2): 240–257.

Locka, Christian. 2016. A Trail of Blood from the CAR to Cameroon: The Players Who Trade in Illegal Diamonds. September 7. https://mg.co.za/multimedia/2016-09-07-a-trail-of-blood-from-the-car-to-cameroon-the-players-who-trade-in-illegal-diamonds/

Lombard, Louisa. 2016. *State of Rebellion: Violence and Intervention in the Central African Republic*. London: Zed Books.

Lujala, Paivil, Nils Petter Gleditsch, and Elizabeth Gilmore. 2005. "A Diamond Curse? Civil War and a Lootable Resource." *Journal of Conflict Resolution* 49 (4): 538–562.

Maconachie, Roy. 2009. "Diamonds, Governance and 'Local' Development in Post-Conflict Sierra Leone: Lessons for Artisanal and Small-Scale Mining in Sub-Saharan Africa?" *Resources Policy* 34: 71–79.

Maconachie, Roy, and Gavin Hilson. 2018. "'The War Whose Bullets You Don't See': Diamond Digging, Resilience and Ebola in Sierra Leone." *Journal of Rural Studies* 61: 110–122.

Mailey, J. R. 2015. The Anatomy of the Resource Curse: Predatory Investment in Africa's Extractive Industries. National Defense University, Africa Center for Strategic Studies. https://africacenter.org/wp-content/uploads/2015/12/Africa-Center-Special-Report-No.-3-EN.pdf

Malaquias, Assis. 2001. "Making War & Lots of Money: The Political Economy of Protracted Conflict in Angola." *Review of African Political Economy* 28 (90): 521–536.

Malpeli, Katherine C., and Peter G. Chirico. 2014. "A Sub-national Scale Geospatial Analysis of Diamond Deposit Lootability: The Case of the Central African Republic." *Extractive Industries and Society* 1 (2): 249–259.

Malunga, Siphosami. 2018a. Zimbabwe: Six Issues That Must Be Fixed for Elections to Be Free and Fair. *African Arguments*. June 14.

2018b. Were Zimbabwe's Elections Free, Fair and Credible? The Final Scoresheet. *African Arguments*. August 21. https://africanarguments.org/2018/08/21/zimbabwe-election-free-fair-credible-final-score-sheet/

Mambo, Elias. 2017a. Jinan Diamond Saga Mystery. *Zimbabwe Independent*. August 11. www.theindependent.co.zw/2017/08/11/jinan-diamond-saga-mystery/

2017b. CIO Company Looted Marange Diamonds. September 22. www.theindependent.co.zw/2017/09/22/cio-company-looted-marange-diamonds/

Mamdani, Mahmood. 2009. "Lessons of Zimbabwe: Mugabe in Context." *London Review of Books* 30 (23). www.lrb.co.uk/the-paper/v30/n23/mahmood-mamdani/lessons-of-zimbabwe

Manayiti, Obey, and Elias Mambo. 2017. Mbada Diamonds Drowns in Debt. *Zimbabwe Independent*. www.theindependent.co.zw/2017/03/17/mbada-diamonds-drowns-debt/

Manenji, Tawanda. 2017. "The Trajectory of Zimbabwean Marange Diamond Revenue Remittances from 2006 to 2013." *Scholedge International Journal of Business Policy and Governance* 4 (6): 56–70.

Marques, Rafael. 2005. Lundas – The Stones of Death: Angola's Deadly Diamonds: Human Rights Abuses in the Lunda Provinces, 2004. www.medico.de/fileadmin/_migrated_/document_media/1/lundas–the-stones-of-death-angolas-deadly-dia.pdf

Marshall, Monty, and Gabrielle Elzinga-Marshall. 2017. State Fragility Index and Matrix. Center for Systemic Peace. www.systemicpeace.org/inscr/SFImatrix2017c.pdf

Martin, Alan, and Bernard Taylor. 2010. *Diamonds and Clubs: The Militarized Control of Diamonds and Power in Zimbabwe*. Ottawa: Partnership Africa Canada.

2012. *Reap What You Sow: Greed and Corruption in Zimbabwe's Marange Diamond Fields*. Ottawa: Partnership Africa Canada.

Matimaire, Kenneth. 2017. ZCDC Starts Exploration of DTZ Diamond Claim. *The Financial Gazette*. August 3. www.financialgazette.co.zw/zcdc-starts-exploration-of-dtz-diamond-claim/

Matthysen, Ken, and Iain Clarkson. 2013. Gold and Diamonds in the Central African Republic. IPIS Report. http://adamasswiss.com/en/pdf2/Gold%20and%20diamonds%20in%20the%20Central%20African%20Republic.pdf

Mbwale, Lorna. 2010. Analysis of Namdebs's Turnaround Strategy to Improve Its Financial Performance in View of Declining Carats Profile. MA thesis. University of Namibia.

McIntyre, Chris. 1998. *Namibia: The Bradt Travel Guide*. Old Saybrook, CT: Bradt Publications.

Mearsheimer, John. 2004. "The False Promise of International Institutions." *International Security* 19 (3): 5–49.

Melber, Henning. 2015. *Understanding Namibia: The Trials of Independence*. Oxford: Oxford University Press.

Melman, Yossi. 2010. U.S. Ties Israeli Billionaire with Chinese Intelligence. *Haaretz*. www.haaretz.com/1.5091133

Meredith, Martin. 2008. *Diamonds, Gold, and War: The British, the Boers, and the Making of South Africa*. London: Hachette UK.

Merriam, Sharan. 2009. *Qualitative Research: A Guide to Design and Implementation*. San Francisco, CA: Jossey-Bass.

Mezzofiore, Gianluca. 2014. Israel: London-Based "King of Diamonds" Lev Leviev Pulls Out from West Bank Settlement Construction. *International Business Times*. October 29. www.ibtimes.co.uk/israel-london-based-king-diamonds-lev-leviev-pulls-out-west-bank-settlement-construction-1472249

Mhaka, Tafi. 2018. Is Chiwenga on a Path to Transform Zimbabwe into Sisi's Egypt? *Al Jazeera*. May 4. www.aljazeera.com/indepth/opinion/chiwenga-path-transform-zimbabwe-sisi-egypt-180503131043364.html

Mighty Movies Online. 2018. Ask the MP #Where Is the $15 Billion. January 25. www.youtube.com/watch?v=WfDEwLH0spw

Mining Weekly. 2014. Angola Wants Mining to Broaden Its Economic Base. May 2.

Ministry of Labour and Social Welfare. 2012. *The Namibia Labour Force Survey 2012 Report*. Windhoek: Namibia Statistics Agency.

Mitchell, Ronald. 1994. "Regime Design Matters: Intentional Oil Pollution and Treaty Compliance." *International Organization* 48 (3): 425–458.

Mitchell, Sara McLaughlin, and Cameron Thies. 2012. "Resource Curse in Reverse: How Civil Wars Influence Natural Resource Production." *International Interactions* 38 (2): 218–242.

Moyo, Dambisa. 2009. *Dead Aid: Why Aid Is Not Working and How There Is a Better Way for Africa*. New York: Farrar, Straus and Giroux.

Munier, Nathan. 2014. From Passiveness to the Presidency! The Changing Nature of Angolan Responsiveness to Conflict Diamond Regulation. Presented at the International Studies Conference-Midwest. November 7–9.

2016a. "The One Who Controls the Diamonds Wears the Crown! The Politicization of the Kimberley Process in Zimbabwe." *Resources Policy* 47: 171–177.

2016b. "Diamonds without Blood: A Look at Namibia." *African Security* 9(1): 21–41.

2016c. "Diamonds, Dependence and De Beers: Monopoly Capitalism and Compliance with the Kimberley Process in Namibia." *Review of African Political Economy* 43 (150): 542–555.

Murphy, Shannon. 2011. "Clouded Diamonds: Without Binding Arbitration and More Sophisticated Dispute Resolution Mechanisms, the Kimberley Process Will Ultimately Fail in Ending Conflicts Fueled by Blood Diamonds." *Pepperdine Dispute Resolution Law Journal* 11 (2): 207–228.

Muronzi, Chris. 2013. Ghanaian Tycoons "Fleeced of $10m." *Zimbabwe Independent*. September 27.

Nam News. 2014. British Foreign Under-Secretary of State Briefed on Kimberley Process in Angola. 6 August.

Newitt, Malyn. 2008. "Angola in Historical Context." In *Angola: The Weight of History*, ed. Patrick Chabal and Nuno Vidal. 19–92. New York: Columbia University Press.

Newsday. 2014. ZMDC Holding "Missing" Gye Nyame Diamonds. August 5.

2017. G40 Cabal Responsible for Chiadzwa Diamond Looting. March 22.

New Zimbabwe. 2014. Grace: Mujuru Formed Marange Rights Company ACR. https://allafrica.com/stories/201410240405.html

Niño, Helena Pérez, and Philippe Le Billon. 2014. "Foreign Aid, Resource Rents, and State Fragility in Mozambique and Angola." *ANNALS of the American Academy of Political and Social Science* 656 (1): 79–96.

Now Daily. 2016a. Security Forces on High Alert as Mugabe Clashes with China over Diamonds. February 25.

2016b. Anger as Mugabe Drives Army Generals out of Marange Diamond Mines. March 31.

Ntali, Elia. 2018. "The Situation Is Unbearable": Life under Zimbabwe's Economic Crisis. *African Arguments*. October 1. https://africanarguments.org/2018/10/31/zimbabwe-economic-crisis-situation-unbearable/

Nujoma, Sam. 2001. *Where Others Wavered*. Bedford: Panaf Books.

Nyamunda, Tinashe, and Patience Mukwambo. 2012. "The State and the Bloody Diamond Rush in Chiadzwa: Unpacking the Contesting Interests in the Development of Illicit Mining and Trading, c. 2006–2009." *Journal of South African Studies* 38 (1): 145–166.

Nyaungwa, Mathew. 2012. Why LLD Diamonds Namibia Failed to Renew Its Sightholder Contract? *Rough and Polished*. www.roughpolished.com/en/expertise/65161.html

2013. Alrosa, De Beers in Race for Unexplored Angolan Diamonds. April 22. www.rubel-menasche.com/en/alrosa-de-beers-in-race-for-unexplored-angolan-diamonds/

2018. Sierra Leone to Review Mining Law, Contracts – Report. May 29. www.rough-polished.com/en/news/110827.html

Nyokabi, J. K., E. Ikpe, and A. Alao. 2017. Building the State without Peace or Making Peace without the State: A Baseline Study on the Paradox of State-Building and Peace-Building in Sierra Leone. African Leadership Centre. https://idl-bnc-idrc.dspacedirect.org/bitstream/handle/10625/56346/IDL-56346.pdf?sequence=2&isAllowed=y

Nyota, Shumirai, and Fortune Sibanda. 2012. "Digging for Diamonds, Wielding New Words: A Linguistic Perspective on Zimbabwe's 'Blood Diamonds'." *Journal of South African Studies* 38 (1): 129–144.

Obale, Offah. 2016. From Conflict to Illicit:Mapping the Diamond Trade from Central African Republic to Cameroon. Partnership Africa Canada. https://impacttransform.org/wp-content/uploads/2017/09/2016-Dec-From-Conflict-to-Illicit-Mapping-the-diamond-trade-from-Central-African-Republic-to-Cameroon.pdf

Office of the High Commissioner for Human Rights. 2013. Letter of Allegation Concerning the Prosecution of Rafael Marques de Morais by the Government of the Republic of Angola. August 2.

Oliver, Francios. 2011. N$25 Million Diamond Polishing Factory in Katutura. *Namibian Sun*. August 2.

Partnership Africa Canada. 2006. Killing Kimberley? Conflict Diamonds and Paper Tigers. Ian Smille and Josee Letourneau. Occasional Paper # 15. November. https://impacttransform.org/wp-content/uploads/2017/09/2006-Nov-Killing-Kimberly-Conflict-Diamonds-and-Paper-Tigers.pdf

2010a. From Tragedy to Farce: Zimbabwe Flouts Us Still. https://impacttransform.org/

2010b. Diamonds without Borders: An Assessment of the Challenges of Implementing and Enforcing the Kimberley Process Certification Scheme. A Report to the 2010 KPCS Plenary. https://impacttransform.org/wp-content/uploads/2017/09/2010-Nov-Diamonds-Without-Borders-An-assessment-of-the-challenges-of-implementing-and-enforcing-the-Kimberly-Process-Certification-Sc.pdf

2013. Diamond Watchlist: Lebanon. www.pacweb.org/en/

Peltzman, Sam. 1976. Toward a More General Theory of Regulation. *Journal of Law and Economics* 19 (2): 221–240.

Pensador, Daniel Garelo, and Philippe Alfroy. 2018. Angola Still Waiting for Promised "Economic Miracle." www.yahoo.com/news/angola-still-waiting-promised-economic-miracle-035509529.html

Peskin, Victor. 2008. *International Justice in Rwanda and the Balkans: Virtual Trials and the Struggle for State Cooperation*. Cambridge: Cambridge University Press.

Pisani, Andre du. 2003. "Liberation and Tolerance." In *Re-Examining Liberation in Namibia: Political Culture since Independence*, ed. Henning Melber. 129–137. Stockholm: Elanders Gotab.

Polack, Peter. 2013. *The Last Hot Battle of the Cold War: South Africa vs. Cuba in the Angolan Civil War*. Philadelphia, PA: Casemate.

Political Analysis South Africa. 2018. CAR's Decline in Diamond Production Blamed on Fraud, Other Factors. December 28. www.politicalanalysis.co.za/cars-decline-in-diamond-production-blamed-on-fraud-other-factors/

Poteete, A. R. 2009. "Is Development Path Dependent or Political? A Reinterpretation of Mineral-Dependent Development in Botswana." *Journal of Development Studies* 45 (4): 544–571.

2012. "Electoral Competition, Factionalism, and Persistent Party Dominance in Botswana." *Journal of Modern African Studies* 50 (1): 75–102.

Potoski, Matthew, and Aseem Prakash, eds. 2009. *Voluntary Programs: A Club Theory Perspective*. Cambridge, MA: MIT Press.

Public Law 108-19. 2003. Clean Diamond Trade Act. April. www.treasury.gov/resource/center/sanctions/Documents/pl108_19.pdf

Regan, Patrick, and Daniel Norton. 2005. "Greed, Grievance, and Mobilization in Civil Wars." *Journal of Conflict Resolution* 49 (3): 319–336.

Reno, William. 1995. *Corruption and State Politics in Sierra Leone*. Cambridge: Cambridge University Press.

1998. *Warlord Politics and African States*. Boulder, CO: Lynne Rienner.

Report of the Review Mission of the Kimberly Process to the Central African Republic. 2003. http://archive.niza.nl/docs/200309111248463183.pdf

Responsible Jewellery Council. 2014. Certified Members. www.responsiblejewellery.com/members/certified-members/

Reuters. 2012a. Central African Republic Rebels Threaten to Resume Fighting. www.reuters.com/article/2013/02/25/us-car-rebels-idUSBRE91O1122013 0225

2012b. Liberia Says Lacks Cash Not Will to Fight Blood Diamonds. September 14.

2016. Zimbabwe's Mugabe Says Government Will Take over All Diamond Operations. March 3. www.reuters.com/article/us-zimbabwe-diamonds/zimbabwes-mugabe-says-government-will-take-over-all-diamond-operations-idUSKCN0W52J3

Rieckmann, Johannes. 2008. *Two Dynamic Export Sectors (Diamonds, Tourism) in Namibia and Botswana: Comparison of Development Strategies*. No. 112. Bremen: Institute for World Economics and International Management.

Rodney, Walter. 1974. *How Europe Underdeveloped Africa*. Washington, DC: Howard University Press.

Roberts, Brian. 2016. *The Diamond Magnates*. London: Thistle Publishing.

Ross, Michael. 2003. "The Natural Resource Curse: How Wealth Can Make You Poor." In *Natural Resources and Violent Conflict: Options and Actions*, ed. Ian Bannon and Paul Collier. 17–42. Washington, DC: World Bank.

2004a. "What Do We Know about Natural Resources and Civil War?" *Journal of Peace Research* 41 (3): 337–356.

2004b. "How Do Natural Resources Influence Civil War? Evidence from Thirteen Cases." *International Organization* 58 (1): 35–67.

2006. "A Closer Look at Oil, Diamonds and Civil War." *Annual Review of Political Science* 9: 265–300.

Rough and Polished. 2013. Israel Ranks Leo Schachter as Top Diamond Exporter in 2012. January 7. www.rough-polished.com/en/news/72508.html

Ruggie, John Gerard. 1998. "What Makes the World Hang Together? Neo-utilitarianism and the Social Constructivist Challenge." *International Organization* 52 (4): 855–885.

2002. "The Theory and Practice of Learning Networks: Corporate Social Responsibility and the Global Compact." *Journal of Corporate Citizenship* 5: 27–36.

Santiago, Anne. 2014. "Guaranteeing Conflict-Free Diamonds: From Compliance to Norm Expansion under the Kimberley Process Certification Scheme." *South African Journal of International Affairs* 21 (3): 413–429.

Saunders, Richard. 2008. "Crisis, Capital and Compromise: Mining and Empowerment in Zimbabwe." *African Sociological Review* 12 (1): 67–87.

Scherer, Andreas Georg, and Guido Palazzo. 2011. "The New Political Role of Business in a Globalized World: A Review of a New Perspective on CSR and Its Implications for the Firm, Governance, and Democracy." *Journal of Management Studies* 48 (4): 899–931.

Scherer, Andreas Georg, Guido Palazzo, and Dorothée Baumann. 2006. "Global Rules and Private Actors: Toward a New Role of the Transnational Corporation in Global Governance." *Business Ethics Quarterly* 16 (4): 505–532.

Schneider, Gabi. 2008. *Treasures of the Diamond Coast: A Century of Diamond Mining in Namibia*. Windhoek: Macmillan Education Namibia Publishers.

Schroeder, Richard. 2010. "Tanzanite as Conflict Gem: Certifying a Secure Commodity Chain in Tanzania." *Geoforum* 41 (1): 56–65.

Schure, Jolien, Verina Ingram, Julius Chupezi Tieguhong, and Cleto Ndikumagenge. 2011. "Is the God of Diamonds Alone? The Role of Institutions in Artisanal Mining in Forest Landscapes, Congo Basin." *Resources Policy* 36 (4): 363–371.

Schott, Jeffrey. 1994. *The Uruguay Round: An Assessment*. Washington, DC: Institute for International Economics.

Scott, Jeffrey, and Jayashree Watal. 2000. "Decision Making in the WTO." In *The WTO after Seattle*, ed. Jeffrey J. Schott. 283–285. Washington, DC: Institute for International Economics.

Shejavali, N. 2009. Nam Diamonds' Reputation at Risk. *The Namibian*. March 16.

Shishlo, Alex. 2016. The KP Warns about Fake Certificates from Sierra Leone. April 18. *Rough and Polished*. www.rough-polished.com/en/news/102215.html

Sibeene, Petronella. 2008. Namibia: Liberians Eager to Learn Namibia Diamond Management. *New Era*. July 15.

Siegel, Dina. 2009. *The Mazzel Ritual: Culture, Customs and Crime in the Diamond Trade*. Utrecht: Springer.

Simmons, Beth. 1998. "Compliance with International Agreements." *American Review of Political Science* 1 (1): 75–93.

2009. *Mobilizing for Human Rights: International Law in Domestic Politics*. Cambridge: Cambridge University Press.

Sinclair, Upton. 1906. *The Jungle*. New York: Doubleday.

Smillie, Ian. 2010a. *Blood on the Stone: Greed, Corruption and War in the Global Diamond Trade*. New York: Anthem Press.

2010b. Paddles for Kimberley. An Agenda for Reform. Partnership Africa Canada. https://impacttransform.org/wp-content/uploads/2017/09/2010-Jun-Paddles-for-Kimberley-An-Agenda-for-Reform.pdf

2012. Going the Distance: Striving and Thriving: Annual Report 2012. Diamond Development Initiative. http://ddiglobal.org/wp-content/uploads/2019/05/ddi-annual-report-2012-english.pdf

2014. *Diamonds*. Cambridge: Polity Press.

Smillie, Ian, and Josee Letourneau. 2008. *Diamonds and Human Security Annual Review*. Ottowa: Partnership Africa Canada.

2009. *Diamonds and Human Security Annual Review*. Ottowa: Partnership Africa Canada.

Smith, Ben. 2007. Meet the Mogul: The Putin Pal Who Just Bought the Old New York Times Building. October 24. *New York Magazine*. http://nymag.com/news/intelligencer/31549/

Smith, Julia, and Kelley Lee. 2018. "From Colonisation to Globalisation: A History of State Capture by the Tobacco Industry in Malawi." *Review of African Political Economy* 45 (156): 186–202.

Snyder, Richard. 2006. "Does Lootable Wealth Breed Disorder? A Political Economy of Extraction Framework." *Comparative Political Studies* 39 (8): 943–968.

Snyder, Richard, and Ravi Bhavnani. 2005. "Diamonds, Blood and Taxes: A Revenue-Centered Framework for Explaining Political Order." *Journal of Conflict Resolution* 49 (4): 563–597.

South African Development Community. 1997. Protocol on Mining in the Southern African Development Community (SADC). www.sadc.int/documents-publications/show/Protocol%20on%20Mining%20(1997)

Southhall, Roger. 2013. *Liberation Movements in Power: Party and State in Southern Africa.* Woodbridge: University of KwaZulu-Natal Press.

Spar, Debora. 2006. "Markets: Continuity and Change in the International Diamond Market." *Journal of Economic Perspectives* 20 (3): 195–208.

Spar, Debora L., and Lane T. La Mure. 2003. "The Power of Activism: Assessing the Impact of NGOs on Global Business." *California Management Review* 45 (3): 78–101.

Spiegel, Samuel. 2015. "Contested Diamond Certification: Reconfiguring Global and National Interests in Zimbabwe's Marange Fields." *Geoforum* 59: 258–267.

Stein, Nicholas. 2001. The De Beers Story: A New Cut on an Old Monopoly: The Company That Has Ruled Diamonds for a Century Wants to Polish Its Image … and Dominate as Never Before. *CNN Money*. http://archive.fortune.com/magazines/fortune/fortune_archive/2001/02/19/296863/index.htm

Sterling-Folker, Jennifer. 2013. "Historical Materialism and World System Theory." In *Making Sense of International Relations Theory*. 2nd edn. 217–227. Boulder, CO: Lynne Rienner.

Stewart, Frances, and Graham Brown. 2009. Fragile States. Centre for Research on Inequality, Human Security and Ethnicity, Working Paper No. 51. https://assets.publishing.service.gov.uk/media/57a08b62e5274a27b2000af7/wp51.pdf

Stigler, George. 1971. "The Theory of Economic Regulation." *Bell Journal of Economics and Management Science* 2 (1): 3–21.

Strange, Susan. 1982. "Cave! Hic Dragons: A Critique of Regime Analysis." *International Organization* 36 (2): 479–496.

1996. *The Retreat of the State: The Diffusion of Power in the World Economy*. Cambridge: Cambridge University Press.

1998. *Mad Money*. Manchester: Manchester University Press.

Tamm, Ingrid. 2004. "Dangerous Appetites: Human Rights Activism and Conflict Commodities." *Human Rights Quarterly* 26 (3): 687–704.

Taylor, Celia. 2012. Conflict Minerals and SEC Disclosure Regulation. *Harvard Business Law Review Online*. www.hblr.org/2012/01/conflict-minerals-and-sec-disclosure-regulation/

Taylor, Ian. 2016. "Dependency Redux: Why Africa Is Not Rising." *Review of African Political Economy* 43 (147): 8–25.

Taylor, Ian, and Gladys Mokhawa. 2003. "Not Forever: Botswana, Conflict Diamonds and the Bushmen." *African Affairs* 102 (407): 261–283.

Tempelsman, Maurice. 2008. Lazare Kaplan International Inc. Commitment to Higher Standards

Thomas, Abdul Rashid. 2018. President Bio Wants Diamonds to Be Cut and Polished in Sierra Leone. *SierraLeoneTelegraph*. November 6. www.thesierraleonetelegraph.com/president-bio-wants-diamonds-to-be-cut-and-polished-in-sierra-leone/

Thornycroft, Peta, and Aislinn Laing. 2014. Zimbabwe's Ruling Zanu PF Split as Robert Mugabe Ejects His Vice-President Joice Mujuru. *The Telegraph* [online]. www.telegraph.co.uk/news/worldnews/africaandindianocean/zimbabwe/11258451/Zimbabwes-ruling-Zanu-PF-split-as-Robert-Mugabe-ejects-his-vice-president-JoiceMujuru.html

Tinhu, Simukai. 2016. What Does G40 Want? *Zimbabwe Independent*. www.theindependent.co.zw/2016/03/18/what-does-g40-want/

Titley, Brian. 1997. *Dark Age: The Political Odyssey of Emperor Bokassa*. Montreal: McGill-Queen's University Press.

Towriss, David. 2013. "Buying Loyalty: Zimbabwe's Marange Diamonds." *Journal of Southern African Studies* 39 (1): 99–117.

Tsebelis, George. 2002. *Veto Players: How Political Institutions Work*. Princeton, NJ: Princeton University Press.

United Nations Development Program. 2018. Human Development Index. http://hdr.undp.org/en/2018-update

United Nations Security Council. 2014. Letter Dated 28 October 2014 from the Panel of Experts on the Central African Republic Established Pursuant to Security Council Resolution 2127 (2013) Addressed to the President of the Security Council. October 29. https://reliefweb.int/sites/reliefweb.int/files/resources/N1453897.pdf

UN News Centre. 2003. Annan Strongly Condemns Coup in the Central African Republic. United Nations. March 17. www.un.org/apps/news/story.asp?NewsID=6483ID=6483&Cr=central&Cr1=african

United States Department of State. 2010. Background Note: Central African Republic, Bureau of African Affairs. www.state.gov/r/pa/ei/bgn/4007.htm

US Department of State. 2014. Remarks with Angolan Vice President Manuel Domingos Vicente before Their Meeting. August 4. www.state.gov/secretary/remarks/2014/08/230201.htm

Vines, Alex, and Markus Weimer. 2011. Angola: Assessing Risks to Stability. Center for Strategic and International Studies. http://csis.org/files/publication/110623_Vines_Angola_Web.pdf

Vircoulon, Thierry. 2015. "Cameroon: Africa's Pivot." *World Policy Journal* 32 (2): 113–119.

Vlassenroot, Koen, and Steven Van Bockstael, eds. 2008. *Artisanal Diamond Mining: Perspectives and Challenges*. Ghent: Academia Press.

Vorrath, Judith. 2018. "What Drives Post-War Crime? Evidence from Illicit Economies in Liberia and Sierra Leone." *Third World Thematics: A TWQ Journal* 3 (1): 28–45.

Wall Street Journal. 2010. The "Blood Diamond" Resurfaces. June 19.

Wallerstein, Immanuel. 1974. "Dependence in an Interdependent World: The Limited Possibilities of Transformation within the Capitalist World Economy." *African Studies Review* 17 (1): 1–26.

2004. *World Systems Analysis: An Introduction*. Durham, NC: Duke University Press.

Weimer, Markus, and Alex Vines. 2012. "China's Angolan Oil Deals 2003–2011." In *China and Angola: A Marriage of Convenience?*, ed. Marcus Power and Ana Cristina Alves. 85–104. Cape Town: Pambazuka Press.

Weinthal, Erika. 2002. *State Making and Environmental Cooperation: Linking Domestic and International Politics in Central Asia*. Cambridge, MA: Massachusetts Institute of Technology.

Wilson, Sigismond. 2011. "Sierra Leone's Illicit Diamonds: The Challenges and the Way Forward." *GeoJournal* 76 (3): 191–212.

World Diamond Council. 2013. Diamond Facts. www.diamondfacts.org/index.php?option=com_content&view=article&id=86&Itemid=133&lang=en

Wright, Clive. 2004. "Tackling Conflict Diamonds: The Kimberley Process Certification Scheme." *International Peacekeeping* 11 (4): 697–708.

Yifu Lin, Justin. 2012. *The Quest for Prosperity: How Developing Economies Can Take Off*. Princeton, NJ: Princeton University Press.

Young, Oran. 2010. *Institutional Dynamics: Emergent Patterns in International Environmental Governance*. Cambridge, MA: MIT Press.

ZBC. 2018. Breaking: ED Romps to Victory. August 3. www.zbcnews.co.zw/page/555/?s%2F

Zikiti, B. 2016. How Can Zimbabwe Leverage Its Mineral Resources for Economic Recovery and Sustainable Growth. http://wiredspace.wits.ac.za/bitstream/handle/10539/21775/Beauty%20Zikiti%20Masters%20Thesis-%202015.pdf?sequence=1

Zimbabwe Daily. 2010. We Can Sell Our Diamonds Elsewhere: Mugabe. www.thezimbabwedaily.com

Zimbabwe Independent. 2017. Mbada Diamonds Drowns in Debt. March 17.

Zimnisky, Paul. 2014. Marange May Not Be the World's Largest Diamond Producer for much Longer. Kitco Commentary. February 19. www.kitco.com/ind/Zimnisky/2014-02-10-Marange-May-Not-Be-The-Worlds-Largest-Diamond-Producer-For-Much-Longer.html

2018. Global Diamond Supply Expected to Decrease 3.4% to 147M Carats in 2018. Paul Zimnisky Diamond Analytics. www.paulzimnisky.com/global-diamond-supply-expected-to-decrease-3-4-to-147m-carats-in-2018

Zoellner, Tom. 2006. *The Heartless Stone: A Journey through the World of Diamonds, Deceit and Desire*. New York: St. Martin's Press.

Index

For EU product safety concerns, contact us at Calle de José Abascal, 56–1°,
28003 Madrid, Spain or eugpsr@cambridge.org.

www.ingramcontent.com/pod-product-compliance
Lightning Source LLC
LaVergne TN
LVHW022212200926
848481LV00006B/1940

* 9 7 8 1 1 0 8 8 1 3 5 8 7 *